At Any Cost

Morton Mintz

AT ANY COST

Corporate Greed,

Women, and the

Dalkon Shield

PANTHEON BOOKS · NEW YORK

Library of Congress Cataloging in Publication Data

Mintz, Morton.
At any cost: Corporate greed, women, and
the Dalkon Shield.

1. Intrauterine contraceptives industry. 2. Dalkon
Shield (Intrauterine contraceptive) 3. Intrauterine
contraceptives—Complications and sequelae.
4. A.H. Robins Company. I. Title.
HD9995.C62M56   1985   338.7′616139435   85-6389
ISBN 0-394-54846-9

Book design by Joe Marc Freedman

For Anita,
for our daughters and sons-in-law,
Margaret and John Birdsall and
Roberta and Harry Levine,
and for our son, Daniel.

Contents

Acknowledgments

I cannot possibly name here all of the men and women who graciously encouraged and helped me in the preparation and writing of this book. The bulk of the credit must go to several plaintiffs' lawyers.

More than in any other country, trial lawyers in America are a potent check-and-balance against conscienceless corporate power, which has increasingly translated into political power. They are a particularly valuable resource in an era in which the President and Vice-President have contrived to strip away many of the hard-won but inadequate protections that were put in place by the federal government. Trial lawyers achieve a measure of rough justice. They frequently draw press attention that usefully alerts millions of people to hazards that otherwise would not come to light and that people in other countries, to their sorrow, discover only the hard way.

The press, by itself, has only limited power. A board chairman or CEO can make corporate records and himself inaccessible to a news reporter inquiring into a matter of high importance to the public's health, safety, or purse, or to the environment. But plaintiffs' lawyers, armed with subpoenas, can compel a recalcitrant corporate board chairman, a secretive chief executive officer, a cautious staff scientist, or a frightened employee privy to terrible truths to reveal documents and to testify—and perhaps to testify again and again. It is important that such documents and testimony, fairly used, be made public without fear of retribution.

For more than a decade, starting in the early 1970s, plaintiffs' lawyers representing Dalkon Shield victims did the bulk of the hard digging for the truly massive stock of records on which this book is based, and without which such a book could not have been written. I particularly want to thank: Bradley Post and Arden Bradshaw of Wichita, Kansas; Roger P. Brosnahan, Michael V. Ciresi, Dale I. Larson, Sidney Abramson, Martha K. Wivell, Thomas C. Kayser, and Roberta Walburn, all of Robins, Zelle, Larson & Kaplan of Minneapolis and St. Paul; Aaron M. Levine of Washington, D.C.; Sidney L. Matthew and S. Lindsey Gorman of Tallahassee, Florida; Robert E. Manchester of Burlington, Vermont; Nicole Schultheis and Michael A. Pretl of Baltimore; John T. Baker and Douglas E. Bragg of Denver; Jane I. Fantel of Seattle; and Dennis B. Conklin, John J. Davids, and Paul V. Melodia of San Francisco.

Two congressional hearings were also invaluable sources of information. The first, an excellent five-day hearing on regulation of intrauterine devices, was held in 1973 by a House Government Operations subcommittee led by former Representative L. H. Fountain (D–N.C.) and staffed by Delphis C. Goldberg and the late Gilbert S. Goldhammer. The second hearing was held in 1975 by Senator Edward M. Kennedy (D–Mass.), who was at that time chairman of the Senate Health and Administrative Practices subcommittees, and two aides, Dr. Larry Horowitz and Walter J. Sheridan. The two hearings, along with many others in which Fountain, Kennedy, and their aides focused on the regulatory performance and nonperformance of the Food and Drug Administration, have made large, if insufficiently appreciated, contributions to the public weal.

The accomplishments of lawyers and legislators can be trees falling unheard in the forest unless the press, as surrogate for the public, listens. The *Washington Post,* where I have been a reporter since 1958, listened. *Post* editors sponsored my extensive investigation of the Dalkon Shield disaster for a series of articles. Benjamin C. Bradlee, the *Post*'s executive editor, let me harvest the fruits of the investigation for this book and granted me a leave of absence in which to write it. His approach to book-writing and advanced study by members of his staff is enlightened and generous, and I am pleased to have reason to say so.

Among the many other *Washington Post* friends and colleagues I would like to thank are Ted Gup, who edited my series of articles with dedication and patience, and Charles R. Babcock, who gave me wise guidance in a stressful period. My thanks go also to Sara Bershtel, my superb editor at Pantheon Books, and to David Sternbach, her assistant; to my beloved wife, Anita, who helped me with research and was my first reader; and to Victoria T. Dawson, for indispensable typing and other help.

Preface

The story of the Dalkon Shield lays bare the perils inherent in a system that allows corporations to profit even if they put human beings at risk. The Dalkon Shield created a disaster of global proportions because a few men with little on their minds but megabucks made decisions, in the interest of profit, that exposed millions of women to serious infection, sterility, and even death.

The problem is not simply that corporations have no conscience, but that they are endowed by law with rights beyond those allowed to individuals. Corporations too often act without compassion and, no matter what damage they cause, without remorse. Even worse, they cannot be held accountable, as people can be. You cannot lock up a corporation, or sentence it to hard labor or the electric chair. And too often the law fails to look behind the corporate veil, to prosecute the individuals who make decisions and act in the name of the corporation.

In 1962, I wrote the story of thalidomide, the sedative-tranquilizer that caused several thousand children to be born without arms or legs. This was my unforgettable introduction to a brutal fact: corporations run by human beings regularly and deliberately undertake activities that cause grave environmental damage, or lead to large-scale disease, injury, or death to those who make, use, or are exposed to their products.

In the ensuing quarter-century, in the *Washington Post* and in books and articles, I have reported many more cases of knowing and willful misconduct involving a broad spectrum of industry: producers of medicines, contraceptives, mechanical heart valves, anesthesia machines, agricultural and industrial chemicals, food additives and colorings, infant formulas, toys, automobiles, tires, asbestos, coal, uranium, space heaters, washing machines, weapons systems. But not until my investigation of the Dalkon Shield did I have access to a factual record so panoramic in scope and so complete that I could reconstruct in faithful detail the origins and evolution of a catastrophic episode and could identify precisely who had done and who had concealed each morally dubious or indefensible act.

By mid-1985, more than 14,000 American women who had worn Dalkon Shields had filed lawsuits and claims against the manufacturer, the A. H. Robins Company of Richmond, Virginia. This flood of litigation has by now produced several hundred thousand pages of pretrial "discovery" materials, particularly company records and sworn testimony in depositions, as well as transcripts of trial testimony and other court documents. Starting in September 1982, and for more than two years thereafter, I reviewed literally tens of thousands of pages of these materials. I also conducted more than one hundred interviews and attended Shield-related judicial proceedings in three Minnesota cities and in Washington. Since 1973, when I covered a five-day hearing on IUDs held by Representative L. H. Fountain (D–N.C.), I have also tracked the Dalkon Shield in hearings held by panels of outside advisers to the Food and Drug Administration.

These materials illuminate every aspect of the Dalkon Shield saga, from its origins in the mid- and late 1960s to the present. They tell what happened, and how and why; what Robins executives knew, and when they knew it; which Robins officials contradicted each other (and, on occasion, themselves) under oath; and what evidence disappeared or was destroyed, falsified, or covered up.

The documents do more: they take the observer to a vantage point from which he can peer into the chasm between the flesh-and-blood person and the paper corporate person. This chasm is widely perceived but rarely examined, for the fact is that the human being who would not harm you on an individual, face-to-face basis, who is charitable, civic-minded, loving, and devout, will wound or kill you from behind the corporate veil. He may do this without qualm because he has been conditioned to drop a curtain between his private moral and religious self and his corporate immoral and irreligious self. And society at large accepts and, if only by its silence, *validates* such compartmentalization.

Is it not an atrocity and a sin—and should it not be a crime? —to commission, devise, or implement an advertising campaign designed to induce children to smoke? To warn American but not foreign physicians that an antibiotic which causes an often fatal blood disease at significant rates should be used only in rare circumstances? To certify shoddy work on a nuclear power plant? To sell faulty weapons to the armed services? To sell in the Third World drugs that are banned in the United States for want of evidence that they are safe and effective? Such questions are rarely discussed in classrooms, schools of theology and business administration, or newspaper editorials or opinion columns. Such questions never arise in presidential elections and probably never in congressional races. Perhaps most dismaying, they seldom become sermon topics for mainstream clergymen and never for television evangelists. From Lynchburg, Virginia, the Reverend Jerry Falwell leads the Moral Majority in its crusade against abortion. In Lynchburg, too, Robins made millions of Dalkon Shields, thousands of which caused spontaneous septic abortions. Might Falwell have by now found this grist for a sermon?[1]

The paradox by which immersion in the corporation washes away personal responsibility is perfectly captured in the figure of E. Claiborne Robins, builder and chairman of the Fortune 500 company that bears his name. A towering presence in American philanthropy, he has given away truly astonishing sums in gifts to a broad array of worthy causes. In 1969 he gave $50 million to the University of Richmond, an unrestricted gift said by the university to have been the largest gift ever made by a living person to an institution of higher education. Since then, Robins and his family have given at least $50 million more to the unviersity, and additional millions to other universities and to diverse other causes. In December 1983, *Town and Country* magazine listed him among the top five of "The Most Generous Americans."

A Baptist, Robins was nominated by the Richmond chapter of B'nai B'rith International for the Jewish service organization's Great American Tradition Award. At the presentation banquet in June 1982, E. Bruce Heilman, president of the University of Richmond, was the principal speaker. "Truly the Lord has chosen you as one of His most essential instruments," he told Robins. "We applaud you for the high accomplishment of always exhibiting a steadfast and devoted concern for your fellow man. . . . Your example will cast its shadows into eternity, as the sands of time carry the indelible footprints of your good works."

But with the power to do great good goes the power to do great harm. Edward Alsworth Ross, sociologist and author of the brilliant, pithy *Sin and Society: An Analysis of Latter-Day Iniquity* (1907), saw this years before Claiborne Robins was born, and observed:

> The grading of sinners according to badness of character goes on the assumption that the wickedest man is the most dangerous. This would be true if men were abreast in their opportunities to do harm. In that case the blackest villain would be the worst scourge of society. But the fact is that the patent ruffian is confined to the social basement, and enjoys few opportunities. He can assault or molest, to be sure; but he cannot betray. Nobody depends on him, so he cannot commit breach of trust—that arch sin of our time. He does not hold in his hand the safety or welfare or money of the public. He is the clinker, not the live coal; vermin, not beast of prey. To-day the villain most in need of curbing is the respectable, exemplary, trusted personage who, strategically placed at the focus of a spider-web of fiduciary relations, is able from his office-chair to pick a thousand pockets, or imperil a thousand lives. It is the great-scale, high-voltage sinner that needs the shackle.[2]

Decades later, Miles W. Lord, chief United States District Judge for Minnesota, had to spell it out again in reprimanding E. Claiborne Robins, Jr., chief executive officer and president of A. H. Robins, and two other officers of the company:

It is not enough to say, "I did not know," "It was not me," "Look elsewhere." Time and again, each of you has used this kind of argument in refusing to acknowledge your responsibility and in pretending to the world that the chief officers and directors of your gigantic multinational corporation have no responsibility for the company's acts and omissions. . . .

Today as you sit here attempting once more to extricate yourselves from the legal consequences of your acts, none of you has faced up to the fact that more than 9,000 [at that time] women claim they gave up part of their womanhood so that your company might prosper. It has been alleged that others gave their lives so you might prosper. And there stand behind them legions more who have been injured but who have not sought relief in the courts of this land. . . .

If one poor young man were, without authority or consent, to inflict such damage upon one woman, he would be jailed for a good portion of the rest of his life. Yet your company, without warning to women, invaded their bodies by the millions and caused them injuries by the thousands.

Edward Ross warned—in 1907—that the insistence on defining sin and misconduct in an industrial society in the same way as it was defined in the past was exacting a terrible price. He saw the absurdity of condemning what a man did in a bedroom but not what he did in a boardroom. Miles Lord repeated—in 1984—that we still haven't grasped that the man who assaults women from an office chair is as grave a sinner as the man who assaults a woman in an alley. Surely the time has come to extend the definition of immoral conduct into the boardroom and the corporate office. Ross said that the public "beholds sin in a false perspective, seeing peccadilloes as crimes, and crimes as peccadilloes." Heeding Ross's admonition, I try here to behold the Dalkon Shield catastrophe in a true perspective.

—MORTON MINTZ

Washington, D.C.
August 1985

At Any Cost

Introduction:
The Toll

In January 1971, the A. H. Robins Company began to sell the Dalkon Shield, promoting it as the "modern, superior," "second generation," and—most importantly—"safe" intrauterine device for birth control. Robins, a major pharmaceutical manufacturer in Richmond, Virginia, distributed 4.5 million of the IUDs in eighty countries before halting sales in the mid-1970s. There followed a catastrophe without precedent in the annals of medicine and law.

The seriously injured victims number in the tens of thousands. Nearly all suffered life-threatening forms of the infections known as pelvic inflammatory disease (PID).[1] In the United States alone, PID killed at least eighteen women who had been wearing Shields. Most of the infections impaired or destroyed the women's ability to bear children.

Not only was the Shield unsafe, it was surprisingly ineffective. The number of wearers who became pregnant with the devices in place was on the order of 110,000, or 5 percent—a rate nearly five times the one falsely claimed in advertising and promotion to physicians and women, and a rate sharply higher than that for many other IUDs.[2] More than ordinary commercial puffery, the exaggerated and bogus claims led women to reject more effective birth control in favor of the Shield; and this led directly to consequences far worse than unwanted pregnancies. Statistically, half of all women who become pregnant with an IUD miscarry. But in fact, of the estimated 110,000 women who conceived while wearing the Dalkon Shield, 66,000—or 60 percent—miscarried. Most suffered the previously rare miscarriages called *spontaneous abortions* in either the first or second trimester. Others, in the fourth to sixth months of pregnancy, experienced the still rarer infected miscarriages, or *septic spontaneous abortions.* By the count of the Food and Drug Administration, 248 women just in this country endured this dangerous, Shield-related complication; for 15 of them, these septic abortions were fatal.[3]

Moreover, hundreds of women throughout the world who conceived while wearing the Shield gave birth prematurely, in the final trimester, to children with grave congenital defects including blindness, cerebral palsy, and mental retardation, or that were stillborn. No one can pinpoint the exact number of such women, partly because no one knows how many times women or their doctors failed to make a proper connection between the Shield and the premature birth of a defective baby.

Robins distributed about 2.86 million Shields in the United States, and doctors implanted them, by the company's estimate, in 2.2 million women. Abroad, Robins distributed about 1.71 million Shields, and in June 1974 it estimated that 800,000 to one million were implanted.[4] The Agency for International Development (AID) bought more than 697,000 Shields for use in the Third World, slightly more than half of them for the International Planned Parenthood Federation and most of the rest for the Pathfinder Fund, the Population Council, and Family Planning International Assistance. AID said in a report in 1985 that nearly half of the Shields it had bought were returned unused to Robins and that a review of cables to the agency left the impression "that very few Dalkon Shield insertions were made." But whatever the precise numbers of Shield insertions in African, Asian, Middle Eastern, Caribbean, Latin American, and South American countries, poor medical conditions made lethal complications more likely. My guess is that Shield-related PID killed hundreds—possibly thousands—of women outside of the United States. Dr. Richard P. Dickey, a former member of the Food and Drug Administration's obstetrical and gynecological devices advisory panel, has seen at first hand the conditions faced by a woman who suffers PID. An infected Shield wearer, "where there are no doctors, no antibiotics, she's going to die," he told me.

In 1974, increasing numbers of Shield-related spontaneous septic abortions became known to the FDA, and the agency asked Robins to suspend Shield sales in the United States. It did so on June 28, 1974. After the sales suspension, the company retrieved unsold Shields from supply channels in this country. Plaintiffs' lawyer Dale I. Larson asked company chairman E. Claiborne Robins why this had been done. Because "it was the proper thing to do," the chairman swore. Larson, trying to find out if the retrieved devices may have been exported, asked if the Shields had been destroyed, and how and when—and why "the proper thing" had not also been done for less-developed countries—where product-liability lawsuits and adverse publicity about a defective product are rarities. To all such questions the chairman's answer was that he did not know.

In fact, after halting domestic sales, the company continued to distribute Shields abroad for as long as nine months—"at the request of . . . specific governments," Robins swore at a deposition in January 1984. Asked who had told him that, he replied, "I don't know that. It seems to me I saw a memo somewhere, but I don't remember when or where."

In El Salvador in 1975—a year after the suspension of Shield sales here—Martina Langley was a volunteer in a family-planning clinic. Now a lawyer in Austin, Texas, she recalls that the only IUD the clinic's doctors were inserting was the Shield, and that some clinics in El Salvador continued to implant Shields until 1980. "Sometimes the doctor would say to the patient, 'This is from the United States and it's very good,'" Langley told David Phelps, a Washington correspondent for the *Minneapolis Star and Tribune*. Then, she said, the doctor would motion toward her and tell the woman, "She is from the United States and people [there] use it."[5]

Today, more than a decade after Shield sales officially ended, its legacies of death, disease, injury, and pain persist. Even women who have had the Shield removed are not out of danger. Because

PID is not an affliction that is simply treated and is then over and done with, large numbers of former Dalkon Shield wearers suffer chronic pain and illness, sometimes requiring repeated hospitalization and surgery; many have waged desperate battles to bear children despite severe damage to their reproductive systems. More cheerless news came in April 1985 from two studies funded by the National Institutes of Health. They showed that childless IUD wearers who have had PID run a far higher risk of infertility if their devices were Shields than if they were other makes.[6] Not even women who currently wear the Shield with no apparent problem are safe: they run the risk of suddenly being stricken by PID. In the words of Judge Lord, they are wearing "a deadly depth charge in their wombs, ready to explode at any time."

The exact number of women still wearing the Shield is unknown. By early 1983, some Food and Drug Administration officials and OB-GYNs were confident that few American women, probably only hundreds, still used it. Other qualified observers, however, were estimating the figure to be much higher, anywhere from 80,000 to more than half a million. Certainly the response to Robins's own call-back campaign of October 1984 suggests that the higher figures are closer to the mark. By February 1, 1985, a $4-million advertising drive, which urged women still wearing the Shields to have them removed at Robins's expense, had drawn more than 16,000 phone calls on toll-free hotlines; by the end of March, 4,437 women had filed claims for Shield removals. The claims were flowing in at the dramatic rate of more than one hundred a week.

And what of women in the seventy-nine other countries where the Shield was distributed? The company told the FDA that it had notified first the countries' ambassadors in Washington and then their senior health officials at home of its Shield-removal campaign in the United States, and had "sought direction on whether a similar program would be appropriate in those countries." By early April 1985, Australia, Canada, and the United Kingdom had requested, and the company had put into effect, one or another kind of removal program. New Zealand, too, was considering a program. Sixteen other countries had simply acknowledged receipt of Robins's letter. Eight others—Denmark, Mexico, Norway, Pakistan,

the Philippines, South Africa, Tanzania, and Zambia—had declined any removal program. From the rest of the countries, of
which there were fifty-one, Robins had received no response almost a half-year after inviting one. If this record suggests indifference to the health and safety of women, at least a partial explanation may be found in the company's adamant refusal to admit to
the special dangers inherent in its device. "Robins believes that
serious scientific questions exist about whether the Dalkon Shield
poses a significantly different risk of infection than other IUDs,"
it said in an interim report to the FDA.

Another measure of the extent of the damage is provided by the
lawsuits and unlitigated claims filed by Shield wearers in the
United States. Nearly all of these women had suffered PID followed by damage to or loss of their ability to bear children. The
large majority had not been pregnant when stricken.[7] Through
June 30, 1985, by the company's own count, the total number of
cases was 14,330, and new ones were being filed at a rate of fifteen
a day. The company continues to experience a dramatic upsurge
in the number of new Shield claims, president E. Claiborne Robins, Jr., told the annual stockholders' meeting on May 30, 1985.
"I want to emphasize that the company anticipates that a substantial number of new claims will be filed in the future," he said.
Through June 30, 1985, Robins and its former Shield insurer,
Aetna Life & Casualty Company, had paid out $378.3 million to
dispose of cases, plus $107.3 million in legal expenses. Juries have
awarded $24.8 million in punitive or exemplary damages, which
are intended to punish wanton or reckless behavior and to deter
its repetition or emulation.

Still, no summary of suits and claims can come close to account-
ing for the total number of Shield injuries. By Robins's own
conservative estimate in April 1985, 4 percent of the wearers were
injured—that is, nearly 90,000 women in the United States alone.
Of course, only a fraction of these will file suit. It is conventional
wisdom among medical scientists that adverse reactions to drugs
are always grossly underreported, and this is surely true of Shield
injuries, too. Also, some Shield victims who stood to win substan-

tial damages chose not to sue, either because they wanted to put a horrifying experience behind them, or because they placed a higher value on avoiding public disclosure of a matter as private and sensitive as the impairment or destruction of their ability to bear children. Other victims did not know or had forgotten the makes of their IUDs, as confirmed by Robins in its report to the FDA. By January 17, 1985, it said, 3,939 calls had come in on its special phone lines "from women presently wearing an IUD but of unknown type."

Furthermore, some of the women who might have sought compensation were certainly intimidated by Robins's brutal invasions of privacy and courtroom techniques. Judge Lord charged:

> When the time came for these women to make their claims against your company, you attacked their characters. You inquired into their sexual practices and into the identity of their sex partners. You exposed these women—and ruined families and reputations and careers—in order to intimidate those who would raise their voices against you. You introduced issues that had no relationship whatsoever to the fact that you planted in the bodies of these women instruments of death, of mutilation, of disease.

Again, if the claims against Robins in the United States represent only a fraction of the incidence of injury, they represent an even smaller fraction worldwide, since figures are simply unavailable from most of the countries where the Shield was used.

But even the true number of injuries is an inadequate measure of the harm done. Behind the statistics, court judgments, and sums are the stories of the women themselves, and how they suffered. Here I relate just a few of the many I have heard. Unfortunately, the experiences they describe are all too common.

Peggy J. Mample, thirty-two years old when I interviewed her in February 1985, conceived while wearing a Dalkon Shield, and gave birth prematurely, in the third trimester, to a child with a grave birth defect. Mrs. Mample was nineteen when she had

Melissa, who has cerebral palsy and will be in a wheelchair for life. "Melissa is very intelligent," she told me. "Her only disability is that she can't walk." At home, the child moves about by crawling, but she attends regular classes in a public elementary school.

Peggy Mample is among the hundreds of women who were themselves physically unharmed, or not seriously harmed, by the Shield while, unknown to them, it seriously injured their unborn children. She learned she was pregnant in February 1972. At the time, the medical profession was divided as to the wisdom of removing an IUD from a pregnant woman, and her obstetrician was among the physicians who believed the odds were fifty-fifty that removal of the Shield would induce a miscarriage. Also at that time, the Robins Company, which had made no studies of the IUD's potential to induce premature births, or of the possible consequences of such births, was making a soothing promotional claim that it would abandon two years later. As the fetus grew, it claimed, the Dalkon Shield would be "pushed gently aside" and no harm would befall either the fetus or the mother. The obstetrician's advice was to leave the Shield in place and go to term, and Mrs. Mample agreed. She then gave birth—prematurely, as was noted—to Melissa on July 22, 1972.

She had no basis for suspecting the Shield until almost nine years later. On April 19, 1981, when Mrs. Mample was living in Seattle, the CBS investigative news program "60 Minutes" did a segment on "the disaster of the Dalkon Shield." A friend who saw the television program phoned to tell her about it and to ask if the IUD she had worn was a Shield. This led her to consult a lawyer, and, shortly, to sue Robins. Under Washington State law, which does not permit punitive awards, she sued for compensatory damages to redress, insofar as money can, the harm done to her by the misrepresentations of Shield efficacy that led her to bear a cerebral-palsied child. In the same lawsuit, she also sought separate compensatory damages for Melissa.

About two-thirds of the way through the jury trial, Robins offered to settle Melissa's case for $1.4 million. Mrs. Mample turned down the offer, but, anxious to assure that money sufficient for her daughter's lifetime care would be provided, she reached an agreement with Robins that a jury verdict for the child, should one be returned, would not be appealed, while the sum of money fixed by the jury would be forever sealed.

The Mamples' lawyers, Jane I. Fantel and John J. Davids, argued to the jury that the cerebral palsy was the ultimate result of Robins's false effectiveness claims, of its failure to do studies on the Shield's potential to cause premature births, and of its related failure to investigate the consequences of such births. Checking around the country before and during the trial, Fantel and Davids found thirty more Shield wearers' children who had been born prematurely in the third trimester with major congenital defects. They told me that Robins initially resisted their demands for data on such children, but finally confirmed the number. Actually, according to trial testimony by Dr. David A. Eschenbach of the University of Washington, an expert on the adverse effects of IUDs, the true total of such children in the United States was two to three hundred.

The jury awarded damages to Mrs. Mample, but nothing to Melissa, holding that a casual relation had not been established between the Shield and her premature birth and cerebral palsy. Mrs. Mample then filed a new lawsuit for damages for Melissa. In June 1984, when Melissa was almost twelve, a second jury awarded her damages. Although the sum is secret, it was well over the rejected $1.4 million offer.

Peggy Mample now lives in Boise, Idaho, where she runs a cabinet shop. Her life is more settled now, but she is still enraged when speaking about the company. "I just think it's absolutely incredible that a large corporation can do this to the American public, using us as guinea pigs," she says. "Needless to say—I don't buy Robins's products anymore. I just experienced so many emotions, the anger, the shock, of knowing what large corporations —what *this* corporation—did to my child . . . it's absolutely incredible that the American public puts up with it, that they don't do something about it."

Joan Smith is among the millions of Americans who believe that abortion is murder. For a woman who holds this belief, becoming pregnant with an IUD in place could have shattering psychological consequences even if it inflicts no physical harm on her.

Joan agreed to tell me her story on the condition that I withhold her real name. We talked in March 1985, when she was forty. Her husband is a law enforcement officer. They live in the upper Midwest with their five children, who range in age from twelve to nineteen. The story began in 1974, when they decided they did not want a sixth child. As practicing Catholics, Joan and her husband gave the birth-control issue serious consideration. She recalled reading about the Dalkon Shield in a women's magazine and being impressed with the claims for its effectiveness and safety. "I decided on the Shield because it was a once-to-the-doctor thing, and I just felt with the Pill that if I had to take [it] every day, I just wouldn't do it."

Joan was fitted with a Shield in 1974 and became pregnant— without knowing it—several months later. That she was unaware of her pregnancy "sounds so foolish," she said, but although her five previous pregnancies had been "very healthy, normal," what she felt this time was a "terrible burning in my gut." She went to the general practitioner who had cared for her in her previous pregnancies and whom she continues to praise. He gave her a pregnancy test. When he told her the results, "the whole bottom dropped out of my world. I knew that they were correct, but I still didn't think that would happen."

Her physician told her she had to have an abortion, explaining that the Shield had to be removed but that removal would imperil the baby because of its proximity to the device. She recalled him saying, "If you don't have this removed, it will perforate your uterus. You will die." Another doctor, his younger colleague, said that, yes, the IUD had to come out, but "we can try to save the baby."

Joan talked the situation over only with her husband. "We thought we had no other option," she said. "The way the doctors made it seem is, if I didn't have this [surgery], either the IUD would perforate the uterus, or perforate the fetus, and I remember the [older] doctor saying I could possibly get peritonitis; and I remember him saying, 'You don't want to leave five children without a mother, do you?' . . . He is an excellent doctor, and I know he had to say those things." After talking with her husband, she went back to the doctors to tell them, "Well, if you do everything that you can to save the fetus, I'll come; otherwise I won't."

She was certain that they would be (and is certain that they were) "very careful."

I asked her why, having resorted to contraception, she wanted so much to have the baby. "I'm very opposed to abortion," she said. "It's always a baby. It just is always human life. It is not a 'nothing,' as far as I am concerned. It doesn't have to move within you, or whatever, before it becomes a baby."

On a February morning in 1975, after her children had gone off to school, Joan Smith went to a hospital to have her Dalkon Shield removed. "I'm sure I knew in my heart what the outcome would be," she said. "But I couldn't go in, I don't think, knowing what was going to happen. I had to think maybe they could just remove the IUD and I could have my baby." She was in her first trimester.

She was given a general anesthetic. When she awoke in the recovery room, she asked the nurse what happened to the baby, but was put off. What had happened was that the Shield came out with placenta tissue clinging to it. Later, when she saw her physician, he told her that they "had to take everything, they had to take the fetus."

Joan was out of the hospital before the children were out of school. But she was devastated. "I felt terrible about myself. I felt I had done a terrible, unforgivable thing. I felt that I had murdered a child. . . . And I was so ashamed of what I had done that I didn't ever want to tell anybody. . . . My mother does not know about this. My sister, my four younger children do not know. . . . I guess I felt it was between me and God, and I had to work it out eventually between me and God."

For years afterward, Joan had suicidal thoughts and marital problems:

> We had virtually no intimate relationships for an awfully long time, because anything would remind me of what had happened. I had terrible recurring dreams, nightmares. I used to dream I would be in surgery, but I would be the patient, and I would be the physician, and I would be the anesthesiologist, and I would be absolutely all of them. And it wasn't the fetus I was aborting, it would be my children.
>
> I couldn't get away from it. . . . It was always there. . . .

I kept trying not to think about it, but it was always there. For several years, if I saw a pregnant lady walking down the street, I'd cross the street. I still don't pick up anybody's baby. . . . I guess I'm not really over it. . . . A person sometimes punishes herself more than God would, but it took a long time to figure this out.

In 1984, Joan Smith became one of 198 women who jointly received a record settlement of $38 million. Among them were eleven whose children had major birth defects, including hydrocephalus, and two whose children were stillborn. Joan said she had become a litigant "feeling I didn't care about any amount of dollars. I felt that the A. H. Robins Company knew what they were doing to these women. They knew. I wouldn't care if I hadn't gotten two cents out of it, if the publicity would make people realize what a crummy company that is." Only after the settlement was reached did Joan reveal her experience to someone other than her husband. She told her nineteen-year-old daughter "because I feel she will have to make adult decisions in her lifetime, and I don't want her ever to use an IUD."

Mary Beth Kornhauser is a screenwriter in West Hollywood, California, who was thirty-one when I interviewed her in December 1984. In its essentials, her story is similar to that of countless other women whose quest for safe and effective birth control led them to trust their physicians, who in turn trusted the manufacturer.

Mary was first fitted with a Shield in February 1972, when she was eighteen. She began having dangerous, extremely painful, and recurring pelvic infections within a few months. From the start, her misfortune was compounded by physicians whose incompetent diagnoses, such as that she was experiencing a nervous breakdown, destroyed her chances for a full and swift recovery. In October 1972, one of them pronounced her seriously infected and removed her Shield; he did not properly treat the infection, and intimated that she had gotten it because of a promiscuous life-style. After seven terrible years of misdiagnosis and illness she was finally deprived of her ability ever to bear a child. Here is her description of the events directly preceding the "total hysterectomy" she suffered at age twenty-five.

In 1978, I started getting sick cramps, vomiting, high fever, the same spells that had come up periodically. I went to a doctor, and he gave me oral antibiotics, which didn't work. So I went back to the University of California at Los Angeles Medical Center, where a doctor recommended me to . . . Dr. Charles E. Hamrell in Santa Monica, and he immediately put me in the hospital. I was very infected with tubo-ovarian abscesses, one the size of a grapefruit, one the size of an orange. I was apparently about ready to explode. To try to control the infection to prevent it from spilling into the abdominal cavity, Dr. Hamrell put me in Santa Monica Hospital for serious intravenous antibiotic therapy—by which I mean that three different antibiotics were pumped into me, one each hour.

After eight days in the hospital, Mary returned to her apartment, sensing that she was having only a reprieve: Hamrell had prepared her for the possibility of a radical hysterectomy. She took antibiotics orally and was cared for by her sister, who flew in from the Midwest, and her mother, who came from Maryland. Two weeks later, Hamrell had to operate. It was February 15, 1979—one day less than seven years after her Dalkon Shield had been inserted.

After surgery, Mary needed hormone-replacement therapy to offset the loss of hormones normally produced by the ovaries. The therapy has side effects, one of which is wild mood swings. "One of the problems," Mary said, "is the lack of research on the effects of this on young women. The first pill they had me on, I was way up and then way down, very quickly." Still, she was free of infection, and her good health returned. "Now when I catch a minor flu, I don't have to worry about my ending up in the hospital, because it really is flu."

Mary filed suit in November 1979. When her lawyer, John T. Baker, prepared a "statement of facts," she said,

it read like Watergate, except that this was my life. You know, charges such as reckless disregard of truth, fraud. The reality of seeing this in print—it was staggering. But the real truth was that what they did was criminal, and that criminal charges should have been brought against the persons responsible. . . .

That there was a conspiracy by Robins executives to hide
the truth is what got me. The fact that Americans, especially
in pharmaceutical companies, would so knowingly ravage
women, and get away with it, was staggering. . . . You'd think
that when people deal in pharmaceutical medicine, they'd be
honorable people. . . .

It's worse than abortion. They took away the right of someone to decide to have children. Losing the ability to choose
whether I wanted a family—that was the hardest thing for me
to get over.

Robins sent her pretrial interrogatories, but did not move to take
her deposition. "They went right to trying to settle, because, I
believe, I had a strong case," she said. At the same time, Mary said
she did not want to go to trial. She found herself unable to bear
the prospect of litigating for two to five more years,

never to able to put the pain behind me, wondering when I
would have to completely relive the experience in a trial
situation. . . . I had had enough pain caused by them. . . .

A lot of things had been blown apart by the hysterectomy;
it was an intensely painful period in my life. I was not emotionally stable because of it and its ramifications. I had lost
ten pounds in two days. I wanted to heal myself and I knew
I couldn't if I had to dredge everything up. I had already
waited two years for the setting of a trial date. Money's fine,
but were they going to give me my ovaries back? Like, yes,
Your Honor, ladies and gentlemen of the jury, are you going
to give me a boy child and a girl child? Maybe for that I would
have waited for trial.

In February 1982, Mary settled out of court.

These women and the ones below express the anger of many
other Shield victims toward the company, toward the absence of
personal accountability in a corporation that has inflicted such
massive physical and mental harm, and about the impossibility of

cash being adequate compensation for the loss of the ability to have children.

Lynn W. Schaeffer of Baltimore was fitted with a Shield in 1973, when she was twenty-one, but had it removed after six months of unrelenting pain. Although she did not know it for some time, the device left her with a pelvic infection. She tried but failed to conceive, sought help in an infertility clinic, had corrective surgery followed by a perilous ectopic pregnancy, and had surgery again. Still the pain persisted. Finally, in July 1979, six years after getting the Shield, she "opted for health"—at the cost of a total hysterectomy. "It ends all hope," she told me. "Hope dies hard."

She blames Robins for her "irreparable" injury. "They were dishonest, and people like me have to pay for it. I'm very angry about that, and I'll be angry forever."

Susan Herman teaches emotionally disturbed children in Chicago. She received a Shield in 1972, when she was twenty-three, had what was found to be a tubal pregnancy in which the embryo burst the tube, and ended up with perhaps a 15-percent chance of ever being able to bear a child. "You see other women with their children, and it's a whole loaded thing," she says. "I think the top people who did this ought to be put in jail. They have killed women because they would not come out in the open and say their product wasn't safe."

Carole Mansfield of Minneapolis is a vocalist and percussionist in a rock band. She was fitted with a Shield in 1973 and had no problems until 1981, when she was thirty-one. Stricken by a sudden pelvic infection that she did not initially relate to the Shield, she was found to have a grapefruit-sized tubo-ovarian abscess, and almost died. At the trial of her lawsuit, Robins's attorneys "constantly referred to the fact that I am in a rock band," she said. "The lawyers showed the jury our album covers and read lyrics. But the jury just laughed and the 'sex, drugs, and rock 'n' roll' legal tactic didn't work."[8]

She and her husband had planned someday to have a child, but never will because "all of my organs are glued together by scar tissue." At the trial the Robins attorneys "made a big point that I had been married for a long time and was on birth control, so it just didn't matter . . . but they had no right to play God. . . ."

Carole told me in April 1985 that she felt "violated. I'm just not the same person that I was or could have been." Does the Shield episode teach a lesson? I asked. "I think maybe it brings to light the amount of corporate irresponsibility out there that none of us is aware of," she said. "I don't really believe that A. H. Robins is the only company that markets products that are unsafe for human use."

The anger of these women has been fueled by Robins's consistent stonewalling and professions of innocence and ignorance. In the face of several thousand settlements, multimillion-dollar court awards of punitive damages, and its own Shield-removal campaign, the claims of innocent ignorance seem incredible, but they persist. At a series of depositions taken in 1984 by plaintiffs' lawyer Dale Larson, E. Claiborne Robins swore that he was unable to recall ever having discussed the Shield with his son, E. Claiborne Robins, Jr., the chief executive officer and president. "You certainly knew, when you started marketing this device, that pelvic inflammatory disease was a life-threatening disease, did you not?" Larson asked. "I don't know that," Robins testified. "I have never thought of it as life-threatening." Did he know it could destroy fertility? "Maybe I should, but I don't know that," he swore. "I have heard that," he added. "I am not sure where."

Ernest L. Bender, Jr., senior vice-president for corporate planning and development, was not about to be outdone in embracing ignorance, denying faint stirrings of curiosity, or disclaiming sensitivity to human suffering. He reports to the younger Robins, but swore, "I've had no conversations with him about the Dalkon Shield." Had he ever asked anyone whether the Shield was "safe or unsafe?" "I've never had any reason to." Had he ever heard of a Robins officer or employee asking how many Shield users had suffered from PID? "No. I recall no such questions being asked."

Did the thousands of Shield lawsuits and claims make Bender "wonder at all . . . whether there might be something wrong with the device?" Larson asked. "No, it doesn't make me wonder," Bender testified. "I have no reason to believe that there is anything wrong with the device." "Have you ever . . . asked anybody, 'Gee, why aren't we marketing the Dalkon Shield anymore?'" "I've never asked any questions in that regard."

Had Bender ever heard an officer or employee say he or she was "sorry or remorseful about any infection that's been suffered by any Dalkon Shield wearer . . .?" His reply was, "I've never heard anyone make such remarks because I've never heard anyone that said that the Dalkon Shield was the cause."

Larson drew similar answers from Carl D. Lunsford. Since 1978, when he became senior vice-president for research and development, he has been in charge of the company's medical department and thus the highest-ranking executive with specific jurisdiction over the Shield's safety. He is a chemist whose involvements with the Shield date back to the premarketing year of 1970.

Dr. Lunsford swore he recalled no "expressions of concern" by any company official about PID, and did not remember having "personally wondered" about the toll it was taking. He had not tried to find out how many users died. He had not "personally reviewed" any studies of the Shield's safety or effectiveness in preventing conception. Did he have "any curiosity" about why the company, a few months before, had paid $4.6 million, most of it in punitive damages, to settle seven Shield lawsuits? The answer was no.

Lunsford is a role model of sorts for a high-ranking subordinate, Fletcher B. Owen, Jr., assistant vice-president for medical services. By August 1984, when he testified at a proceeding in U.S. District Court in Minneapolis, Dr. Owen had for a decade been responsible for monitoring the safety of the Shields in the large numbers of women who continued to wear them. This responsibility did not get his full-time attention; he testified that he had been spending nearly all of his time on Shield litigation, saying he had testified at some eighty depositions and at about eighteen trials.

Larson asked Lunsford, "You never even asked Dr. Owen how many women were injured by the device, correct?" The answer was, "I don't recall asking that question, no, sir." That it would have been pointless for Lunsford to ask is a possibility raised by Owen's testimony. He said he had never inserted an IUD and had done "at least one pelvic examination. I don't recall exactly the circumstances." He also said that if on that day the Shield were on the market, he would have "no hesitancy whatsoever" in recommending it to a physician without disclosure of the design characteristics that have been isolated as the causes of PID. He swore that "I wouldn't have any reason" to tell a physician of the thousands of lawsuits that blamed potentially and actually fatal PID on the Shield.

In February 1977, very few of the several hundred thousand American women then believed to be wearing the Shield had the faintest notion that the devices were putting them at graver risk with each passing day. But Bradley Post, a leading plaintiffs' lawyer, did know of the danger, and he wrote a letter to the company. He asked that Robins mail a corrective "Dear Doctor" letter, partly to urge "immediate removal of devices in use." Upon receiving no response, Post sent a second letter. He wrote that he had just learned of the deaths of two young women, that the circumstances were clearly causally related to their Shields, and that he was concerned about how many more fatalities and serious injuries would have to occur before Robins would take preventive action. No response came to this plea, either.

Four years later, a sequence of deaths began to be reported among long-time Shield users who were *not* pregnant. The first, in November 1981, was a woman in Los Angeles; the second, in April 1983, was Eugenie Standeford, thirty-four, of New Orleans.[9] Ten months later, on February 29, 1984, Judge Lord pleaded for a recall in his now-famous courtroom reprimand to three senior company officers. He told Claiborne Robins, Jr., the CEO; Carl Lunsford, the senior vice-president; and William A. Forrest, Jr., vice-president and general counsel, that

> the only conceivable reasons you have not recalled this prod-
> uct are that it would hurt your balance sheet and alert women
> who already have been harmed that you may be liable for
> their injuries. . . .
>
> If this were a case in equity, I would order that your
> company make an effort to locate each and every person who
> still wears this device and recall your product. But this court
> does not have the power to do so. I must therefore resort to
> moral persuasion and a personal appeal to each of you.

. . . You are the people with the power to recall. You are the corporate conscience. Please in the name of humanity lift your eyes above the bottom line. . . . Please, gentlemen, give consideration to tracing down the victims and sparing them the agony that will surely be theirs.[10]

Robins contended, however, that no campaign was needed, because the Shield was no more hazardous than rival IUDs.

Eighteen days after Judge Lord's appeal, Christa Berlin, forty-one, was admitted to the Los Angeles County–University of Southern California Medical Center with lower abdominal pain and fever. The diagnosis indicated a pelvic abscess. Antibiotics in high doses were injected into her, but her condition worsened, requiring drastic surgery including a hysterectomy. After the operation she improved for a time, only to deteriorate again. "Despite intensive care and cardiorespiratory support," said Dr. Charles M. March, the chief gynecologist, in a letter to the company, "she expired on the eighteenth postoperative day." He pointed out that Mrs. Berlin had worn a Shield for many years.[11]

In October 1984, six months after Mrs. Berlin died, Robins finally announced a recall campaign. Surely it is reasonable to suggest that Eugenie Standeford, Christa Berlin, and other women might not have died, and that thousands of other women would not have suffered pain and agony, if Robins had acted earlier. But Robins consistently claimed—and continues to claim—that the Dalkon Shield was safe and effective when "properly used." Robins executives insist that they did not know of any special hazard. But they did know, and they chose to do nothing—until it was much too late.

II

The Road to Richmond

The regimen I adopt shall be for the benefit of my
patients according to my ability and judgment, and not for
their hurt or for any wrong.

—*from the Hippocratic Oath*

1

Hugh J. Davis, M.D.

FATHER OF THE DALKON SHIELD

In the Dalkon Shield story, first one person and then another, and then yet another, became a pivotal, even a transcendent figure. Much or everything depended upon whether any in a succession of actors would avert or limit the disaster, tell the truth or a lie, do the right thing or the wrong thing, put on or take off a black hat. Up to, but not after, May 1970, when the A. H. Robins Company came on stage, Hugh Davis was *the* central character.

Dr. Hugh J. Davis was graduated in 1949 from the University of Georgia and in 1953 from the Johns Hopkins University School of Medicine in Baltimore. At Johns Hopkins he interned, trained in obstetrics and gynecology, and climbed the academic ladder— instructor, assistant professor, associate professor. Eventually he became Director of Family Planning Services, Associate Profesor of OB-GYN, and Associate Professor of International Health, Population, and Family Health in the School of Hygiene and Public Health. Despite these credentials, Hopkins never granted him tenure, and the American College of Obstetrics and Gynecology never certified him as an OB-GYN. He has said that his interests lay elsewhere, in research and inventions. Fluent in Spanish, he was a consultant, mainly on birth control, to several Latin American countries, as well as to the health departments of Maryland and the District of Columbia. In 1961, during a research fellowship in

Copenhagen, he invented a simple, inexpensive test for cervical cancer that came to be used internationally.

Davis returned from Denmark in 1962, in a revolutionary new era of birth control. Enovid, the first oral contraceptive, had won Food and Drug Administration approval in 1960. Women and the medical profession were almost unreservedly enthusiastic about the Pill (an umbrella phrase for all makes of oral contraceptives); it arrived at a time of general relaxation of sexual mores, when there was widespread faith in the notion that science and technology were taking us always onward and upward, and growing concern about the population explosion. The success of the Pill owed much to the lack of curiosity among most prescribing physicians about the adequacy of the data on which claims of safety were based, and to false and misleading promotion by manufacturers.

In 1962, however, a Senate subcommittee headed by the late Hubert H. Humphrey did what the medical profession had not done: it investigated the foundation of the FDA's approval of Enovid, and made some startling, deeply troubling discoveries. The most important, published in early 1963, was that the "entire series of clinical cases," the basis for the agency's conclusion that Enovid was safe, rested on too small a sample and too short a test period—absurdly small and short, considering that each of tens of millions of women would come to use the powerful birth-control hormones continually, for as long as the three decades of her childbearing years. The sample consisted of 132 women who took Enovid in as few as twelve but no more than thirty-eight consecutive menstrual cycles. The press, at the time still in love with the Pill, paid little heed to the subcommittee's finding.[1]

Indeed, the Pill's undoubted efficacy probably built emotional resistance among physicians and women to the doubts about its safety that should have arisen from a series of carefully researched and highly disturbing studies. An example was a pioneering report published in the spring of 1967, in which the British Medical Research Council concluded that there "can be no reasonable doubt that some types of thromboembolic disorder are associated with the use of oral contraceptives."[2]

In this highly volatile period, in which doubts were forming about the Pill even while its popularity was soaring, Hugh Davis came back to Johns Hopkins as an OB-GYN instructor and began to design and experiment with intrauterine devices.

IUDs are among the most ancient forms of contraception, known for more than two thousand years. Exactly how an IUD prevents conception isn't certain. It may interfere with fertilization of the egg, but more often exerts its contraceptive effect on a uterine pregnancy. In animals, foreign bodies in the womb have prevented pregnancy. For centuries, according to an FDA report, "Arabs and Turks inserted small stones through hollow tubes into the uteri of camels before crossing the desert to prevent pregnancy."[3] For women, "materials used in their fabrication included ebony, glass, gold, ivory, pewter, wood, wool, and diamond-studded platinum."

This is not the place to dwell upon the usually ghastly results of primitive IUD designs and materials. Suffice it to say that IUDs acquired a bad reputation and were rarely used or recommended by physicians. In 1909 and again in 1923, reports in medical literature on ring-shaped IUDs made of silkworm gut caused a flurry of interest in these devices, but it soon abated, apparently because of unacceptably high rates of pelvic infection or pelvic inflammatory disease.[4]

Dr. Ernst Grafenberg of Berlin then invented a ring IUD made of silver wire and reported in 1930 that its failure rate in two thousand insertions was only 1.6 percent. The "silver ring," as it came to be known, had a run of popularity and won a reputation —with some doctors—of being harmless. But in 1936, Dr. Howard C. Clark, an obstetrician and gynecologist in Wichita, Kansas, treated a twenty-six-year-old woman who had a severe pelvic infection of undetermined origin; an X ray "showed a metal ring in the pelvis." Clark then searched through the medical literature on the silver ring. One physician had reported seventeen deaths from perforation of the uterus. Two others had found "several cases of damage to the embryo resulting in deformed children, due to the occurrence of pregnancy while the [device] was in the uterus." Another looked into the consequences of ninety-two pregnancies in ring wearers and found seventy-eight miscarriages. Citing still other reports, Clark concluded that the ring and all other IUDs of the day were "unphysiologic, unreliable and dangerous to life."[5]

Clark's condemnation of IUDs came to be widely shared: in 1943, in a standard reference work on gynecology;[6] in 1953, by the American Medical Association's Council on Physical Medicine and Rehabilitation; and in 1957, by 128 of the 129 Diplomates of the American Board of Obstetrics and Gynecology who responded to a Food and Drug Administration questionnaire (101 opposed continued distribution; 18 opposed use of the devices but said that "under certain qualifying circumstances they could be legitimately used"; only one said "unqualifiedly that he considered them to be safe and efficacious").[7]

For nearly three decades after Grafenberg's reports, according to an FDA study, IUDs were in such ill favor in the United States (although not in certain other countries, particularly Japan and Taiwan) that they "ceased to be used."[8] Then, in 1959, Dr. William Oppenheimer reported low failure rates and a lack of serious side effects in extensive experience with two IUDs, the Grafenberg and the Japanese Ota Ring, which was invented by Tenrei Takeo Ota, and which was tried in 20,000 women. Dr. Oppenheimer's report, and another by Atsumi Ishihama on the Ota device, reopened intrauterine contraception for exploration not only because of the results they reported, but also because of two accompanying technological advances. One was the discovery of new, malleable, inert plastics from which IUDs could be made (the Ota was made of polyethylene), and could, in the molding process, be given a "memory" of an intended shape. The other advance was the development of new, small-diameter inserters for plastic IUDs. In addition to these advances, antibiotic therapy for infection had by then been available for many years.

Now the way was open for a whole new wave of IUDs.[9] For example, two new plastic IUDs were patented in 1966—the Lippes Loop and the Saf-T-Coil. The Lippes Loop is also called the Intrauterine Double-S, because it resembles one S joined to and stacked above another. A pair of doctors, A. P. Satterthwaite and Jack Lippes, made the first report on its safety and efficacy in 1962, at a conference in New York City sponsored by the Population Council. The Saf-T-Coil has a stem that splits at the top into two loops of dissimilar configurations; the left one also enlarges at its end,

The Dalkon Shield on its inserter.

more or less like the bulb of an oral fever thermometer. The inventor was Dr. Ralph Robinson.

In 1964, Hugh Davis and his co-worker, Edmund Jones, developed the Incon (intrauterine contraceptive) Ring, a plastic IUD shaped like a wedding band. They applied jointly for a patent, but Davis assigned his rights to Johns Hopkins, while Jones sold his to the Ortho Pharmaceutical Corporation. By 1966, an estimated three thousand Baltimore-area women had been fitted with the Incon. But the device acquired an undesirable reputation after a woman wearing one suffered a perforated uterus and a herniated intestine, and the expulsion rate proved to be very high. Ortho chose not to market the Incon.

During this period, Davis met Irwin S. Lerner of Stamford, Connecticut, an electrical engineer who worked for a hospital-laboratories supply firm. They and their wives became close friends. In 1964, encouraged by Davis, Lerner left his job to join Robert E. Cohn of Hartford, his attorney and friend, in forming Lerner Laboratories. About a year later, Davis acquired a 5-percent interest in the venture. Its first product was a lab chemical on which the patent was issued jointly to Davis and Lerner.

Meanwhile, Davis had continued to experiment, and in 1967 he patented a new IUD. In shape it resembled a policeman's badge, which is why it came to be called a "shield." After it was patented in 1967, the device was modified to include ten blunted lateral fins or claws that attach to the uterus so as to lower the possibility of accidental expulsion of the device, a common IUD problem. This dime-sized, crablike plastic device was the Dalkon Shield.

At Christmastime in 1967, Davis showed the designs for his patented shield-shaped IUD to Lerner. Davis suggested to Lerner that he try to improve it. It was Lerner who added the five fins on either side. "I gave advice when it was asked for," Lerner has testified. "I guess I was flattered that Dr. Davis felt I could make a contribution in this area." He also said that Davis "thought that perhaps with a fresh look from an engineering point of view, one might achieve a new approach to the problem of good IUD design."

The collaboration led to an agreement, signed on June 10, 1968, under which Lerner Laboratories would sell the "footed" Shield and pay Davis 5 percent of the net sales price as a fee for consulting and for the provision of clinical testing facilities by Johns Hopkins. A patent was applied for in November 1968.

In the patent application, Lerner listed himself as the inventor, without any mention of Davis. He and Davis have both sworn that Lerner, the engineer, was the true inventor of the medical device and that Davis, the inventive physician who had previously patented an IUD, was the true developer. If that were not true, a fraud would have been committed on the Patent Office and the patent would have been invalidated.[10] At a stroke, in any case, a patent in Lerner's name released Davis, at least formally, from the ethical obligation he would have had as inventor to share with Johns Hopkins any profits from sales of the device. The profits went entirely to Lerner Laboratories, the venture owned by Lerner, Cohn, and Davis.[11]

In January 1969, Lerner Laboratories became Dalkon Corporation, with Davis increasing his original ownership share sevenfold, to 35 percent. The new name Dalkon—which suggests a synthesis of the names of the three company owners—celebrated the new partnership. Although Davis has denied this derivation of the Dalkon name under oath, he apparently did not suggest a different explanation.

The Dalkon Shield's principal enticement was the claim that it was almost 100 percent effective and safe. In the late 1960s, the increasing numbers of women concerned about the Pill's safety formed an ever-growing potential market for alternatives. Many switched to, or tried for the first time, older "barrier" methods of undisputed safety, particularly the diaphragm, which, when properly used with spermicidal cream or jelly, is highly effective, although inconvenient. Others turned to IUDs, which, though marvelously convenient, had previously been considered unsafe—causing pelvic infections as well as minor complications such as irregular bleeding, uterine cramps, and accidental expulsion.

The FDA's Advisory Committee on Obstetrics and Gynecology, in a report on IUDs in January 1968, said that large numbers of wearers were suffering painful and sometimes lethal infections and injuries. The committee emphasized that although some of this harm was attributable to problems inherent in the process of intrauterine contraception, much of it was attributable to the marketing of IUDs of needlessly dangerous design, and to the fact that "most devices are packaged without adequate instructions for use, and many are not marketed in sterile packages and with disposable introducers." In turn, the report said, women had no protection from the unsafe designs or nonsterile packages because Congress had yet to enact legislation to regulate any medical devices, as it had regulated drugs that served the same purpose.[12]

For Hugh Davis, the implications of all of this were clear and urgent. If the Dalkon Shield was to become an effective challenger to the commercial primacy of the Pill, he would have to mount offensives on several fronts. He would have to convince physicians (though not necessarily demonstrate to them) that the Shield was at least the equal of the Pill. He would have to convince them, too, that his IUD was significantly superior to others, such as the Lippes Loop and the Saf-T-Coil. He would have to show that the Shield was safer or at least no less safe, that it was better designed, and that it afforded enhanced retention, i.e., greater resistance to inadvertent expulsion from the womb. First and most important, however, he would have to persuade them that the Shield was as effective as oral contraceptives, and markedly more effective than other IUDs, in preventing pregnancy. If he could not do that, he would fail, and none of the rest would matter very much.

Davis was almost unimaginably successful in convincing large numbers of physicians that the Shield was uniquely effective. The principal vehicle of persuasion was an article he published in the "Current Investigation" section of the *American Journal of Obstetrics and Gynecology* on February 1, 1970. The headlines were "The shield intrauterine device / A superior modern contraceptive device." The short text described a study conducted at the Johns Hopkins family planning clinic of 640 women who had worn the Shield for one year, and provided a table of data on "experience with shield device at Johns Hopkins for 1968–69." Davis cited five pregnancies, ten expulsions, nine removals for medical reasons, and three removals for personal reasons. His data analysis covered 3,549 woman-months of experience. But the grabber, the claim that made the device all but irresistible, appeared in the second line of the table: "Pregnancy rate, 1.1 percent."

If only 1.1 percent of the 640 women who had used the Dalkon Shield for one year had conceived, then Davis surely had something to boast about. As he pointed out, the FDA-recognized pregnancy rate for the standard oral contraceptives, which combined an estrogen with a progestogen, was 0.7 percent per year, only one-third less. For the so-called sequential versions the rate was 1.4 percent, meaning they were inferior to his IUD by a quarter.[13] For the widely sold Lippes Loop IUD it was 2.7 percent, a failure rate more than twice the Shield's. Davis went on to embellish his facts in much the same way as would an advertising copywriter. He emphasized certain words and phrases (italicized below) that had unmistakable sales appeal and that would become constant themes of the subsequent advertising and promotional campaigns of the A. H. Robins Company, which reprinted no fewer than 199,000 copies of the Davis article for distribution to physicians.[14]

Davis's report had as its first target the sequential oral contraceptives: "Pregnancy rates have been reduced with these *modern* devices to levels superior to the sequential oral contraceptives and only slightly inferior to the protection offered by combined oral contraception." He said that at Johns Hopkins, trials of IUDs "in more than five thousand women" since 1963 had led to "constant improvements" and "to the development of *modern devices of superior performance*. Recent experience with a shield design approaches *the ideal* of combining very low pregnancy rates with minimal side effects. These *modern* devices are demonstrating such *excellence* as to justify a revision of current attitudes toward the efficacy of intrauterine devices." Davis went on to elaborate on the special advantages of the Dalkon Shield:

> Relative to the generally available plastic IUDs, the shield is less bulky, simple to insert and *exceptionally well tolerated.* In our experience, both the protection against pregnancy (99 percent) and the tolerance (96 percent) achieved by this *modern* shield type of IUD is superior to sequential oral contraceptives. . . . Effective protection against pregnancy is achieved with a *modern* IUD without the actual and potential hazards of systemic medication for birth control. Taken altogether, the *superior* performance of the shield intrauterine devices makes this technic *a first choice method* of conception control.

Nowhere in his article did Hugh Davis disclose that he was, and had been for thirteen months, part owner of the Dalkon Corporation and consequently had a clear conflict of interest. Indeed, so crucial was secrecy about his financial stake that he did not so much as acknowledge the *existence* of the company; instead, his first mention of the Dalkon Shield referred the reader to "Dalkon Shield, 341 Shore Road, Greenwich, Connecticut 06830"—the address of the Dalkon Corporation.

Davis's substantive claims were equally questionable. His statistics were based on "data analysis at the end of the first year," or, as he said, "3,549 woman-months of experience." Simple division —3,549 months divided by 640 women—shows that the average participant had worn a Shield not for one year, as Davis suggested, but for less than a half-year: 5.54 months. Dr. Russel J. Thomsen, an army doctor, pointed this out later in congressional testimony, but the disturbing question is why so many physicians apparently failed to notice the huge clue that Davis had put under their noses.

The numbers were confusing from the beginning. Thus it was that Barbara Seaman, a cofounder of the National Women's Health Network and a columnist for *Family Circle* magazine, in her book titled *The Doctors' Case Against the Pill* (1969), wrote that Davis and his colleagues at Hopkins had "inserted Dalkons in 692 women. Of the 679 women who retained the Shield comfortably, only six (one percent) became pregnant."[15] For her discussion of the risks and benefits of intrauterine devices as possible alternatives to the pill, Seaman interviewed Davis and gave special mention to his apparent success with the Dalkon Shield. Indeed, Davis, then in the spotlight as a prominent critic of the Pill, was asked by the publisher to write a foreword to Seaman's book, and his praise was excerpted on the back of the jacket. But if Davis read the manuscript of the book he was praising, he clearly let these figures slip by, since, writing months *after* Seaman, he reported that 640 women had participated in his study (39 to 52 *fewer* "first insertions"), and that there had been one pregnancy fewer than indicated by Seaman's figures.

Even if this inconsistency could be explained as a simple mistake—miscommunication, or typographical error—no such explanation could account for the basic flaws of Davis's study. In his study, Davis cited the late Dr. Christopher J. Tietze, who was regarded as the top expert on birth-control statistics, and whose recommendations for IUD data analysis had set the guidelines for scientifically acceptable studies.[16] Yet Davis's study failed to meet Tietze's basic standards of "average duration of use per patient [of] at least one year," and of maintaining at least fifty women in the study for its duration. As noted, the average duration in the Davis study was 5.54 months, and as he told Dr. Benjamin Viel, of the University of Santiago in Chile, only eight women had been in his study throughout the twelve months it may have lasted.

Viel had told Davis in a letter more than three months before the article appeared "that one thousand insertions will be required to provide meaningful comparative data with regard to pregnancy rates." This was 56 percent more than the sample of 640 on which Davis based his efficacy claims. Furthermore, biostatistical researchers at Johns Hopkins estimated that a study of 1,200 patients would have been the minimum needed to establish with confidence a true pregnancy rate of one or two percent.

Further doubt is cast on the credibility of the Davis research by the haste with which he submitted his data. When a pregnancy occurs, some time usually elapses before the woman knows it, and considerably more time may go by before her clinic knows it. A rush to process the data in a study such as Davis's is therefore more likely to miss some pregnancies than would a study of longer duration, with a longer follow-up period. But as plaintiffs' lawyer Bradley Post discovered, Davis's data went to Johns Hopkins's statisticians within three days after the closing date of the study. Post pointed out that in a valid study, "approximately three *months* should go by before the calculations are made."

A final point: Women who drop out of a contraception study and who can't be followed up for information on what happened to them are the very ones most likely to have become pregnant or to have had medical problems for which they may have sought treatment someplace other than the Johns Hopkins family-planning clinic. "The patients who drop out of the trials . . . are much more important than the patients who stay in them," Professor J. R. A. Mitchell of Oxford University and the British Medical Research Council has said.[17] Apart from Barbara Seaman's reference to Davis's having inserted Shields in 692 women and to 679 of them who retained them "comfortably," there is no hint that Davis's 640 may have been a *residual* figure resulting from the elimination of an unspecified number of dropouts. That there were dropouts cannot be doubted, if only because most of the participants in his study were in the socioeconomic group most likely to drop out (these participants, poor black women from Baltimore's inner city, were the guinea pigs for a product that would ultimately be used by women in all socioeconomic groups). Davis testified vaguely that "less than 5 percent" were lost to follow-up. If one or two of them had become pregnant and had been followed up, the 1.1-percent pregnancy rate he claimed would have been lost, too.

In retrospect, the major strands of Hugh Davis's campaign for the Dalkon Shield were already visible in his foreword to Barbara Seaman's book and in his article in the *American Journal of Obstetrics and Gynecology*. In the foreword, entitled "A Public Scandal," he carefully nurtured existing legitimate doubts about the safety of birth-control pills, while proclaiming only the Dalkon Shield as "more convenient and just as effective."[18] Here he made his pitch directly to women, coaxing them to ask their doctors (as many would do) to fit them with Shields. Author Seaman provided a benign setting, writing that Davis had reported seeing " 'a number of happy brides' with IUDs." In the article, he built demand for the Shield among his professional peers, easily persuading some OB-GYNs while undermining the resistance of their more skeptical colleagues to patients who asked for the IUD.

In both of these texts, Davis emphasized the fictitious 1.1-percent efficacy figure. He cultivated the image of a scientist who was pushing outward the frontiers for the advancement of women. His business interests remained unacknowledged.

The next major building block in Davis's campaign was an announcement that drew much notice in the press, i.e., that he had "successfully tested" a smaller Shield for women who had never given birth. Most physicians rarely inserted IUDs of any design or make in nulliparous women—"nullips"—because the devices caused severe cramps and other problems. For that reason, the announcement held out the promise of a vast new market, particularly among young, unmarried women. The news stories appeared in November 1969, more or less concurrently with publication of the Seaman book, with Davis's submission of his article manuscript—and with the start of Shield sales by Dalkon Corporation. The timing could hardly have been better.

Meanwhile, Davis was writing *Intrauterine Devices for Contraception*, which recast his themes in the terminology, charts, and tables of a medical textbook.[19] "The modern devices come very close to being perfect contraceptives," he wrote. The only "modern" device he named was, of course, the Dalkon Shield. It was the "second generation" IUD, a slick phrase that served to condemn rival devices as obsolete.

Even slicker was Table 13 in that book. It wrapped Davis's data into a single package with what he called "reliable performance data" for nine rival IUDs. Under the heading of "Complications reported per 100 women-years in first year of use for 10 major IUD's" were four columns headed respectively "Pregnancy Rate," "Expulsion Rate," "Medical Removals," and "Total Percent Complications." Of course, the Shield triumphed. Its claimed pregnancy rate was, as before, 1.1 percent, as against 1.3 percent to

10.8 percent for its rivals. Its listed expulsion rate was 2.3 percent, compared with a range of 2.6 percent to 38.2 percent. Shield removals for medical reasons were a mere 2 percent, a fraction of the 7.3 to 22.8 percent reported for the other devices. Finally, the combined complications were an alleged 5.4 percent for the Shield, a spectacular showing against a range of 18.9 to 55.7 percent. Davis did slip in a barely visible clue to the shoddy research that supported his own study, but it was too subtle to be noticed by most readers. He cited as his source for data on the other nine IUDs the Cooperative Statistical Program (CSP) of the Population Council. But in the CSP program, each of the nine rival devices was monitored (on average) in 3,529 women, or 5.5 times as many as Davis claimed for his study; the average wearer in the CSP program wore an IUD for 17.2 months, or 3.1 times as long as the putative average wearer in Davis's study. Table 13, by comparing the IUDs on an equal basis, obscured these significant differences in the sizes of the samples and lengths of the test periods.

One OB-GYN who was not fooled was the U. S. Army's Major Russel Thomsen, whose patients at Fort Polk, Louisiana, had had terrible experiences with Dalkon Shields. He conducted a personal investigation into the causes and then testified at a congressional hearing two years after publication of the book. He said that the Davis study had produced "pathetic statistics," that "the textbook turns out to be but a thinly veiled promotion of the Dalkon Shield," and that in Table 13, "the deception is amazing."[20]

Dr. Thomsen didn't let it go at that. On May 14, 1974, he wrote to Davis's publisher, the Williams & Wilkins Company of Baltimore, to urge an "editorial inquisition" into the "deceptive" book, which he called "a thinly disguised promotion of the Dalkon Shield under the cover of an author who failed to identify his relationship to [the IUD]. . . . I believe that the minimal appropriate action would be a recall of the book from distributors and stores." Three weeks later, while Thomsen was giving a deposition in a Shield lawsuit, a defense attorney showed him a copy of his letter to Williams & Wilkins—although he had received no reply from the publisher. He sent a protest to Williams & Wilkins about this surprising use of his unanswered personal correspondence, but was again ignored. I tried to put inquiries about this and other matters concerning the Davis book to Sara Finnegan, head of the publisher's medical book division, but she refused to provide any information, including the number of copies sold.

By the winter of 1969–1970, public concern about the safety of oral contraceptives was nearing its peak. There had been a steady stream of disturbing reports about links between the Pill and a broad spectrum of diseases, and these reports were drawing increasing attention in the press. In addition, critical books, particularly Barbara Seaman's and the paperback version of my own *The Pill: An Alarming Report,* had appeared and been widely reviewed. It was in this climate that Senator Gaylord Nelson (D–Wis.) announced that he would convene his Subcommittee on Monopoly for a prolonged hearing on birth-control drugs.[21]

The lead-off witness, using this hearing for his own bully pulpit, testifying before television cameras and reporters covering a sure-fire story, was Hugh Davis. The date was January 14, 1970—just eight days before the *American Journal of Obstetrics and Gynecology* would publish his article on the 640-patient study. Once again, but with much greater impact than ever before, Davis built the market for the Shield by inciting fears about the Pill. Reporter Stuart Auerbach's story in the *Washington Post,* representative of many others, began:

> A Johns Hopkins gynecologist warned a Senate subcommittee yesterday that he fears birth control pills, used by 8½ million American women, may cause breast cancer that won't be detected for years.
>
> "Shall we have millions of Americans on the pill for twenty years and then discover it was all a great mistake?" said Dr. Hugh J. Davis, the Johns Hopkins specialist in birth control devices.

For Davis, the Senate forum was an unparalleled opportunity to peddle his wares free of charge. Indeed, he succumbed to the temptation by exaggerating his already unsupportable claim of effectiveness for what was clearly, albeit implicitly, the Dalkon Shield. Within a few minutes he made the following statements, each of which nudged the purported efficacy of the device closer to 100 percent: "In our experience, some modern intrauterine devices provide a *99 percent* protection against pregnancy. . . ." "The intrauterine devices that are available now can give you a *99 percent or better* protection." "Pregnancy rates, depending upon the types of device, range anywhere *from 0.5* [i.e., 99.5 percent effectiveness]. . . ."

When Lee Iacocca goes on television, the viewer knows perfectly well that the chairman of the Chrysler Corporation is trying to sell him a car. What could be fairer? When Davis appeared before the television cameras, viewers assumed he was a scientist from a distinguished academic institution who was motivated by concern for the health and safety of women. Why should they not have?

Toward the end of the hearing, James P. Duffy III, the minority (Republican) staff counsel, gave Davis a bad moment. Duffy had become "aware of the report that [Davis] had recently patented such a device," he said, and asked, "Is there any truth or substance to that report?"

Davis's reply was a model of the smoke-in-your-eyes genre of Capitol Hill testimony: accurate but misleading. "I hold no recent patent on any intrauterine device," Davis said. He went on to say that he had given his patent rights to the Incon Ring to Johns Hopkins, thus turning what could have been a defeat into a victory: he was a principled fellow, one who had rendered unto Hopkins what was Hopkins's, for the sake of the general good.

Hugh Davis's triumph was sealed in Washington. For a fleeting moment the searchlight beam of publicity had shone on the dark secret of his financial stake in the Dalkon Shield—a secret on which much depended—but it moved, barely pausing, to the next question and the next witness. Now the road to Richmond was unobstructed.[22]

2

Thad J. Earl, M.D.

OUTDOING HUGH DAVIS

Hugh Davis had mastered the art of promoting a product while disguising his economic involvement. His success was assured by his academic credentials as assistant professor of obstetrics and gynecology at the prestigious Johns Hopkins University School of Medicine, his Paul Revere role in expressing concern about the hazards of birth-control pills, and his play on the notion that science and technology had come up with a "modern" intrauterine device in a nick-of-time rescue.

Not surprisingly, his announcement of the new, smaller Dalkon Shield received heavy news coverage, including interviews with reporters and a wire-service story that was published by the *Crescent News* in Defiance, Ohio, on November 3, 1969. Probably the most interested reader in Defiance was Dr. Thad J. Earl, medical director of the Family Planning Agency, a local birth-control clinic. "At that time I had two patients in their late twenties [who] had had strokes on pills . . . three months prior to that time, and I was very concerned," Earl said in a deposition in 1977. Earl was also interested because the new device—designed for girls and women who had yet to bear a child—held promise for the many young women who came to his clinic for birth-control help.

The next day, Earl wrote a letter to Hugh Davis. "I would be interested in coming to Baltimore to spend a couple of days with you and/or your clinic for instructions as to inserting of the IUD," he said. "I have a large gynecology practice but up to the present time have been very dissatisfied with the IUDs on the market."

Davis welcomed the proposal, and Earl, who is not a gynecologist, went to Johns Hopkins to learn from the master. "I was interested in finding something . . . of contraceptive efficacy, that I would have confidence in [and] that I didn't think would hurt my patients," he testified. He spent "in excess of four or five days" studying with Davis and watched him insert two or three Shields. "I was very pleased with what I had seen," he said in his deposition. He was also "very impressed" by Davis's insertion procedure, or protocol: "I thought it was a very thorough, complete, logical sequence of events which I had never seen before"; he was also "impressed with [the Shield's] anatomical configuration."

He bought forty-eight Shields from Dalkon Corporation and began to insert them on December 8 or 9, making him one of the first physicians outside of Maryland to implant the device, and also one of the first to encounter alarming problems with it.

When Earl arrived in Baltimore, according to his testimony, he had "no conceptual idea of an investment of anything, period." Less than three weeks later, however, he became convinced that the Shield "had a great future in contraception." Wanting to be part of it, he flew to Greenwich, Connecticut, for a New Year's Eve conversation with Dalkon's two officers, Irwin Lerner, the electrical engineer who had applied for the Shield patent and was president of the company, and Robert Cohn, the lawyer, who was secretary and treasurer. In March, Dalkon made its first sale of nullip Shields. In April, Earl invested $50,000 in Dalkon and became its fourth co-owner and also its medical director. To make room for the new partner, the others—Lerner, Cohn, and (secretly) Davis—each parted with a proportionate number of shares of stock. The new ownership structure was as follows, in percentages: Lerner, 50.875, Davis, 32.375, Cohn, 9.25, and Earl, 7.5. If $50,000 was the fair value of Earl's share, $215,833 was the fair value of Davis's.[1]

Dalkon lacked salesmen, or detailmen, as they are known in the pharmaceutical industry, and this severely constricted the device's sales potential, no matter what its merits or demerits. Principally for this reason, Lerner wanted to try to make a deal with a company that had a sales force. In 1969 he went to Little Falls, New Jersey, to meet with executives of Julius Schmid, Inc. (now Schmid Laboratories), which distributed condoms and the Saf-T-Coil IUD. "Lerner pitched it to us first," retired Schmid president Albert Carroll told me in an interview. "He said it was marvelous, a great opportunity." But Carroll and Dr. Harry Gordon, the company's medical director, were repelled by the Shield's protruding-fins design. A former Schmid officer who asked not to be named recalled being more than repelled. "We thought of it as a grappling hook. . . . This is what we visualized, my God, putting it into a girl."

Lerner next recruited Earl to help him sell the Shield to a major pharmaceutical manufacturer. Earl wrote to five firms, not including the A. H. Robins Company.[2] One of the five, the Upjohn Company of Kalamazoo, Michigan, expressed interest, and Earl introduced Upjohn representatives to Lerner and Cohn.

Meanwhile, Earl touted the Shield at medical meetings, using Hugh Davis's promotional article in the February 1, 1970, *American Journal of Obstetrics and Gynecology* and its claim of a 1.1-percent failure rate as his principal sales tool. "Did you ever reveal to doctors that Dr. Davis had an interest in the device?" a plaintiffs' lawyer asked him. "Anybody that ever asked me, I told them," he replied. Yet Earl's efforts to sell the Shield, which met with increasing if modest success, drew a sneer from, of all people, Davis, his admired mentor. Davis confessed his low regard for Earl to Dr. Frederick A. Clark, Jr., Robins's medical director, at their first meeting. Clark's memo on the meeting said that Davis "commented that he could reach people (e.g., OB-GYN departments, FDA, [the] Population Council) that Earle [sic] could not. I detected feeling toward Earle as a 'Johnny-come-lately' whose 'snake oil approach' would 'turn many people off.' Davis acknowledged that Earle's enthusiasm would be very useful at exhibits and among GPs, however."[3]

In mid-May 1970, the New Jersey General Practice Association held a meeting at Host Farms in Bedford Springs, Pennsylvania. Earl manned the Dalkon Corporation's Shield exhibit booth while John E. McClure manned the A. H. Robins Company's booth nearby. On May 18, Earl approached McClure "concerning AHR's possible interest in an intrauterine device."[4] McClure then phoned senior vice-president C. E. Morton and mailed copies of Shield materials to Richmond for review at the home office.

Morton assigned the task to W. Roy Smith, who, as director of product planning, was responsible for the acquisition of new products. A pharmacist and former owner of a small drug company in Petersburg, Virginia, he had been with the company only eight months; he would rise through the ranks and become a senior vice-president in 1975. Later, when a lawyer suggested that he had become "the hub of the wheel" in deciding whether to buy the Shield, he said, "In large part, I think I was."

Roy Smith was well known in Richmond in a different capacity. Perhaps more than anyone, he personified what Virginians call "the Coalition" or "the Main Street Crowd"—a group of wealthy downstate business and political heavyweights who were stalwarts of the Democratic machine run by Senator Harry F. Byrd, Jr. Starting in 1952, Smith represented the City of Petersburg in the House of Delegates. He became the highly influential chairman of its Appropriations Committee until he resigned the legislature in 1973. He remained politically active, however, becoming Charles S. Robb's key liaison with the state's business establishment in Robb's successful campaign in 1982 to become the first Democratic governor in sixteen years. Later he was appointed chairman of Governor Robb's Economic Advisory Council. In 1984, Smith became a leader of Virginians for Reagan, along with former Senator Byrd and former Governor Mills Godwin, another onetime Democrat. Smith's support of the reelection of a Republican President came as no big surprise; there was finally little practical difference between a putatively conservative Harry Byrd Democrat and a Republican with pro-business and right-wing leanings.

Most Virginians, including some reporters who were assigned to Richmond to cover state government and politics, had no idea that the Smith they saw and dealt with in public life had any connection whatsoever with the implanting of Dalkon Shields in millions of women, even if they knew he worked for Robins. He retired from Robins on January 1, 1982. In 1983 the American Pharmaceutical

Association, the professional organization of pharmacists, recognized his service in politics and public affairs by giving him its Hubert H. Humphrey award.

The Dalkon Shield materials sent to Smith from Bedford Springs consisted of Hugh Davis's 1970 journal article, a file card of the sort that is given to physicians as a handy reference about a product, and a sample order card to be used in ordering the Shield.[5] Smith signed for receipt of the materials on May 21, 1970, and on the same day, Dr. Clark, Robins's medical director, sent Smith a memo "indicating that he had reviewed the Davis article." Meanwhile, C. E. Morton sent Smith a memo saying he didn't know whether the Dalkon Shield was unique, or even different from other IUDs, but directing him to check it out "from a public relations standpoint."

Since public relations were what the company was interested in, the research that led to the purchase of the Dalkon Shield by A. H. Robins took but a small fraction of the time that a check of safety and effectiveness would have taken. In fact, the deal was closed a mere twenty-two days after Smith received Thad Earl's thin package. And that's counting the Memorial Day holiday.

III

A. H. Robins Buys the Dalkon Shield

"I've got to believe that had they known early on what they were dealing with, they wouldn't have touched it with a ten-foot pole. It was just that one step led to another, until they had the grenade spinning in the middle of the floor."

—*Roger L. Tuttle, former A. H. Robins attorney*

3

A. H. Robins

A CORPORATE AND FAMILY PROFILE

In 1866, soon after the Civil War, Albert Hartley Robins, a registered pharmacist, opened an apothecary shop in Richmond, Virginia. He was twenty-three or twenty-four years old. He is said to
have worked seven days a week, filling prescriptions every day, but
not selling over-the-counter products on the Sabbath. In 1896 his
son Claiborne, also a pharmacist, joined the business. Helped by
his wife, Martha, he operated the A. H. Robins Company—the
direct ancestor of the contemporary firm—on the second floor, over
the pharmacy. It sold drugs only to physicians, became legally
separate from the apothecary, and kept separate books. Albert is
said not to have known how Claiborne was doing financially, and
vice versa.

Claiborne died of heart disease in 1912, when he was thirty-
nine, and when his son, E. Claiborne Robins, was two (grandfather
Albert lived to be ninety-two). While still a child, E. Claiborne
began to work in the apothecary, sometimes waiting on customers,
sometimes delivering prescriptions. In 1978, when he was sixty-
eight years old and chairman of what had become the multinational
A. H. Robins Company, he reminisced about those early hard-
scrabble days in a lengthy interview with his "Manager of Public
Information." The company published it in an elegant brochure.[1]

"There was quite a conflict with my father because my grandfa-

45

ther didn't think there was much future in the ethical* side of the business," Claiborne Robins says in the interview. "I remember my mother saying that it was very rough in the first years because Grandfather was selling some products over the counter, advertising them in newspapers, while she and my father were trying to promote them ethically through doctors at the same time. Not under the same names."

The business deteriorated after his father's death, but his mother kept it going for twenty-one years in the hope that he would be interested in it. He was graduated from the University of Richmond and received a degree in pharmacy from the Medical College of Virginia, also in Richmond, in 1933. In that mid-Depression year, Claiborne Robins went into the family business. "The Company was hanging by a thread," he said. "It had only three employees. Mother was one of them, of course, and Miss Alma May Robertson and a black woman were the others." He went on the payroll as a salesman and "detailed" in several states. Even so, the year ended with total sales of $4,800, and a net loss. "One of the strange things [was] that I didn't have sense enough to know I could fail," he said. "In the middle 1930s we were coming out of a depression and a lot of people were unemployed. But you see, I didn't know all this. I hadn't been used to having any money, so the fact I didn't have any was just normal and it didn't seem any harder to me."

Claiborne's mother, who ran the office and packaging and shipping operations because he was on the road, "made me President in 1936." A year later, as shown by the company payroll, which is reproduced in the brochure, weekly salaries totaled $70.50, with Claiborne accounting for $10. While detailing in Waco, Texas, he met his bride-to-be, Lora, and they were married in 1938. "I was working Houston and I lived on about thirty-two dollars for the entire month," he recalled. "I think I paid twenty-eight dollars for a third-floor room up in someone's attic, and this included two good meals a day. The three or four dollars that were left went for what little lunch I ate and a little bit of gasoline for the car."

*"Ethical," in this context, means a drug or medical product generally available only by physician's prescription, as opposed to those medications available over the counter.

In 1942, sales reached $100,000 for the first time, "but we were still putting everything we could back into the business." In 1948, sales hit the million-dollar mark; in 1949, when Robitussin cough medication and two other preparations joined the product line, revenues nearly doubled, and as Claiborne says, "the Company really began to take off." The "product strategy," apparently devised in the 1950s, "was to select therapeutic areas where there was a great market." Always there was an emphasis on aggressive, enthusiastic salesmen, and he repeatedly praised them. The year 1963 was critical. Sales reached $50 million; the company acquired the Morton Manufacturing Company, maker of Chap Stick lip balm, and thus started down the conglomerate path. In that year it offered its stock to the public for the first time. Two years later, a director of international development was appointed. By the time of the interview in 1978, the company had more than fifteen subsidiaries around the world and was selling its products—including drugs, Parfums Caron, and Sergeant's Flea & Tick Collar and other pet-care products—in more than a hundred countries.

The interview is interesting, even though it is—as any such public-relations exercise is bound to be—unremittingly self-serving. Yet it is also an evocative, sometimes touching remembrance of the origins and evolution of a company that, for most of its life, was solely a family enterprise. In it, E. Claiborne Robins unburdens himself of "recollections and observations" on all manner of things, including his attachment to a dying form of paternalistic employee relations ("small checks at Christmas and on their birthday," free coffee in the lunchrooms, and summer Friday afternoons off), and his aversion to federal regulation ("millions and millions of dollars in unnecessary research"). Most important, it captures his ability to dispense pieties and buy public acclaim for good works while at the same time he is busy indulging his lust for profits.

Consider his description of a company magazine for physicians called the *Robins Reader*. "It has no religious message, if that's the word, but it does have a semi-spiritual tone and it's inspirational," he said. "Any number [of doctors] have written in over the years saying, 'This has been very helpful to me and my Sunday School class.'" Such facile religiosity was commonly directed toward doctor-customers in small towns, where Robins had always done much of its business. But the magazine's quasi-spiritual orientation in fact draws attention away from the need for the kind of religious thinking that grapples with serious problems, such as the nature of personal morality in a corporate world.

Certainly there is no evidence of such soul-searching in Robins's interview. His is an American success story. Indeed, although his account is chock-full of names of A. H. Robins products, there is only one unelaborated mention of "disappointments" (of which there have been "very few"), and not a word about the Dalkon Shield.

With company prosperity came vast personal wealth—in 1968, *Fortune* listed Claiborne's worth at $150 million—and, on a stunning scale, philanthropy. In Richmond, Robins's personal and corporate goodness became legendary. On June 9, 1969, George M. Modlin, president of the University of Richmond, announced that Claiborne Robins had made an unrestricted gift that was one of the largest, if not the largest, ever made by an individual to a private institution of higher education, and one that was five times the total endowment of the severely strapped, Baptist-affiliated university. The gift—four-fifths of it in common stock in the A. H. Robins Company—was $50 million. Modlin made the announcement of the gift at commencement exercises, after degrees had been conferred. "The audience of several thousand responded with a whoop and most persons in the auditorium arose and applauded," a Richmond newspaper reported the next day. By the end of 1983 the university was valuing its gifts from the Robins family (Claiborne and Lora Robins have a son and two daughters) at more than $100 million.

In addition, Claiborne and Lora and their children had made numerous large gifts to a cross-section of educational and cultural institutions, organizations, and causes. Such philanthropy was not restricted to the immediate family; the average A. H. Robins employee's gift to the United Way of Greater Richmond in 1983 was $185.40, which E. Claiborne Robins, Jr., called "probably the highest for our type of firm in the nation."[2]

Robins's beneficiaries vied with each other in their praise of the man. In 1982, the Richmond chapter of B'nai B'rith, the Jewish international service organization, presented Robins with an award the international organization gives each year "to an individual who has distinguished himself in his community." As Sidney H. Closter, B'nai B'rith's director of development, told me, "E. Claiborne Robins is strongly identified with every major cultural and charitable institution in Richmond."[3]

The presentation of the award was set for the night of June 3, 1982. In an afternoon fanfare, the *Richmond News Leader* reprinted an effusive eighteen-inch column of praise that had been put into the appendix of the *Congressional Record* by Representative Thomas J. Bliley, a Republican congressman from Richmond. "Claiborne Robins has put service to his state and country and, above all, his fellow man, well ahead of material pursuits," Bliley said. "By his unswerving attention and devotion to people, he has inspired others like him to help their fellows."

The award banquet, at the Richmond Hyatt House, was practically a canonization. E. Bruce Heilman, president of the University of Richmond, delivered a eulogy in which he said that Claiborne Robins's life "reflects values worthy of emulation not only by young Americans but by the rest of us, as well." He then went on:

> I know of no one who has earned and who deserves more respect than Claiborne Robins. He is sensitive, sympathetic, honest, and generous. His concern is for everybody and he expects nothing in return. . . . His church, his business, his university, and everything else deserving his attention are beneficiaries of his special human qualities. . . .
>
> I proudly proclaim that no one else has deserved the Great American Tradition Award more than you. Your example will cast its shadow into eternity, as the sands of time carry the indelible footprint of your good works.
>
> We applaud you for always exhibiting a steadfast and devoted concern for your fellow man. Truly, the Lord has chosen you as one of His most essential instruments.

A lesser man than Claiborne Robins might have been embarrassed by the beatification. But only two weeks earlier he had offered this encomium to himself in the public prints: "I always try to make decisions based on the Golden Rule, how a question would strike me if I were sitting on the other side of the desk. That sometimes gives you a different perspective."[4] He surely didn't mean that he would have had the women injured or killed by the Dalkon Shield do unto him what he had done unto them.

Richmond was the capital of the Old Confederacy, and antebellum attitudes still linger there. It is the city where, in the time of the Harry Byrd political machine, the strategy of massive resistance to desegregation of the public schools originated. It is, along with Dallas, one of the most "conservative" cities in the country ("conservative" in the sense of an ethic that seeks to conserve the power and wealth of the already powerful and wealthy) and a bastion of antifederalism (the federal government is "evil"; "we're above the government"; "Washington is the capital of sin" are sentiments commonly expressed there). Richmond is, finally, a city with an unusually inbred establishment, and Claiborne Robins, his company, and his university were thoroughly integrated into it.

Bruce Heilman, the president of the University of Richmond, has been on the board of A. H. Robins since 1975. In turn, Robins had been a UR trustee for many years before Heilman joined the company board. In 1969, less than five months after Robins's $50-million gift to the university was announced, UR made seventeen new appointments to its forty-member board of trustees. A six-sentence news story began, "The under-thirty generation will be represented on the University of Richmond's revamped board of trustees, not by students, but by the three children of E. Claiborne Robins, who recently gave the institution $50 million." The story ended by saying that the fourteen other new appointees "include bankers and industrialists, all from Virginia," and that "this is the first time the trustees have nominated fellow board members."[5]

Most major pharmaceutical manufacturers, like other large corporations, draw outside directors from beyond their home cities and states. Not A. H. Robins; it has three outside directors, and all are from Richmond. In addition to Heilman, they are Stuart Shumate, retired president of the Richmond, Fredericksburg and Potomac Railroad Company, and Carroll L. Saine, chairman of

Central Fidelity Banks, Inc. The outside directors of Central Fidelity include E. Claiborne Robins and Bruce Heilman.

Two of the four "inside" directors are E. Claiborne Robins senior and junior, who, the company says in its proxy statements to stockholders, "may be considered as control persons of the Company." A third is George E. Thomas, retired executive vice-president and first director of international development. The fourth, William L. Zimmer III, was associated with McGuire, Woods & Battle of Richmond, one of Virginia's largest law firms, which has coordinated as many as 150 other firms across the country in defending Dalkon Shield litigation. In 1952, while a partner in McGuire, Woods's predecessor law firm, Zimmer became a director of A. H. Robins. In 1970 he left the law firm to become the company's president. When, in 1975, Claiborne senior reached the age of sixty-five, he relinquished the post of chief executive officer to Zimmer until Claiborne junior took over as CEO in January 1978. Zimmer returned to McGuire, Woods and served until 1982; he remains a Robins director.

Throughout all of these corporate interrelationships, E. Claiborne Robins, Sr., and his company remained almost indistinguishable. "The A. H. Robins Company has been my father's life," Claiborne junior testified in 1983. And Claiborne senior gave the identification a special moral tinge when he swore at a deposition in January 1984, "We have always acted responsibly and with integrity. I will stake the reputation of our company for integrity [against that] of any company in the United States. We are known not only as a company that does the right thing, but we are known as a company who are more compassionate and more concerned with getting good products than we are concerned with profits." Indeed, Robins had reason for his pride.

For more than a century, the A. H. Robins Company had done business without having a single product-liability lawsuit filed against it. To be sure, it did not until relatively recent times sell the potent—and therefore sometimes unavoidably hazardous—products that are the stock-in-trade of many often-used pharmaceutical manufacturers. Still, as Roger Tuttle put it, "They had always gone by the book, and had been a great success. . . . They had no problems with the therapeutic areas in which they were engaged, unlike many other major drug companies. . . ." It was understandable that Claiborne Robins scorned federal regulation; his company demonstrably didn't need it.

But the Dalkon Shield would change all that, and ultimately drive a potential wedge—of sorts—between family and company. In 1983, investors who had bought stock in the company during the approximately three years preceding the suspension of Shield sales filed a class-action suit that named the company, Claiborne Robins senior and junior, and director and former CEO Zimmer as defendants. The suit, which has now been settled, alleged that the defendants, in violation of the securities laws, had made material misrepresentations and withheld material facts about the IUD, thereby artificially inflating stock prices.

The defendants denied the charges. But at the 1984 annual stockholders' meeting, the seven directors unanimously requested and got approval for a drastic reduction in the personal liability of present and former officers and directors. This got them off a very sharp hook. The resolution amended Robins's corporate charter to say that the company would pay the fines, penalties, attorneys' fees, and other costs of an officer or director who was finally held liable "for gross negligence or willful misconduct in the performance of his duties. . . ."

More bluntly, the two Robinses—the "control persons" who voted enough of the stock to accomplish whatever they wanted— and the other directors, most notably E. Bruce Heilman, arranged that the company, not the perpetrators, would pay for proven "gross negligence or willful misconduct." Is it not astonishing that such a resolution was necessary in a company led by a man willing to stake its reputation for integrity against that of any in the United States? A man said to have been chosen by God as "one of His most essential instruments"?

4

Anatomy of a Decision

The A. H. Robins Company twice explored the possibility of buying the rights to an intrauterine device. The first time was in 1965, when Dr. Jack Freund, the vice-president who headed the medical department, became interested in the Lippes Loop. The second time was, of course, in 1970, when the Dalkon Shield became available. The Loop episode was a dry run, in a sense; it offers a glimpse of the considerations that influenced the Robins executives.

Dr. Freund asked Dr. Frederick Clark, the medical director, for what Clark called "preliminary comment on the IUCD [intrauterine contraceptive device], with specific attention to the Lippes Loop." In a two-and-a-half-page memo on July 12, 1965, Clark said that "only a few references have been located for review." Whoever had searched the medical literature would have flunked a test in library science, for there was no shortage of dire warnings about IUDs.[1]

"The larger question undoubtedly is the potential of the IUCDs as a group," Clark wrote, making it clear that he meant *marketing* potential. He went on to list the pros and cons. One favorable entry was, "Trend is up and likely to continue. Old fears on use receding." A second "pro" was that a new-drug application (NDA) would not have to be filed with the Food and Drug Administration. The absence of an NDA requirement arose from an absurdity in the Food, Drug, and Cosmetic Act that needs a bit of explanation, particularly because it would play a crucial role in the Dalkon Shield disaster.

As originally enacted in 1938, the law required a manufacturer seeking to sell a new prescription product to file an NDA demonstrating that it had established relative safety with reliable and sufficient animal and clinical testing. The 1962 Kefauver-Harris Amendments, in addition to tightening safety requirements, made a direct attack on the literally thousands of false and misleading advertising and promotional claims by pharmaceutical manufacturers, which sometimes resulted in the use of potent, hazardous drugs to treat medical conditions for which they were ineffective. The amendments required a manufacturer to submit to the Food and Drug Administration an expanded NDA showing "substantial evidence"—derived from adequate and well-controlled clinical investigations—of effectiveness in the uses for which the company was recommending the product.[2]

But the law had a ridiculous loophole: with no premarket clearance, a manufacturer could put on sale an untested, hazardous *device*. Only *after* it had caused injury or death could the FDA— if it was prepared to carry the legal burden—go to court for an injunction to halt interstate sales. What it came down to was that the attitude of Congress toward drugs was preventative: try to avert harm to people. Toward devices, the approach was laissez faire and punitive: let people be harmed, and then—maybe!—go after the transgressor (or, more likely, after some small change in his bulging pocketbook).

Not that Congress hadn't been alerted: starting in 1962, three years before A. H. Robins would consider the Lippes Loop, Presidents Kennedy, Johnson, and Nixon sent eight consecutive annual messages to Capitol Hill urging premarketing clearance of medical devices for safety, efficacy, and reliability. But a device bill, like so much legislation that would benefit the public rather than special interests that finance political campaigns, had always lacked an active constituency. This made it easy for Congress to turn its back on the fundamental contradiction; if it required the FDA to regulate a drug taken into the body for a specific purpose, such as birth control, how could it not compel the agency to regulate a device inserted into the body for the identical purpose?

The FDA, too, was troubled by the situation and asked its Advisory Committee on Obstetrics and Gynecology to review the record on IUDs, particularly since increasing numbers of women were using them, often retaining them in their bodies for years at a time. The committee reported in 1968 that it found significant evidence of death and injury and placed the blame on the inherent design defects of some IUDs, as well as non-germ-free packaging and deficient instructions. The Task Force on Inflammatory Reactions and Warnings said: "Without any concerted effort we have obtained four case reports of deaths associated with overwhelming infections following the insertions (without [uterine] perforations) of the IUDs. None of them have been reported in the medical literature. We wonder how many more such tragedies may have occurred that have not come to our attention." The committee concluded—in a detailed report two and a half years before A. H. Robins would decide whether to buy the Dalkon Shield—that device legislation was essential. In a judgment that would prove to be prophetic, Dr. R. B. Scott, who headed the task force, wrote that "the complications from the use of IUDs provide a fertile field for medicolegal suits."[3]

The indications are overwhelming—from the history of the Robins company, from the words of both the elder and the younger Robins, and from innumerable documents—that had a device law been on the books, the company would never have seriously considered the Dalkon Shield, and Thad Earl would have had to go elsewhere. A. H. Robins had not shown interest in regulated birth-control pills; why would it have been interested in a regulated birth-control device? Without regulation, the company could be in the birth-control market in a matter of months. With regulation, it would have to monitor 1,500 to 2,000 users for no less than two years, submit the results to the Food and Drug Administration, and delay marketing until the FDA flashed the green light. Without regulation, it would have a free hand to do a host of things that, under regulation, would be violations of the law, punishable by civil and criminal penalties. It could put the Shield on sale without prior testing for safety in either animals or humans. It could sell the new, small nullip Shield that had been tested for *neither* safety nor efficacy. It could make false and misleading claims in advertising and labeling, such as the 1.1-percent pregnancy rate for the untested nullip Shield. It could withhold reports of unexpected, grave adverse reactions from the FDA. It could deny FDA inspectors access to its Shield complaint file. In short, if the Shield had been regulated, it would either have taken as much as four years to get it on the market, or, as Bradley Post said, it "never would have made it to the market at all."

Noticeably missing from Dr. Clark's balance sheet on the Lippes Loop was any concern about the possibility of IUDs creating serious hazards for women. On the negative side of his July 1965 memo to Dr. Freund, Clark cited some reasons why the company should not go into the IUD business: "mild discomfort and excessive bleeding (14 percent severe enough to remove device) experienced by some women, particularly during first 3–4 menstrual periods," and "spontaneous expulsion of the device (6 to 9 percent in first year), sometimes unrecognized, particularly during first 3–4 menstrual periods." But he dismissed such grave safety issues as pelvic inflammatory disease ("not proven with current devices and techniques"), and was simply wrong about ectopic pregnancies ("not so—and actually lower than without use"). On the contrary, he saw it as an advantage for IUDs that they need not be shown to be safe, effective, and reliable—shown, in particular, to the evil regulators in Washington, D.C.

In separate assessments, neither Clark, the medical director, nor Dr. Lester W. Preston, Jr., the director of scientific information, dwelt exclusively on the medical or scientific aspects of IUDs. Clark concluded in his memo: "Small profit margin, small turnover (can wear for year or so), only nonprofit organizations now promoting the IUCDs. . . . Although IUCDs are medically sound and rational, strong marketing questions exist." Preston, in a memo to Freund three days later, recommended consideration of the Lippes Loop on the basis of its " 'investment potential' . . . in relation to the alternative investments consonant with corporate goals."

In the end, the highest levels of the company decided that the answers to the "strong marketing questions" were unsatisfactory, and to pass on the Lippes Loop. Rights to the device were acquired by the Ortho Pharmaceutical Corporation, a large supplier of diverse products for birth control. By 1969 the Loop, while not without major problems, had become what a government report termed "the standard IUD of international use. It was a known, *tested* entity." [Emphasis added.][4]

A year later, in 1970, the chance encounter in Bedford Springs, Pennsylvania, between Thad Earl and John McClure gave Robins, which had specialized in bowel and cold medications through most of its first century, a second crack at the IUD market.

As we have seen, Earl's materials were received in the Robins home office on May 21, 1970, and checked out "from a public relations standpoint." On May 25, W. Roy Smith had a long phone conversation with Thad Earl. William Forrest, vice-president and general counsel of A. H. Robins, summarized the conversation much later in a confidential memo on the acquisition and marketing of the Shield. Earl, Forrest said, claimed that in the seven months that Dalkon had been selling the device, "there were no pregnancies, no expulsions, and no removals." Possibly none were *reported* to Earl, who, in any event, was out hustling Shields. Possibly he was misquoted. But, bearing in mind Earl's tendencies toward promotion rather than science, it is not out of the question that this is indeed what he said. Subsequently, in a welcome contribution to a Shield publicity blitz, Earl claimed a sensationally low pregnancy rate of 0.5 percent—less than half of Davis's famous 1.1 percent.[5] Forrest's summary, prepared in February 1975, also contained cryptic references to "several thousands" of case histories, to negotiations with the Upjohn Company, and to "Upjohn's arrangement—exclusive license in return for royalty plus cash payment." In any case, the phone conversation ended with Earl inviting representatives of Robins to come to his Northwestern Ohio Family Planning Agency in Defiance with "an impartial specialist in the field of obstetrics and gynecology so that they could get an unbiased opinion about the product."

The specialist turned out to be Dr. Solon E. Davis III, a board-certified OB-GYN who was an assistant professor at the Medical College of Virginia. "We discussed the implications of the [Hugh] Davis paper and the fact that it was obviously a preliminary report," he has testified. "But obviously there wasn't a way of our vouching for either the correctness or anything else concerning it."

Robins "was interested in something which had a real growth potential and had the potential for being a real worldwide seller," he added. "Robins's management believed the Shield had the potential to take over the IUD market."

On May 28—the day before a deal with Upjohn was to be signed —Smith and Drs. Clark and Davis flew in a chartered aircraft to Defiance. Earl met them at the airport and drove them directly to his clinic. He told them he had inserted about two hundred Shields since October 1969 and had had no difficulties.[6] While Smith waited in an anteroom for about an hour, Davis and Clark watched Earl insert perhaps eight or ten Shields, and then Davis inserted two or three. Earl and Smith have testified that the visiting physicians were enthusiastic, although Davis testified that he never told Robins officials that the Shield was safe. The men discussed business at lunch and at Earl's farm. Earl said he told Smith that a Robins offer "would have to be larger than the one from Upjohn," which was reportedly for $500,000 plus a 6-percent royalty on sales. In an apparent bargaining gambit intended to get him on the Robins payroll, he also told Smith that Upjohn had not offered to retain him as a medical consultant. Smith, he said, commented that he "felt that I would be very useful in that capacity." At some point, Forrest's memo said, the Robins representatives caucused "and agreed that they were interested in the Shield." The visit lasted six or seven hours.

On returning to Richmond, Smith, who testified that his role was restricted to assessing the business aspects, told vice-president C. E. Morton that the Shield was "an economic opportunity" and urged that the company "go forward." Now developments came swiftly, starting on May 29, the day after the trip to Defiance.[7] But the climactic moves occurred over a period of five days starting on Monday, June 8, when Fred Clark, the medical director, drove to Baltimore to see Hugh Davis at the Johns Hopkins School of Medicine.

Clark described the mini-summit in a three-page, single-spaced memo dated June 9. The initial paragraphs evoked the atmosphere and Davis's personality. A "not overtly enthusiastic person," Clark wrote of Davis, adding that he was "talkative but seemingly guarded in glorifying the Dalkon Shield and in volunteering information germane to the Dalkon Company. Most information [was] elicited by questions—on a couple of points, he suggested that information be obtained from Lerner, only to later come through with the answer."

But a few paragraphs down, there were two sentences that should have sent shock waves through the Robins executives; indeed, they would later prove highly damaging to A. H. Robins's defense against Dalkon Shield lawsuits:

> Davis' first paper on his first year experience mentions 640 insertions with five pregnancies. However, data given me for first 14 months (Sept. '68–Nov. '69) covers 832 insertions with 26 pregnancies (none after 11th month).

The memo went on, however, without missing a beat, a testimonial to the promotional cast of mind of the two physicians:

> Davis stated that the company which takes the Dalkon Shield must move fast and distribute much merchandise and really make an inroad in "the next 8 months." My feeling was that others might be working on similar improvements for IUDs.
>
> He stated that a company not having other OB-GYN products could be a plus or a negative factor—for the latter, he cited the training job required for [sales] representatives and the fact that no other entrée [to physicians] is available.
>
> Davis writing book on IUDs—80 percent completed.

Clark sent a copy of the memo to his boss, Jack Freund, who had asked him to go to Baltimore, and who, as vice-president for research, was the highest-ranking physician at Robins. He also sent copies to Roy Smith and Ernest L. Bender, Jr., vice-president for administrative staff. A stream of information was percolating up to Bender, who reported to president William Zimmer; Zimmer, in turn, reported to Claiborne Robins.

In a memo to Bender two days later, on June 11, Dr. Freund summarized "comments on the performance of this device and a synthesis of available information concerning the IUD's [sic] in general and the Dalkon Shield, obtained by discussions with Doctors Ed [Solon] Davis, John Board, Hugh Davis, Dr. Earle [*sic*] and other OB-GYN specialists contacted by Doctors Clark, John Board and myself during the past week." Next came three sentences that rivaled Clark's in shock value:

> Definitive information on the Dalkon Shield is available primarily from Dr. Hugh Davis' studies. The follow-up period for the published pregnancy rate is not long enough (1 year) to project with confidence to the population as a whole. More recent conversation with Mr. Lerner indicates that the pregnancy rate of the group published by Dr. Davis has increased from 1.1 percent to 2.3 percent with a longer follow-up period.

The final sentence read: "The need for continuing the research effort initiated by Dr. Davis and Mr. Lerner and added studies to support the effectiveness and safety of this device should be emphasized." Freund sent copies of the memo to Zimmer, Clark, and four other executives.

By now only the formalities—the signing of papers and the shaking of hands—remained. Robins and Zimmer had probably approved the purchase days earlier—possibly right after the visit to Defiance on May 28, possibly following Clark's trip to Baltimore to see Davis. Or maybe the purchase was locked in on June 9, when Thad Earl came by for lunch with an array of Robins brass: Zimmer, Bender, Smith, Freund, Clark, Morton, and Forrest. "This meeting," the general counsel said in his chronology, "was devoted to the details of an agreement for purchase of the Dalkon Shield. In addition to discussions with Dr. Earl, there was at least one telephone conversation with Cohn, Dalkon Corporation's counsel." In any case, it seems that the deal could only have been stopped by a drastic turn of events. That is why two executive memos that might well have given pause had no apparent impact.

On June 8, the day Clark visited Davis, Oscar Klioze, director of pharmacy research and analytical services, wrote a memo to Freund. Would the polyethylene matrix and the nylon tail string be stable, Klioze asked, or would either or both degrade and leach into the woman's body? The Shield "has not been subjected to any formal stability testing," Klioze wrote. "No accelerated aging tests were conducted . . . nor was there any study of the 'leeching' [*sic*] effects of the *in vivo* environment." In a deposition years later, Klioze said he had not really been disturbed. "After all," he explained, "Dr. Davis was on the faculty of the Johns Hopkins medical school. . . ."

Then, on June 10, Roy Smith wrote a memo that explicitly raised ethical considerations. His focus again was on the problem of leaching—in this case of copper—into women's bodies. Heavy metals were thought to be biologically "active" in the body, chemically enhancing birth control, and the Shield patent application filed by Irwin Lerner in 1968 specifically mentioned copper in the context of efficacy. An "important aspect of the device is that it may be coated with a suitable film of material [to] enhance its effectiveness," the application said. The material could be a heavy metal: "gold, platinum, silver, copper." The choice was copper. In October 1969, the Dalkon Corporation began to mix copper into the plastic that became the Shield matrix—a fact unacknowledged by Davis in his article in the *American Journal of Obstetrics and Gynecology*. Indeed, his results were based on a Shield that contained no copper.

Smith's memo referred to a discussion he had had about the presence of copper with vice-presidents C. E. Morton and Ernest Bender, and clearly stated his misgivings:

> I am concerned that we may not have given sufficient consideration to all the problems involved in marketing the Dalkon Shield with the composition presently being distributed by Dalkon.
>
> At the luncheon yesterday we discussed the possible implications of utilizing the Davis paper for promotional purposes, while marketing a device not identical in composition to that on which the paper was based. I understand the conclusion that was reached and the reasons therefor, i.e., that the composition is not mentioned either in the paper or on the product package, and that the effectiveness rate is even

better than that cited by Dr. Davis, but I am not sure that these are the principal considerations.[8]

We have relatively limited information on the Dalkon Shield in terms of length of usage, overall cases published, etc. Even with his relatively limited total case history, the bulk of the experience to date and the bulk of the available data is on the Shield made from the plastic with barium sulfate added [to permit X-ray detection of the device in the uterus by giving it what is called radiopacity], but without either copper or copper sulfate.

From what Dr. Freund said, I understand that statistics are continuing to be developed on pregnancy rates, expulsions, etc., the same as for the original material.

I am less clear, however, about what type of patient follow-up, if any, is being done to determine specifically whether the copper sulfate may have some deleterious effect on the patient. Copper salts are irritant and astringent. This would seem to me to indicate a danger of causing increased discomfort. According to Goodman and Gilman [a reference to a standard work entitled *The Pharmacological Basis of Therapeutics*], copper in small amounts is a normal constituent of the diet and can be detected in the blood. Its physiological function is apparently concerned chiefly with hematopoiesis [a blood disorder].

My principal "hang-up" goes beyond any of the above and is related to what I would term as "implied warranty."

If we sell a doctor a *device* with no mention that the content of the material includes a copper salt which may contribute to the overall effectiveness, then it would seem clear that the doctor was buying a device and expecting the results to be attributable to that device. What troubles me is our implication to him—in the absence of "full disclosure"—that a device is doing the job, whereas we would actually be selling a *device* to which we have added copper sulfate for the express purpose of getting an added "drug effect."

As I understand it, metallic copper was first added for the purpose of improving radio-opacity and to improve the physical qualities of the plastic (i.e., by using copper, the desired degree of radio-opacity could be obtained without increasing the barium content to a point that made the plastic difficult to mold).

Then, according to my understanding, they observed that the material with copper was apparently lowering the pregnancy rate, and at this point they reasoned that a more soluble form of copper would further improve effectiveness, so they added copper sulfate for the express purpose of improving effectiveness.

It seems to me that the use of *copper* perhaps can be justified. Whether it is or is not a good change is, I feel, a medical judgment matter.

However, the inclusion of copper sulfate, in my judgment, carries with it certain implications that I have tried to point out and which I feel should be very carefully considered before a final determination is made.

I discussed this with Ernie Bender following our luncheon meeting and you may recall that he expressed similar reservations at the meeting.

Roy Smith, who had given the Shield a thumbs-up as a business proposition fourteen days earlier, now sounded a deferential but powerful warning: the tested Dalkon Shield was not the Dalkon Shield that would be sold; he was not sure that the effectiveness rates claimed by Hugh Davis should be the controlling consideration; clinical experience with the device was relatively limited; and the Shield under consideration contained a copper salt that might be injurious. Finally, he warned, by selling this Shield, the officers of the A. H. Robins Company were breaching the trust put in them by the physicians who would insert Dalkon Shields in the women who placed *their* trust in those physicians.

Even on the day the deal was struck, Friday, June 12, 1970, there was a warning flag in a report filed by David E. Jones of the Marketing Research Department on telephone interviews with twelve physicians, seven of whom had inserted varying small numbers of Shields purchased from the Dalkon Corporation, and five "randomly selected" OB-GYNs "to provide some basis of comparison." "In summary," Jones said, the findings tend to reflect our previous knowledge or expectations in that physicians expressed mixed opinions concerning the use of IUDs. Some physicians do not use any IUD's for a variety of reasons: religious, medical, personal experience, etc. Other physicians use IUD's, but have not had any experience with the Dalkon Shield. Previous Shield users had different views ranging from enthusiasm to displeasure. *No severe complications were reported, but it is important to note that experience with the Dalkon Shield in all physicians contacted was limited to a matter of months.* [Emphasis added.]

If the Dalkon Shield can approximate its claims for effectiveness in widespread use—barring unforeseen complications—it will in all probability be a significant factor in the IUD market in the near future.

Actually, as Jones's memo shows, none of the seven physicians who had inserted Shields had expressed enthusiasm. Dr. Marvin H. Grody of Hartford, Connecticut, came closest. The Shield was "his first choice of contraceptive devices or medication," Jones said. "His use to date, however, is very limited."9

The six other Shield-using OB-GYNs refrained from making final judgments or hailing the device as superior to other IUDs, because their experience with it was too limited and because they preferred to see more data than was then available. Two of the six had difficulties inserting the Shield, and one found insertion no less difficult than with rival IUDs.

In short, everybody had reason for concern, yet nothing dampened the spirits of the men who assembled in A. H. Robins's executive offices on June 12, 1970. The signing of papers was a ceremonial affair. Robins bought the patent rights to the Shield for $750,000, to be shared by the Dalkon Corporations's co-owners in proportion to their holdings. Lerner got $381,562.50, Davis $242,812.50, Cohn $69,375, and Earl $56,250 (for a $6,250 capital gain in two months). Robins also retained Earl at $30,000 a year (making him its highest-paid consultant), Davis at $20,000 a year, and Lerner at $12,500 the first year and $2,500 thereafter. In addition, Robins agreed to pay the Dalkon Corporation a royalty of 10 percent on net sales in the United States and Canada. These ultimately totaled $1,840,640 from June 1970 through March 1974, and Lerner, Earl, and Davis shared them in proportion to their ownership of Dalkon.

It is, of course, normal for such transactions—and certainly the details of them—to go unpublicized. In this case, however, there were reasons for shrouding the arrangements in secrecy. Above all, it was beneficial to conceal the royalty arrangements giving Hugh Davis of the Johns Hopkins University School of Medicine a direct financial interest in every Shield that Robins would sell. Sales and profits, after all, would hinge on advertising and promotion emphasizing the claims of this "independent" academic physician (and, to a lesser extent, of the equally "independent" Thad Earl). Only secrecy could sustain the fragile credibility of his claims—or sustain it long enough to let the A. H. Robins Company earn a large return on its investment.

Another provision in the purchase agreement gave Robins financial protection—a sharp cut in North American royalties—if it should ever be required "to prove safety or efficacy of the product." Finally, the agreement provided that, at least through December 1970, Dalkon would continue to manufacture Shields— but with profits accruing to Robins—in its small, two-story factory at 207 Greenwich Avenue in Stamford, Connecticut. Meanwhile, Robins began to prepare to manufacture the devices itself and to meet the myriad challenges posed by its grand plan for global marketing of the Dalkon Shield under its own name.

On June 23, 1970, the A. H. Robins Company issued a press release in which Claiborne Robins announced the purchase of the Dalkon Shield, said that it heralded the company's entry into the medical-device field, and applauded the Shield's claimed efficacy and other virtues. He testified in 1984 that his principal advisers in the purchase had been Dr. Freund, who by then had retired as senior vice-president for research and development, and Dr. Clark, who had retired as a vice-president and medical director.

Neither Freund nor Clark was a gynecologist. Indeed, no physician employed by Robins, then or during the entire period in which it marketed the Shield, was a gynecologist. Neither Ellen J. Preston, who was the company's liaison with physicians, nor Fletcher Owen, Jr., the director of medical services, had ever inserted an

IUD. Never before in its 104-year history had Robins made or sold an OB-GYN product or a medical device.

In 1983, William Zimmer, the director and former president and CEO, recalled how the situation had appeared to him at the time of the purchase of the Dalkon Shield. Stressing that the Shield "had been developed by a Johns Hopkins obstetrician, Hugh Davis," he told me, "knowing what we knew then, we would make the same decision."

IIII

The Launch

Northern Division will not be humiliated by a lack of
Dalkon sales. If you have not sold at least 25 packages of
eight, then you are instructed to call me. Be prepared to
give me your call-back figures. No excuses or hedging will
be tolerated, or look for another occupation.

*—Telegram to A. H. Robins Company salesmen from E. D.
Hood, Northern Division sales manager, February 26, 1971.*

5

Deceiving Doctors

By late December 1970, the A. H. Robins Company had trained an aggressive force of several hundred salesmen—who had never sold a gynecological product and who seldom if ever called on obstetrician-gynecologists—to sell Dalkon Shields. Robins also had brought fifteen district managers to Richmond for an intense orientation course and had sent them around to physicians to "pretest" their new sales techniques. In addition, the company had begun to promote the Shield to physicians by preparing nontechnical informational brochures that they could put in their waiting rooms for women seeking guidance about birth control. It was also getting ready to advertise the intrauterine device in medical journals, an effort on which it would eventually spend $373,527. While Robins geared up to make the IUDs itself at its Chap Stick plant in Lynchburg, Virginia, it had stocked regional warehouses with large supplies of the IUDs produced by the Dalkon Corporation.[1] At Chap Stick, Robins estimated, the production cost of a Shield, to be priced at $4.35, would be only twenty-five cents, labor and overhead costs being about 40 percent less than at the main plant on Cummings Drive in Richmond.[2] But although they carefully examined marketing and manufacturing, A. H. Robins, like the Dalkon Corporation before it, had not undertaken to test the Shield for safety in either animals or women. The only study of efficacy—done by Hugh Davis—had been questioned by Robins's own senior physicians.[3]

In January 1971 (formally on January 1), Robins began to sell Dalkon Shields in the United States, and ultimately in seventy-nine other countries. The marketing campaign was a dazzling success. Over the next twelve months, according to company estimates made for internal purposes, 56 of each 100 IUDs inserted in American women were Shields; in 1972, 59 of each 100. In the three-year period ending December 31, 1973, the Dalkon Shield vastly outsold its two leading rivals—the Lippes Loop 2 to 1, the Saf-T-Coil 4 to 1, and the two of them combined 1.3 to 1.[4]

Hugh Davis's article in February 1970 in the *American Journal of Obstetrics and Gynecology*—which advertised the Shield as "a superior modern contraceptive," with a pregnancy rate nearly as low as the Pill's, without "the actual and potential hazards of systemic medication for birth control"—was the foundation for Robins's feat of worldwide marketing. But piled onto that foundation were many other market-building blocks without which Robins would not have distributed or sold a reported 4,570,291 Shields worldwide. Some of the tactics were marked by what can only be called inventive forms of disregard for any standards of honorable conduct.

For a roaring start on promotion to the medical profession, Robins bought 199,000 reprints of the Davis article and 122,000 of "Dalkon Shield May Carry the Day for IUDs," a report published by *Medical World News,* that was wholly uncritical of Davis's claims. The date of the report—May 16, 1969—is yet another nail in the coffin of the credibility of Hugh Davis's study, not that it does much for the reputation for perspicacity of the physicians who received it from Robins in 1971. Assuming zero lead time for publication, May 16, 1969, was approximately eight months after Hugh Davis purportedly began his year-long study, and four months before he has testified he ended it. Yet even then, months before his study was completed, Davis claimed a 1.1-percent pregnancy rate.[5]

By August 1973, the company had printed more than 5 million pieces of Shield literature. They included 3.8 million "patient-oriented" brochures and 365,000 "patient aid" pads intended for distribution via doctors to women, and 819,000 cards for physicians' files on pharmaceutical products.

These large numbers reflect an audacious decision by Robins to reach beyond OB-GYNs, the traditional customers for IUDs because of their special knowledge, training, and practice, to the much larger market of general practitioners, osteopathic as well as medical. Thad Earl, himself not an OB-GYN, had proposed this tactic at a meeting with company executives on June 14, 1970, two days after Robins had bought rights to the device. Two months later, however, the marketing research department, after interviewing twenty-eight members of the Robins Medical Advisory Board, severely questioned the wisdom of Earl's suggestion. George J. Mancini and David E. Jones told five executives in a report:

GP's and D.O.'s [doctors of osteopathy] who do not routinely do pelvic examinations can constitute risky business. An IUD in the hands of a physician who is not familiar with reproductive anatomy is almost certain to have problems. Enough problems arise when competent physicians perform insertions. Under no circumstances should the Dalkon Shield be "pushed" on a physician who is just casually familiar with pelvic anatomy. Such sales could be very detrimental to the establishment of this product.[6]

The prevailing mood in the executive suites, however, was unreceptive to cautionary advice from almost anyone. Indeed, in August 1970—the very month of the Mancini-Jones warning— "Dalkon Shield: Orientation Report No. 2" reiterated a promotional strategy directed at "the OB/GYN, G.P., and D.O. specialties." The report was signed by R. W. Nickless, product management coordinator for the pharmaceutical division. In another status report two and a half months later, Nickless again said, "Total promotion to physicians [is] to begin about mid-January."

According to Roger Tuttle, there was no "iniquitous design" behind the marketing strategy. "I think that the conscious decision was to promote the hell out of this thing . . . and to make money out of this thing. . . . If you confine promotion through OB-GYNs, I can make a strong case that that eliminates the majority of the [female] population of the country, because out here in Sapulpa, Oklahoma, and Podunk, Iowa, you may not find an OB-GYN, but you'll certainly find a GP." Still, that Robins should press the GP to insert Dalkon Shields—contrary even to the warnings of its own market researchers—is another matter.

In September 1970—the month following the Mancini-Jones recommendation that the Shield not be "pushed" on GPs—Robins did precisely that, and on a large scale. At the annual meeting of the American Academy of General Practice in San Francisco, the company set up exhibits that contrasted awesome results in users of the Shield with much less impressive results in wearers of competitive IUDs, particularly the Saf-T-Coil and the Lippes Loop. This comparison was, of course, false, because it pitted the single study done by Hugh Davis, which Robins's executives knew to be gravely flawed, against multiple studies of the other IUDs done to meet accepted scientific standards. On October 8, 1970, Albert Carroll, president of what is now Schmid Laboratories, protested in a letter to Claiborne Robins. He wrote that A. H. Robins,

in its effort to enter the IUD market, is disseminating false, misleading and deceptive information to the medical profession on our Saf-T-Coil IUD and IUD's of other companies. . . . The data your company produced at the meeting was taken out of complete context. . . .

As a former President of the Pharmaceutical Manufacturers Association, you will be shocked to find that your company is engaging in activities that are of great concern today. . . . Half truths, out of context data and improper comparisons have no place in the medical profession. Such activities leave the industry vulnerable to dangerous attack.

We consider the activities of your company to constitute trade libel [and] unfair competition and [to be] in violation of several statutes and . . . regulations.

From my knowledge of your reputation in the pharmaceutical industry, I can only assume you were not aware of the activities of certain representatives of your company because I cannot imagine you would lend your name or reputation to the type of misrepresentation that occurred. . . .

Carroll probably did not expect his rhetorical flourishes—that Claiborne Robins would be "shocked"; that he was "unaware" of what was going on—to be taken seriously. But the substance of his letter was dead serious. Here was a fellow manufacturer putting the chairman on the spot, personally. And the mention of the Pharmaceutical Manufacturers Association was meant to hurt. Robins had been president of the PMA, the organization of most trade-name makers of prescription drugs, in 1968–69. Its voluntary Code of Fair Practices contains these provisions:

> Complete and accurate information concerning marketed drug products should be made available promptly to the medical profession. . . .
>
> Statements in promotional communications should be based upon substantial scientific evidence or other responsible medical opinion. Claims should not be stronger than such evidence warrants. Every effort should be made to avoid ambiguity. . . .
>
> Any comparison with other drug products should be made upon a valid scientific basis.

"Would you be willing to have the Robins Company judged by the principles of that code?" lawyer Bradley Post asked Robins in a deposition several years later. "I assume so," Robins replied. "Would you consider the use of false, misleading, or deceptive advertising or promotional material for promotion of the company's products, including the Dalkon Shield, as unethical business conduct?" Post asked. "We wouldn't consider using any tactics of that kind," Robins testified. Had anyone told him that his company had used deceptive and misleading promotion? Robins's reply was that he had "absolutely not" been told. There were problems with that testimony given under oath. For instance, there was Claiborne Robins's response to Carroll on October 14, in which he said:

> I was frankly surprised and disturbed to receive your letter of October 8. I trust that Robins' reputation confirms the fact that it would not knowingly engage in the dissemination of

false, misleading or deceptive information to any profession or to the public. . . .

We intend to immediately review the activities of our authorized representatives at the meeting of the American Academy of General Practice. . . . To that end, and in order that we might be fully apprised of events during this meeting, I have requested our Vice President of Medical Affairs, Doctor Jack Freund, to call you to discuss your allegations.

To the extent that any Robins representatives may have engaged in any activities of a questionable ethical nature, you can rest assured that those involved will be reprimanded and steps taken in order that there will be no repetition of these activities.

It was, of course, Robins's designated investigator, Freund, who had said four months earlier that the follow-up period for Davis's "published pregnancy rate is not long enough (one year) to project with confidence to the population as a whole," and that "the pregnancy rate of the group published by Dr. Davis had increased from 1.1 percent to 2.3 percent with a longer follow-up period."[7] The rate claimed in San Francisco, and nearly everywhere else, was, needless to say, 1.1 percent.

In an interview, Carroll said that he could not remember a call from Freund or, for that matter, from anyone at A. H. Robins. His protest went the way of all the others. In 1970, Dr. William S. Floyd, an associate professor of OB-GYN at Wayne State University in Detroit, was consulted by A. H. Robins about the Davis study. Floyd, applying his experience and analytical abilities to the study, divined from the internal evidence that it was biased and that the Shield was not superior to other IUDs. He suggested instead that the true pregnancy rate in users of the Shield would more likely be on the order of 5 percent. Robins ignored his warning: it could, after all, chill the go-get-'em-or-you'll-be-fired ethic of its sales managers. Better that the salesmen should tout the Shield as did Gene Lukas of Southfield, Michigan. In an early report to his boss, Lukas wrote: "My opening statement is, 'Doctor, this is the Dalkon Shield, an IUD that's as effective as the Pill.' "

In a letter to Claiborne Robins in December 1972, Russel

Thomsen, then an army OB-GYN at Fort Polk, Louisiana, denounced as "deceptive" the claims the company was making for the Shield in an advertisement. Robins testified he had not seen the letter. In July 1973, the Food and Drug Administration, in yet another letter to Claiborne Robins, asked him to reconcile the very low pregnancy rates claimed in his company's ads with the much higher rates being reported by researchers. Robins testified that he had received the letter but could not recall it.

Despite all these objections, the Dalkon Shield sales pitch did not change; it sounded more and more like one of those old-time boasts for patent medicines: "No general effects on the body, blood or brain . . . safe and trouble-free . . . the safest and most satisfactory method of contraception . . . truly superior."

Hugh Davis's ostensibly objective text on IUDs for the guidance of physicians was yet another piece of Shield puffery. *Intrauterine Devices for Contraception* was published by the Williams & Wilkins Company of Baltimore in September 1971, about nine months after Robins had begun global Shield sales. It was reissued in 1973, and also appeared in a Spanish edition.[8] The book rounded up the usual suspects—the 1.1-percent pregnancy rate, the "distinctly superior" performance of "this second generation IUD"—but is also significant for what Davis did *not* say.

Davis named Irwin Lerner as the Shield's inventor; he acknowledged nothing of his connection to Lerner, of his role in designing the device, or of his financial interest in it. Bradley Post asked him at a deposition if he had submitted galley proofs to Robins. "I submitted a copy of my book for educational purposes to the Robins Company," Davis swore. He also testified that Robins had picked up the bill for artwork in the book but that he had not disclosed this to the late Dick M. Hoover, editor-in-chief and vice-president of Williams & Wilkins. Davis had urged Robins to buy copies of the book in bulk lots for distribution to its salesmen, but, he said, the company had done bulk buying only for some of its overseas representatives. From Paris, an official of Laboratoires Martinet, a firm retained by Robins, wrote to product coordinator Nickless on September 9, 1971, that he had received a copy of this "excellent book of propaganda that we may give away. A great number of physicians will certainly be most interested. . . . We will need forty copies. . . ." Six weeks later, Nickless wrote a thank-you to Davis: "I have had some warm letters from doctors to whom we sent your book, and I will continue to send copies of such letters for your reading."

The year 1973 began with a stepped-up promotional campaign. As George Mancini, Robins's group product manager, reported in the *National ale & Marketing Review,*

> Our strategy in 1973 will be to continue to highlight:
> 1. Effectiveness (Remember, the DALKON SHIELD wouldn't be NUMBER ONE in sales if it wasn't NUMBER ONE in effectiveness.)

In May 1972, A. H. Robins had shipped 114,600 Dalkon Shields; in June it had shipped 79,300, or 35,300 fewer, and in July, only 53,500.[9] The explanation for this sag in sales was mainly that an increasing number of physicians who had believed the Davis-Robins claim of a 1.1-percent pregnancy rate were experiencing pregnancies in their Shield patients at much higher rates, some of them startlingly higher.[10] The first of Robins's two principal responses was to perpetuate the real but unspoken theme of the Shield sales campaign: whatever goes wrong, it's the fault of the doctor, not of the device. That theme was in the air in July 1971, when three Robins physicians met to review complaints from the "field," including the "apparent high pregnancy rate in the hands of some practitioners." Robert S. Murphey, vice-president and director of scientific development and international research, said in a memo on the meeting, "Some investigators insist that pregnancy and removal rates can be kept extremely low by proper placement of the Shield [in the uterus]." He expanded on this as follows:

> An extra effort should be made to transmit to the physician the problems of insertion and the use of proper technique in placing the Shield. Our printed literature, exhibits, and other instructional methods should be re-examined to determine if there is a better way to inform the physicians on how to use

the Shield, what pitfalls may rise from use and how to cope with them.[11]

The second major response to declining Shield sales was to step up advertising in medical journals. In September 1972, Robins began four months of publication of "A Progress Report," a multicolor, eight-page advertisement that was reportedly the largest and costliest in the history of Robins and of the IUD business as a whole. A bold, page-one headline proclaimed "The IUD That's Changing Current Thinking About Contraceptives. . . ." The text, precleared by Ellen Preston, the Shield physician monitor, and Roger Tuttle, the company attorney, laid primary emphasis on four published studies that purported to "substantiate" very low pregnancy rates. On their face, the rates quoted in these studies would seem to be irreconcilable: the highest was four times the lowest. The ad did not deal with this statistical oddity, possibly because Robins correctly assumed that many or most physicians wouldn't notice it. The ad said plainly, too, that 3,174 women in the four studies had worn Shields for 17,222 months. Simple division is—again—a wondrous tool. It shows that the average was 5.43 months. Any careful physician could have easily spotted such faults; what he or she could not have seen—because they were well concealed—were the deceptions involving each of the four studies cited in the ad.

The first study cited was Hugh Davis's original report claiming a 1.1-percent pregnancy rate over twelve months. The second was Thad Earl's report in *American Family Physician* claiming a sensational 0.5 rate over fifteen months. How would our conscientious physician have detected Davis's and Earl's secret financial ties to Robins? What reason would he have had to suspect that the company had known even before it bought the Shield that Davis's data were shaky at best? The Davis and Earl studies have already been dissected and they need no further attention now. But the two remaining studies, by Donald Ostergard and Mary Gabrielson, add some highly unusual aspects to the Dalkon myths.

Dr. Donald R. Ostergard was an assistant professor of OB-GYN at the University of California School of Medicine at Los Angeles and "head physician" in the OB-GYN department at Los Angeles County Harbor General Hospital. He and the Family Planning Clinic at Harbor General participated in Robins's so-called "ten-investigator" clinical study in which selected investigators filled out forms provided by Robins and returned them for statistical analysis to Lester Preston, Jr., director of scientific information at A. H. Robins, and to Dorothy K. Ervin, manager of data management analysis. Preston found Ostergard's data "sloppy" and "intolerable"—and said so in a scathing memo, which he sent to medical director Frederick Clark, by now a vice-president, with a copy to Jack Freund, by now a senior vice-president:

> By copy of this memo, I am confirming my instructions to Miss Ervin that *all* Data Management and Analysis activities should be immediately suspended on both prospective and retrospective Dalkon Shield data from Dr. Donald Ostergard. . . .
>
> I find it difficult, without producing a compendium, to say exactly what the problems are that we all seem to be facing, but they include such facets as multiple data sheets, not agreeing in content, from the same patient; many, many obvious "errors" in completing the forms (i.e., obvious inconsistencies), as well as ambiguities; gross deviations from protocol instructions . . . with respect to such things as [patients in the study] "Lost to Follow-up" and "Release from Follow-up"; questionable patient selection; administrative aspects (e.g., designating re-insertion patients as a new patient); etc. Our experience with the retrospective data that we have handled indicates that it, too, is flagrantly different and fraught with the *most obvious* errors. Even Dr. Ostagard's [*sic*] publication (viz. *Contraception* 4(5) 313–317, 1971) is "sloppy" to say the least—Dr. Ellen Preston concurs on this assessment. Frankly, my biggest fear is that we . . . can only see the "tip of the iceberg." I dislike the expression, but this could well turn out to be a clear-cut case of GIGO [a computer acronym for "garbage in, garbage out"].
>
> As you well know, we expect "problems" with all clinical data, but, as compared to other Dalkon Shield investigators,

Dr. Ostergard's has created an essentially intolerable situation. I do not feel that I can jeopardize other activities of the Data Management and Analysis Section in order to cope with the problems created by this one man nor do I feel that you [Dr. Clark] can do so either.

Since this is "your problem," I have no definitive recommendations. However, I would like to be assured by you that these gross problems have been reasonably resolved prior to our reinitiating any activity on Dr. Ostergard's retrospective or prospective data. Please let me know your views on this matter.

The Ostergard article in *Contraception* that Lester Preston derided as " 'sloppy' to say the least" appeared in November 1971. It claimed a pregnancy rate of 1.1 percent over a period of nine months. Preston wrote his memo on February 4, 1972, three months after the article appeared. The "Progress Report," citing the *Contraception* article and the 1.1-percent figure as if they were credible, ran without change from seven to ten months afterward —September through December 1972.

On June 12, 1973, more than sixteen months after Preston had heaped scorn on Ostergard's work, a Robins delegation defended the Shield at a hearing held by Representative L. H. Fountain, chairman of a House Government Operations subcommittee. In the delegation, appearing to put a University of California imprimatur on his glowing report on the Shield, was Donald Ostergard. It goes without saying that the company members of the delegation— including Jack Freund and Lester Preston's wife, Ellen Preston— were mum about the Preston memo.

I interviewed Ostergard in March 1985, after he had been promoted to associate professor at UCLA and full professor at the University of California at Irvine. "We did have some difficulty in getting the data in the form they liked," he said. "But after a personal visit by myself to the Robins headquarters in Richmond, Virginia, it was my impression that all of these problems had been resolved." But how? The question seems to have been answered in a series of depositions taken mainly by two plaintiffs' lawyers, Bradley Post and Dale Larson.

Dr. Clark, the sole addressee of the Preston memo, testified in 1976 that he recalled neither Preston's statement that Ostergard's work could be "GIGO," nor Preston's appeal for a suspension of data-processing, nor Freund's admitted order to Preston's department to continue to process Ostergard's data, nor—if the reader's credulity is not already overstrained—an effort by Freund, testified to by Ellen Preston, to have Ostergard named a member of an FDA advisory panel on IUDs.[12] Finally, Post showed Clark a copy of the memo. *Now* did he recall it? "I do not precisely," Clark swore. He did agree with Post's characterization of it as a "red flag."

Freund's memory was similarly fogged. "Have you ever heard that term, GIGO, 'garbage in, garbage out,' applied to the studies of Dr. Donald Ostergard?" Post asked. "I've not heard that." "Don't you recall a discussion about the use of Dr. Ostergard's data that occurred back in 1971?" "I don't recall that discussion, no." Freund took a different tack in 1984, after he had retired as senior vice-president for research and development to practice medicine in Richmond. Lester Preston was "a very hyperkinetic individual," a man who "has a very short fuse," he said in a deposition.

Would Ellen Preston agree with such an appraisal of her husband? She had, according to him, shared his assessment of Ostergard's data. Lester "didn't overreact to the data, did he?" she was asked in 1984. "In my opinion, he probably did," she swore.

Finally, what of Lester Preston himself? His testimony, given in 1978, needs close attention:

> Q: And the reason you wrote that memorandum was that you were concerned that Dr. Ostergard's data might turn out to be a clear-cut case of GIGO, is that true?
>
> A: No, sir; that is not true.
>
> Q: Did you include a statement in the memoranda where you ordered a suspension of all data analysis of Dr. Ostergard's data that you disliked the expression but this could turn out to be a clear-cut case of GIGO?
>
> A: I think I made that statement; yes, sir.
>
> Q: What does GIGO mean?
>
> A: It's an acronym for garbage in, garbage out.[13]

Dr. Mary O. Gabrielson and her colleagues at birth-control clinics in San Francisco and Oakland inserted Shields in 756 women, and she reported her results to the Ninth Annual Meeting of the American Association of Planned Parenthood Physicians in Kansas City, Missouri, in April 1971. She told the AAPPP that the 756 women, all of them nullips, some of them in their mid-teens, had accumulated 3,625 woman-months of use over a period of nine months. Removals for medical reasons (pain and/or bleeding) ran 14.9 percent (seven times Davis's rate). The pregnancy rate was 1.9 percent (four times Thad Earl's rate). The "Progress Report" reported all of this accurately, citing the published proceedings of the AAPPP's annual meeting. Where was the shell game?

Gabrielson's full study lasted eighteen months, or twice as long as the segment summarized in the "Progress Report." The number of nullips had risen to 1,209, although 31 percent of them could not be followed up. In the remaining 937, the pregnancy rate was 5.1 percent. The rate of medical removals had increased to 26.4 percent from the nine-month figure and was now thirteen times the rate claimed by Hugh Davis. These were not the kinds of figures Robins would care to advertise. Gabrielson reported them at the AAPPP's next annual meeting, in Detroit. In the audience was Kenneth E. Moore, the Shield project coordinator; several days after Gabrielson spoke, Moore detailed what she had said in a memo to several Robins physicians, led by Drs. Freund and Clark. The date on the memo was April 17, 1972—four and a half months before the "Progress Report" began its four-month run. A few weeks later, *Family Planning Digest,* a publication of the Department of Health, Education, and Welfare, reported her results. Congressman Fountain, at his hearing in June 1973, asked Jack Freund about "the propriety" of ignoring the report in the HEW publication. "There is no question of propriety," Freund testified. "This was not a published study; this was a report." It was, he explained, company policy, a matter of ethical principle: A. H. Robins was too scrupulous to cite any but published studies in its ads.[14]

The "Progress Report" came in for increasing criticism. At

Congressman Fountain's hearings, Russel Thomsen challenged another claim in the "Progress Report," that "the secret of the Dalkon Shield's high degree of contraceptive effectiveness" is that it is "the *only* IUD which is truly 'anatomically engineered' for optimum uterine placement, fit, tolerance, and retention." Thomsen testified, "Of course, this gets down to semantics, but, gentlemen, when I examine the patient, I cannot tell whether the inside of her uterus is average, and neither can the A. H. Robins Company. . . . There is no way." Methodically decimating one claim after another, Thomsen characterized the "Progress Report" as "a calculated effort to mislead the doctors." Was it a "fraud"? asked Representative Benjamin S. Rosenthal (D–N.Y.). In response, Thomsen delivered a broadside against *all* IUD advertising in that period of nonregulation of medical devices: "I would have to classify as fraud," he said, both the "Progress Report" and an ad for the LEM, a rival IUD made by G. D. Searle & Company.[15]

Others disagreed, notably Robins's Jack Freund, who, testifying after Thomsen, said, "We categorically refute the charge of fraud and deceit in the selection of studies for citation in the ad,"[16] and David M. Link, director of the FDA's Office of Medical Devices, who wrote in a memo, "The most that one can say is that there are a few statements included which fall into the mild puffery category."[17]

In July 1973, a month after the hearing, Robins began to feel more heat. The *British Medical Journal* published a study showing a 4.7-percent pregnancy rate in Shield users, and the FDA asked Claiborne Robins to answer the "serious questions" raised by the "Progress Report" and also by numerous complaints of high pregnancy rates. He didn't reply. In August, Dr. Max Elstein, a company consultant in Great Britain, reported the same 4.7-percent rate to Richmond. On October 31, about ten months after the "Progress Report" had appeared for the last time in the United States, Allen J. Polon, the newly installed Shield project coordinator, wrote a three-paragraph memo that tied a hangman's knot around Robins's efficacy claims. He sent it to Robert A. Hogsett, manager of promotional services, and the following is its text (emphasis added):

SUBJECT: Destruction of Dalkon Shield Literature

This memo is written referencing two pieces of Dalkon Shield literature which you questioned me about. The first is the eight-page advertisement titled "A. H. Robins—A Progress Report—The IUD that's changing current thinking about contraceptives. . . ." In this advertisement there is a table entitled "Clinical Results to Date" which is outdated *and parts of which are no longer valid.* Also, the labeling on the back cover is not considered complete and could cause trouble for AHR if we continued to use this advertisement.

The other advertisement in question is the earlier two-page ad with a large picture of a uterus with the Dalkon Shield inserted. This, too, is out of date for two reasons. *A pregnancy rate of 1.1 percent is stated which is not valid* and the labeling at the bottom of the second page is incomplete and no longer used.

Therefore, please *do not continue to use the two advertisements in question since both are outdated and both contain statements which are either incomplete or invalid.*

The A. H. Robins Company never told the medical profession or the FDA, and certainly not the public, that its Dalkon Shield project coordinator had repudiated the claims with which it had induced physicians to implant the devices in millions of women. Nor did Robins reveal that no senior executive, so far as is known, took serious issue with Polon.

A year later, *The Australian & New Zealand Journal of Obstetrics & Gynaecology* published a full-page ad in which Robins said that it was "making today's medicines with integrity. . . ." The headline was, "When you compare the Dalkon Shield to other contraceptives there's almost no comparison." The text contrasted the "highly sophisticated" Shield with five " 'older generation' " IUDs. A table dominated the page. It repeated as if still in their virgin state the old claims that the Shield had a pregnancy rate of 1.1 percent, a medical-removal rate of 2 percent, and a continuation rate of 94 percent. The citation was to Hugh Davis's February 1970 article. The "Progress Report" had at least told American

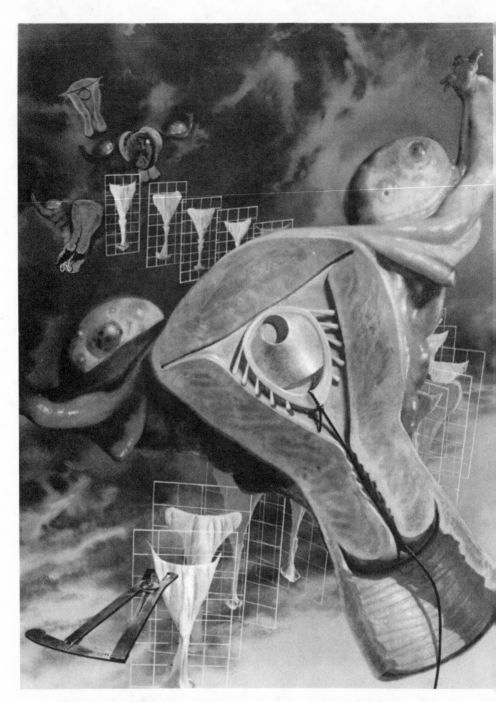

This bizarre advertisement, which appeared in several OB-GYN journals and other medical publications, was an apparent effort to lend an extraterrestrial aura to the Shield. "The Flying Uterus ad" was the apt description adopted by trial lawyers.

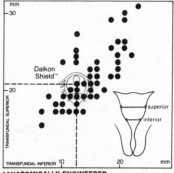

85

physicians of Dr. Gabrielson's interim nine-month results, including a pregnancy rate almost twice 1.1 percent and a medical-removal rate seven and a half times 2 percent. Not even this information was given to physicians in Australia and New Zealand, and probably not to those in many other countries.

Roger Tuttle, the former Robins lawyer who defended Shield cases from 1971 to 1975, has said, "The Robins medical department knew by 1972 that Hugh Davis's data were patently wrong, or should have known they were patently wrong." "What hung Robins out to dry," Tuttle continued, "was that the [Davis] data on effectiveness were untrue, and the courts and juries came to say that if you lied to us about effectiveness, why shouldn't we believe you lied to us about safety?"

On the eve of the purchase of the Shield, it will be recalled, vice-president Jack Freund had cited a need for "added studies to support the effectiveness and safety" of this IUD. Given the possibility of federal regulation of medical devices in the future, such a study would have to observe the guidelines for IUD studies that Dr. Christopher Tietze, associate director of the Population Council's biomedical division, had established, and that were followed for testing of rival devices.[18] The hope was that the Dalkon Shield would do well; the reality was that even if it did not, sales would continue during the lengthy period before the testing would be completed and the results analyzed and submitted to the government. Thus, even if the results should be bad, the momentum of Shield advertising and promotional campaigns would outweigh them, and the expected high return on investment would be realized. This was the background for Robins's ten-investigator (or ten-clinic) study. The final results, which Robins has never disclosed to the medical profession or, for that matter, to its own salesmen, turned out to be fatal to its claims of high effectiveness.

Seven clinics were in the United States: in Defiance, Ohio (Thad Earl's—while he was a Robins consultant receiving Shield royalties), New York City, Philadelphia, and Chapel Hill, North Carolina; there were three in the greater Los Angeles area. Three clinics were in Canada: Quebec City, Quebec; Halifax, Nova Scotia; and Vancouver, British Columbia. The first of the 2,391 women who participated were fitted with Shields at three clinics in December

1970, the month preceding the opening of Robins's worldwide sales campaign. Another clinic entered the study in February 1971, five more between July and September 1971, and the tenth in January 1972. By then, the company has calculated, 830,000 women were already wearing Shields. Three studies ended on June 30, 1973, three more on December 31, one on June 30, 1974, and three on December 31, 1974—six months after Robins had suspended domestic sales, and after doctors had inserted Shields in an estimated 2.2 million women in the United States alone.

In the scientific information department, Lester Preston and Dorothy Ervin were receiving the forms from the ten clinics, and crunching the numbers. They made their initial report in November 1972—before all of the women had been enrolled. It showed a sixteen-month pregnancy rate of 1.6 percent. "This is an excellent result," Ellen Preston told salesmen in the *National ale & Marketing Review* in January 1973.

But a bleak result followed thirteen months later, after additional experience had been accumulated. The more realistic semifinal report showed that the pregnancy rate after six months was 2.1 percent; after twelve months, 3.2 percent; after eighteen months, 3.5 percent; and after twenty-three months, 4.1 percent.[19]

Even the higher semifinal rates grossly understated the realities, because so many women dropped out of the study. Dropouts can be the most important participants of all, because pelvic infections or pregnancy could account for their disappearance. Under the guidelines set by Tietze, a woman was to be classified as a dropout —i.e., lost to follow-up—if she was at least three months late for a scheduled clinic visit and had supplied no information by mail, phone, or home visit. The guidelines set 15 percent as the upper permissible limit for loss to follow-up.[20] But among the ten investigators, according to a report in July 1974, only two, Donald Ostergard being one of them, met the permissible limit of 15 percent. The ten-clinic average was 34.5 percent. The record was the astounding 91 percent reported by Dr. Howard Balin of Philadelphia.

Robins submitted the report to the FDA in July 1974, following the company's suspension of domestic sales on June 28. It showed an accidental pregnancy rate of 4.1 percent and a medical-removal rate of 15.8 percent. Lester Preston and Dorothy Ervin then recalculated the data after excluding the results they considered scientifically unreliable—specifically the Ostergard and Balin results. In an internal document in August 1975, Preston and Ervin reported the new, final, and totally devastating findings:

Time Since Insertion	All 10 Studies (2,391 insertions)	Excluding Ostergard and Balin (for a net of 1,789 insertions)
6 months	2.6 percent	3.3 percent
12	4.2	5.5
18	4.9	6.3
24	5.7	7.2

Note, in particular, the eight-investigator, twelve-month pregnancy rate. It was exactly *five times* the false rate that A. H. Robins advertised and promoted so as to catapult the Dalkon Shield to the top of the IUD business. In the absence of federal regulation, nothing—not conscience, not fear of the Almighty, not competition —stood in the path of the false advertising and promotion. It may be remembered that thousands, probably tens of thousands, of women who trusted the doctors who trusted A. H. Robins paid a ghastly price: pelvic infections, impairment or loss of childbearing capacity, defective babies, unwanted abortions, recurring health problems, and persisting pain.

In a deposition in 1984, two years after the president of the University of Richmond had pronounced Claiborne Robins "one of His most essential instruments," lawyer Dale Larson took a final crack at jogging the chairman's memory. They had this exchange at a deposition:

Q: As I understand your testimony, the company has never gone on an advertising campaign to retract those representations, is that correct?
A: I think that is correct, because we didn't think it was necessary.

6

Deceiving Women

The A. H. Robins Company had a double strategy for becoming the dominant supplier of intrauterine devices. On the one hand, it fought for the confidence, trust, and cooperation of the medical profession and of the public and private agencies and clinics that provided IUDs. On the other, it addressed women directly, persuading them to accept the Dalkon Shield if their physicians should recommend it, and to request and even to insist upon the device if their doctors were skeptical or reluctant.

To get to women, Robins planted Shield propaganda in the guise of news in domestic and foreign newspapers, in columns, magazines, and books, and on television and radio programs. Moreover, it persuaded honorably motivated physicians and birth-control providers to make the company's Shield brochures available to patients in waiting rooms and clinics. Like the information in advertising and promotion aimed directly at doctors, the information in the planted stories and the brochures was not federally regulated. A. H. Robins let its conscience be its guide.

Still, the effort to sell the Shield simultaneously to doctors and to women was not without problems. Robins always stressed the medical and prescription aspect of the device. After all, only doctors were qualified by training and experience to insert it; only doctors could order it, by writing prescriptions. But traditionally, a prescription product, according to the code of the Pharmaceutical

Manufacturers Association, is "promoted and advertised to the medical profession rather than directly to the lay public."[1]

How, then, could the Shield properly be promoted and advertised to both doctors *and* women without stripping it of the prestige reserved for prescription products? Robins's way out of the dilemma was simple and also economical: promote and advertise to doctors; promote *but don't advertise* to women.

Of course, promotion amounts to free advertising, and Robins's efforts to have it both ways yielded some truly vertiginous distinctions. Thus, Claiborne Robins, in a deposition in 1976, insisted that the Shield was "not a prescription product, no, but it's a product that could be used only by the physicians." Jack Freund, the company's foremost physician and a vice-president, had testified before a House Government Operations subcommittee on June 12, 1973: "It [the Shield] is promoted only to the medical profession." In a deposition in 1976, he agreed that Shield promotion was "ethical," meaning that it was "promoted and described to the physician laymen directly . . . it was not an over-the-counter product."

Frederick Clark also agreed in a 1976 deposition: Robins considered the Shield a prescription product because "it could not be used by the patient without an intervening party." Plaintiffs' lawyer Bradley Post asked him, "If in fact all promotions of the Dalkon Shield were ethical in nature, that would mean that Robins had not promoted the Shield directly to the consumer, is that correct?" "Yes," Clark replied. "That would be the connotation, yes."

What Robins did, in fact, was to hire a matchmaker to woo the general press. In the fall of 1971, Richard A. Velz, the vice-president for public relations and a confidant of Claiborne Robins, consulted Richard L. Wilcox, president of Wilcox & Williams, a Manhattan public-relations firm that had previously done some work for Robins. Velz sent Shield literature to Wilcox and talked with him on the phone. Wilcox's response, in a letter on September 30, laid out a whole publicity program. The Shield, he told Velz,

> provides an excellent subject for the sort of favorable coverage you are looking for. Rather than approach a medical

writer, you will probably be better served by stimulating interest directly with the editor of a large woman's interest magazine who, in turn, will assign the piece to one of his staff or to a contributor qualified in the medical field. Since you have a new, effective and superior product of considerable significance to modern life, the attractiveness of this being offered to a magazine editor on an exclusive basis is high, and the chances of it being assigned and published [are] consequently better than through the free-lance channel.

We are on very good terms with a number of such editors and are prepared to approach them on your behalf. As a top priority, I would name the *Ladies' Home Journal* since it has wide circulation among the women you wish to reach, and its editorial policy is currently receptive to your kind of a story.[2]

The next day, Velz sent a memo on his "promotional activity" to vice-president Jack Freund, the highest-ranking physician, and other executives. Velz's opening line was of a kind that was likely to get men in a corporation to snap to attention: "As you know, Mr. Robins has assigned top priority to special promotion of the Dalkon Shield in other than medical and trade magazines. . . ."

Two weeks later, on October 15, Velz returned a signed contract to Wilcox, saying, "This project was approved by the Chairman of our Board. . . ." Wilcox would be paid $2,500 a month in expenses; the sales department would pay the bill. In November, Velz argued that publicity efforts had to be carefully coordinated and centralized. But, he said, two self-appointed promoters, Hugh Davis and Thad Earl, could cause "what might be a very embarrassing situation":

Mr. Wilcox, in talking with Dr. Davis in Baltimore, found that he had prepared an article for *Family Circle* magazine which had been "shelved" by the magazine. Mr. Wilcox talked with the editor of the magazine, and they have now "pulled it out" and it has been beefed up by additions Mr. Wilcox has supplied, and there is the prospect that it will run in the spring of 1972. . . . Mr. Moore [Kenneth Moore, the Shield project coordinator] has just come back from a visit with Dr. Earl, and finds that Earl has submitted a story to *Woman's Day*, based on the enclosed story which he had previously placed in *American Family Physician*. [3]

It is essential that there be one central control point and one organization seeking the placement of stories on the Dalkon Shield other than those intended for medical publications. . . . There must be some semblance of order, as magazine editors get very upset if they find a story they have scheduled for an issue has already appeared in one form or other in another publication and they are not aware of it. I think this can be taken care of if all of our internal promoters are advised that Mr. Wilcox and Wilcox & Williams are mounting an all-out campaign to publicize the product and that they should correlate all of their efforts through Mr. Wilcox. If we do not, the whole program will be in jeopardy. I assume that this word should come from someone in the Sales Department.

On January 27, 1972, Dr. A. N. Chremos, Robins's director of clinical pharmacology, attended a round of meetings arranged by Robins's PR firm, by then renamed Wilcox & Company. He "met first with Louis Berg of our staff who is preparing an article giving high marks to the Shield for *Midwest* magazine, a popular supplement of the *Chicago Sun-Times*," Richard Wilcox wrote Dale R. Taylor, Robins's marketing vice-president, the next day. The magazine never published the article.

Chremos and Wilcox next had a long meeting at the offices of *Mademoiselle* magazine with editor Edith Locke and managing editor Mary Cantwell. "I believe that we were very successful," wrote Wilcox, "and that good coverage of the Dalkon Shield will result." *Mademoiselle*'s "college issue" in August 1972 did carry an article entitled "Contraception: What You Don't Know and Must Ask," and Wilcox later claimed that the Chremos visit had "largely inspired" it. Wilcox possibly was doing some PR for himself here; the article reasonably summarized contemporary knowledge about contraception and gave the pros and cons of various forms of birth control, including IUDs in general and the Shield in particular.[4]

Wilcox also arranged a lunch meeting with an editorial colleague of Barbara Seaman at *Family Circle* magazine. Seaman's
book, *The Doctors' Case Against the Pill,* it will be recalled, cited
Davis's original study and had a foreword by Davis. On May 25,
a few weeks after the luncheon, Velz sent Claiborne Robins, William Zimmer, and seven other company executives an exultant
memo about Seaman's new book, *Free and Female: The Sex Life
of the Contemporary Woman:*[5]

This probabl[e] best seller will be released next week, and
Mr. Wilcox has worked with Barbara Seaman to introduce the
Dalkon Shield into the text. You will note that in the coverage
of the IUD, Mrs. Seaman quotes Dr. Davis and that the
Dalkon Shield is the only device mentioned. . . .

This is the more medically oriented part of the book, but
some of the other chapters with their interesting titles will
certainly lead readers into going through the whole book, and
the Shield will have a good presentation. All of the women's
lib "characters," including Betty Friedan, have given the
book rave reviews.

The book introduced Davis as "the author of the recent medical
book *Intrauterine Devices for Contraception*"—which, as we've seen,
recycled his false statistics about the Shield and concealed his
financial interests in it. The book's false representations and its use
by Robins as a sales tool no doubt helped Davis gain the attention of
so committed an activist for women's health as Barbara Seaman.
She devoted a full page in *Free and Female* to excerpts from
Davis's book in which the phrase "modern devices" appeared four
times. There could be no doubt about which was the "modern"
device; Davis was identified as "a developer of the Dalkon Shield,
a new intrauterine device which has been tried at [Johns] Hopkins
and elsewhere." Nevertheless, Seaman gave the last word on IUDs
to Dr. Christopher Tietze, who said that their only advantage was
that their "mischief" was "confined to the female organs," as
opposed to the more widespread effects of the Pill.

Wilcox & Company filed a progress report with Robins, apparently in July, on "the most significant developments," including:

Books—Barbara Seaman's *Free and Female* has received excellent reception among the book-buying public. . . . The book contains two and a half pages on Dr. Hugh Davis and the Dalkon Shield, the only IUD or contraceptive favorably mentioned. . . .

Television—During June the National Broadcasting System *[sic]* ran a month-long series of more than 170 programs on population and its control. Several of these programs made use of Dalkon Shield material made available to Barbara Walters of the *Today* show and other producers and editors at both NBC and its local New York outlet, Channel 4.

In a subsequent memo, Velz said that Wilcox had "established contact with Dr. Irwin [J.] Polk, a New Jersey physician who writes a column distributed by the Copley News Service. As a result, Dr. Polk devoted a recent column to IUDs, mentioning only the Dalkon Shield by name." The column, which appeared in many newspapers in June 1972, said: "A report from Johns Hopkins University details trials with this Shield on more than 5,000 women. Of this overall group, only one percent became pregnant while about 2 percent had the devices removed by the doctors for medical reasons."

Kenneth Moore, Robins's Shield project coordinator, sent the Polk column to seven executives and physicians with a note calling it "a little favorable publicity on the Dalkon Shield which was sent to me by Dick Wilcox." The note, dated July 19, 1972, continued: "Evidently this resulted in part from Dick's efforts. Dr. Polk's column appears in a number of newspapers around the country including the *New Orleans Times-Picayune,* the *St. Louis Post-Dispatch* and the *Sacramento Bee.*" "Dick's efforts" apparently included the Hopkins study of "more than 5,000 women," which, of course, existed only in someone's imagination.

By fall, Moore was saying that the publicity was paying off. Citing a new report by the marketing research department, he told Velz in a memo on October 12 of a sharp increase in the number of Shields being inserted:

Although the sample size is small, I think we can conclude that patient requests play an important part in Dalkon Shield sales.

The jump [in the Shield's share of IUD prescriptions] from 12 percent in 1971 to 33 percent in 1972 under OGyn's [*sic*] is encouraging. It appears that we are beginning to reap some benefits from Dick Wilcox's efforts. I trust the Dalkon Shield lay publicity program will continue at least through 1973.

Was the "lay publicity program" intended to promote the Dalkon Shield directly to women? On May 31, 1973, seven months after approving the program, Moore somehow could write a memo saying, "All Dalkon Shield promotions have been ethical in nature in that Robins has not promoted directly to the consumer."

Roger Tuttle, who defended Shield lawsuits for Robins from 1971 to 1975, told me that the Wilcox firm ghost-wrote and "planted" some articles. A memo bearing on Tuttle's allegation went from Velz to Claiborne Robins and nine other officers and officials on December 28, 1972. "The attached article is a family health column ["Health Highlights"] which goes to over 1,000 newspapers—small dailies and suburban weeklies," Velz wrote.[6] "Material was provided to the syndicate by Dick Wilcox."

The unidentified writer, using phrases identical to some that had popped up in Dr. Polk's column, emphasized a Johns Hopkins trial "on more than 5,000 women," and claimed that "of this overall group, only 1 percent became pregnant."

Claiborne Robins, asked if he had ever heard of such a huge trial, testified, "I don't know that there was such a study."

Neither Velz nor the unsigned column named the "syndicate" to which Wilcox, according to Velz, provided "material." In advertising and PR agencies, "syndicate" is commonly a code word for a conduit through which they feed understaffed newspapers unsolicited, free, and production-ready advertising and promotional matter that appears to be authentic news, written by reporters with no economic interest in the subject.[7]

Ernest Bender, Robins's senior vice-president for corporate affairs, was asked about the family health column at a deposition in February 1984. "I don't know whether you would call it intentionally unbalanced or not," Bender told plaintiffs' lawyer Dale Larson. While he could not swear it was Wilcox who "put that information together for us," he testified that the PR man "would have to be supplied information in order for him to know what to publish." The supplier of the information, he conceded, was A. H. Robins.

Some of the good news periodically reported by Wilcox concerned stories planted in the foreign press, a subject of particular interest to R. W. Nickless, by now Robins's international marketing director. "You will be pleased to see the beginning of international coverage . . . as evidenced by the attached copy of a clip from the so-called 'provincial' English press," Wilcox told him. "I understand from my colleague [in London], W. K. B. Hamilton, that this was widely carried outside of London."

Later, Robins's representative in Kenya reported another achievement: "Enclosed is a clipping from the *Sunday Post* of January 7, 1973, placed through the help of a local PR firm, Ian Raitt Public Relations Limited." The *Sunday Post* article was headlined "A New Alternative to the Pill" and was accompanied by a large photo of the Shield. In the guise of news, an "editor" let an unnamed "reporter" gush Shield advertising copy, much of it false or misleading, at length.

Roger Tuttle told me that even before he knew of the lay publicity program, he had opposed any Shield promotion targeted at women. "Since this product is a prescription product, our duty as a manufacturer is to adequately warn and advise the physician, through 'official' labeling, which includes 'full disclosure,' " he said in an interview. "I felt it was wrong as a matter of morality, and I felt it was absolutely the kind of thing that the plaintiffs' bar would kill [the company] with." He went further in a deposition in the summer of 1984, testifying that he had felt the company's promotion to women was "fraudulent . . . because they . . . weren't telling the truth."

Tuttle said in the interview that he probably learned of the program in 1973 because "someone was running around the shop crowing about it. . . . And Ken Moore comes to me and says, 'Did this have legal approval?' And I took one look at it and said not only did it not have legal approval, but had I known about it, it wouldn't have legal approval unless my boss [general counsel

Forrest] wanted to overrule me. I told him, 'This is shocking, it's horrendous, it's got to be stopped.' " (Forrest testified in 1984 that he had no memory of this episode.)

Tuttle told me he had argued to "anybody who would listen" that they could not take the position that the Shield "is an ethical pharmaceutical, in the terms of the trade, and at the same time send Dick Wilcox out to ghost-write these articles and publish them all across the country. How can you do it?" Finally, he said, he heard from John Taylor, a public-affairs assistant, that the campaign had been halted. "John's response to me was, 'Well, we've called it off. It was probably a mistake, but it would cause more problems now to try to do something to recall it or rectify it than to let it die a natural death.' So I accepted that."

Claiborne Robins, it will be recalled, had "assigned top priority to special promotion of the Dalkon Shield in other than medical and trade magazines. . . ." In 1976, three years after the lay publicity program had ended, Bradley Post asked him if he thought this kind of PR campaign "was in any way unethical or improper?"

"No, we did not, or we wouldn't have done it," he replied.

Aside from inflating the efficacy statistics of the device, Robins made several other false claims for the Shield, designed to increase its appeal to women. For one thing, Robins promoted the claim that the Dalkon Shield was nearly pain-free. In fact, insertion and removal of the finned device inflicted agony on thousands of women who had been led to expect no pain. Some doctors argued that the Shield caused more pain than did any other IUD. Robins had known all along of the need for painkillers and anesthetics, but concealed this from doctors and women for about two years.

After buying the Shield in mid-1970, Robins quickly began to dissociate it from pain. For this effort a key instrument was an Orwellian brochure entitled "Answers to Your Patients' Questions." Company salesmen gave copies to doctors to pass along to women who were seeking information on the various modes of birth control. The brochure posed the question, "Where and how can I have the Shield inserted?" and then provided its own answer: "This is done routinely and quickly (in about two minutes) as part of the regular appointment in the doctor's office. You will not require an anesthetic. The procedure is generally well tolerated by even the most sensitive women."

What the brochure failed to mention was the Shield's special pain-producing aspects, which sharply distinguished it from other IUDs on the market.

A light, flexible, molded plastic IUD, the Shield was unique in having four or five spicules, or fins, protruding from either side of the matrix. These strengthened the grip of the device in the uterus, decreasing the possibility that it would be expelled either by accident or as a result of pelvic infection. A survey of the Robins Medical Advisory Board in August 1970—two months after Robins bought the Shield, and five months before the beginning of global sales—reveals that some of the twenty-eight members were frightened:

> Reactions to the Dalkon Shield were varied and inconsistent. While many physicians felt that simplicity, flexibility and apparent ease of insertion would definitely be promotionally advantageous, others had serious reservations about the ability of the Shield to pass through the cervix without causing unnecessary pain and trauma. Some were enthusiastic about the design of our unit, the comparative compactness, and the obvious ability of its fins in preventing expulsion. On the other hand, several were appalled by what they considered the "frightening" looks of the device and very concerned with the possibility of these fins tearing into the uterus upon withdrawal.[8]

The company's approach was to emphasize that proper insertion techniques would minimize problems. It made photos showing the flexible fins, which protruded from the matrix at an angle of approximately 120 degrees, folding further downward as the device was thrust through the cervix. On entering the womb, the fins unfolded and gripped the endometrium, or lining, of the uterus. What the company downplayed was the reverse side of the coin: fins angled to fold downward on insertion would *unfold* upward on removal.

The problem of removal came up again in November 1970,

when Robins salesmen were asked at a "debriefing" if their Shield training had been adequate. Notes made at the session by John L. Burke, the general sales manager, indicate that the problem of unfolding received scant attention, although there was much attention to its effect on sales. "Why stress the point of removal when you can reap the benefits of it not coming out when you don't want it to?" Burke said. He added, "Folds when it goes in and folds when it comes out." He did not note that the folding on removal could require a good deal of force.

Such claims increased Shield sales, of course, but they also enraged physicians who met unexpected difficulty in inserting the relatively wide IUD through the narrow cervix, or, more often, in removing the device. Dr. Paul R. Packer, an OB-GYN in New Rochelle, New York, made one of the first protests, in a letter to Robins on February 11, 1971, six weeks after the company had formally begun to sell the Shield:

> I have just inserted my tenth Dalkon Shield and have found the procedure to be the most traumatic manipulation ever perpetrated upon womanhood. (I have inserted thousands of the other varieties [of IUDs] presently available.) . . . I have ordered all Shields out of my office and will do the same in all clinics with which I am affiliated.

Several weeks later, on March 31, Packer received a reply from Ellen Preston, who had recently been put in charge of Shield postmarketing surveillance. She did not mention the claims in the "Answers" brochure; rather, she implicitly repudiated them:

> If difficulty is experienced or anticipated, based on knowledge of the patient's emotional make-up as well as her physical condition, during either insertion or removal, especially nulliparous patients, we can recommend one or both of the following: a. premedication with 50 milligrams Demerol [a painkiller] and 0.5 milligrams [a]tropine [an antispasmodic drug to protect the patient from pain-induced cardiac arrest] . . . b. paracervical block anesthesia [an anesthetic procedure] . . . .

Preston did not tell Packer that she was citing the original labeling, or prescribing instructions, that had been supplied to physicians by the Dalkon Corporation, which had sold some 27,000 Shields in 1969–70 before selling rights to the IUD to Robins. She did not tell Packer that Robins had abandoned the recommendation, or why. Nor did she explain to him why the advice that she was giving him, and that Robins was giving to the physicians who were conducting its so-called "ten-investigator study" in nearly 2,400 women, conflicted with the advice the company was simultaneously promoting to the public, and advertising to the medical profession.

One of Robins's major claims to physicians regarding the Shield was that it was "DESIGNED FOR GREATER COMFORT . . . The Dalkon Shield is a more comfortable IUD." This claim was prominent in the eight-page "Progress Report" that Robins published in the final quarter of 1972 in the United States and as late as November 1974 in Australia and New Zealand. Russel Thomsen denounced the claim at a congressional hearing. "I have seen a number of women pass out from Dalkon Shield insertion," he testified. "If that is designed for comfort, I would hate to see one that was not designed for comfort."[9]

Frederick Clark had learned no later than mid-May 1970 that Shield insertions could be painful. Clark conceded in his 1976 deposition that when he flew to Defiance, Ohio, for the demonstration by Dr. Thad Earl, he had seen Earl using Demerol and atropine in several women. Even Shield developer Hugh Davis openly recognized the possibility of pain, particularly in the case of women who had never borne a child. He sent Clark a copy of a letter in which he told a physician on November 30, 1970, more than a month before Robins began its sales drive: "Using a paracervical block with five cc of 2 percent Xylocaine [anesthetic] . . . is a useful procedure for difficult removals or insertions in nulliparous patients."

In November 1971, Robins quietly deleted the no-anesthetic advice from "Answers to Your Patients' Questions." But it wasn't until July 1972 that it began to amend physicians' promotional materials and labeling to include the instructions regarding pain that the old Dalkon Corporation had offered. Commonly, physicians overlook unemphasized revisions in such materials. In September 1972, while "A Progress Report" was claiming that the Shield "has no general effects on the body, blood, or brain," a panel of Robins scientists was asking Irwin Lerner "to offer suggestions for a new model Shield" that would "reduce the incidence of pain and bleeding." Meanwhile, Clark helped to prepare a new "Answers to Your Patients' Questions." Dated October 1972—twenty months after Ellen Preston, his subordinate, had written to Dr. Packer—it restored the soothing claim that "the insertion procedure is generally well tolerated by even the most sensitive women."

One of the angered doctors was Dorothy I. Lansing, an OB-GYN who practices with her husband in Paoli and Westchester, Pennsylvania. She and Frederick Clark received their medical degrees together from Indiana University in 1947, and she remembers him as having been "very bright" and first in their class. After being out of touch for a quarter-century, she chanced on his name in Shield literature. Later, in 1974, she learned of a mounting toll of fatal infections among Shield wearers who had become pregnant. "Really annoyed" at Clark, as she put it in an interview, she wrote to him to explain why neither she nor her husband had ever inserted a Shield:

When the Dalkon Shield appeared on the scene, we rejected its use on my say-so. Why? Well, it's a gruesome looking little device that I would not allow to be installed in myself, that's why. Furthermore, with those vicious spikes, its installation would present a serious problem for removal.

When I told the Robins salesman "no," he was furious and announced we were the only ones not using the Dalkon Shield —that he had all the general practitioners and osteopaths in the area using it, and I remarked that was fine with me but changed nothing.

We have seen several patients with the Dalkon Shield put in elsewhere and several have been most difficult to extract in the operating room under anesthesia. I regard . . . the Dalkon Shield as a poorly designed IUD and a veritable instrument of torture.

A plaintiffs' lawyer asked Clark in a 1976 deposition if the Shield "had been described to you as 'a veritable instrument of torture'?" The phrase "doesn't ring a bell with me at this time," he testified. Lansing's letter, dated August 23, 1974, and signed "Dottie," went on to say of the Shield:

I am indeed sorry to hear that its use has been responsible for the deaths of seven women, but as a woman physician, I must tell you that the device never should have been marketed in the first place and then to have its use pushed on to GPs and GP osteopaths compounded all the problems involved.

Lansing told me that Clark replied with a letter in which he "begged" Lansing "to have a more balanced view," meaning that problems arise with all IUDs.

Robins's handling of information about pain was part of a general pattern of manipulating sales-sensitive issues to increase Shield profits, with no concern for women's exposure to agony or injury, unwanted pregnancy or infertility.

Thus, for example, the Dalkon Corporation's original prescribing instructions said: "Recent reports from clinical investigators strongly recommend adjunctive use of a spermacidle [sic] foam, jelly or cream to enhance contraceptive effectiveness during the first three months after insertion of the Dalkon Shield."

This recommendation grew out of the belief of Hugh Davis and Thad Earl that in the first two or three months after being fitted, a Shield wearer's chances of pregnancy were considerable, in some cases because she might unknowingly expel the device. The recommendation also reflected the practice that Davis had followed with at least some of the participants in his original study. Neither Davis nor Earl suggested deletion of the recommendation. Nevertheless, Robins omitted it from its initial labeling and promotional materials. A plaintiffs' lawyer asked Lerner if the recommendation "would cause sales resistance among some doctors." "It might," he said.

Gradually, over a nine-month period, the company began to tell physicians and women that the Shield should be supplemented with foam, at least in the beginning. The company had first mentioned and advised use of foam in November 1971, in updated editions of physicians' file cards and of the "Answers to Your Patients' Questions" brochure. In the same month, Ellen Preston said in a letter to a doctor that Robins's medical department recommended foam. Not until July and August 1972, however, did the company begin to include the advice in revised versions of the labeling inside the package, in the patient-oriented promotional folder, and in the pamphlets providing information and instructions to women in both English and Spanish. That was several months after Preston had claimed in a letter to all Robins salesmen that "we have tried to make this Dalkon Shield information as accurate, clear, comprehensive and up-to-date as possible."

Many women would never have been fitted with Shields had their doctors known that the devices they were inserting were not the ones that Robins was promoting. Such knowledge would have generated questions, and possibly suspicions that something was amiss or being covered up. If a manufacturer wants to modify a marketed drug product for which the Food and Drug Administration has approved a new-drug application for marketing, it must get FDA approval. It has been repeatedly shown that even a slight change in, say, the formulation of a product, or the form in which a dose is administered, can make a life-or-death difference in some people. Certain prescription drugs for asthma victims, for example, turned out to be relatively safe in dosages taken more than once a day, but hazardous to some users in a new once-a-day dosage. But Robins, unhampered by federal regulation of the Dalkon Shield, never revealed that the data from Hugh Davis's original study that it was using in advertising and promotion were not for the Shield it was selling. As mentioned in Chapter 4, Davis and Irwin Lerner, upon finishing the study, had quietly modified the plastic used for the matrix, mainly by adding copper salts to try to enhance efficacy. Dr. Clark described the changes in his secret June 1970 internal memo on his visit to Davis a few days before Robins bought the Shield from Dalkon, although, he wrote, the "shape and pattern [were] basically unchanged."

In October, Robins made several more undisclosed changes in the Shield, and it was *only* this altered, untested model that Robins distributed worldwide. One change was made when it was found that an X ray of a woman's pelvic region could miss a Shield because the plastic was insufficiently opaque. This was a serious problem, and Robins tried to augment radiopacity by increasing the amount of barium sulfate in the plastic. Other changes included thinning the central membrane so that it would "fold" for easier insertion and removal, decreasing the width by two millimeters, rounding the tips of the fins into teardrop shape, and thickening the string-attachment area.

Finally, Robins, making a special pitch to women who had never borne children, advertised and promoted the new, smaller nullip Shield. There was no disclosure that such studies as were cited—however inadequate—had been done with the large model, and that *no* safety and effectiveness tests whatsoever had been done with the small version.

As noted earlier, doctors seldom inserted IUDs in nulliparous women because they reacted with high rates of menstrual cramping, bleeding, complications, and expulsions. When Robins acquired the Shield, no IUD maker was recommending its device for nullips, who constituted an obviously huge potential market for a safe, effective IUD.

By Hugh Davis's account of his effectiveness study, the 640 women who participated included 51 nullips who received the original standard-size Shield. He claimed they did well, and for two years thereafter he nourished the claim with ever-larger numbers. Roy Smith, the Robins executive who had recommended that the company buy rights to the device, termed the claim "a big plus" for sales.

On November 1, 1969, after the study ended but three months before its publication, Davis told a *Washington Post* reporter that he had tested the same Shield in 117 nullips, and that it worked as well in them as in women who had had one or more children or who at least had been pregnant. In Davis's book, published in 1971, he claimed "excellent results" in more than 300 nullips at Johns Hopkins. (Notably, he advised medication and anesthesia to minimize the "discomfort" of insertion or removal.)

Meanwhile, in January 1969, Davis had begun a three-year study of a Shield designed expressly for nullips. "The major change," he said under oath, "was simply to scale down the device to have it conform to what was known about the smaller dimensions of a uterine cavity in a woman who had not previously borne children." The scaling-down decreased the number of spicules from ten on the standard Shield to eight on the small model. In late 1970, although no study of the nullip Shield's safety and efficacy was near completion, Robins decided to produce it and then to promote it with claims identical to those that Davis had made for the standard Shield in his 640-woman study—particularly the 1.1-percent pregnancy rate.

Davis completed his three-year nullip Shield study in January 1972, and in April he told a meeting of Planned Parenthood physicians that he had "personally fitted" 337 private patients with the nullip IUD. He renewed the old claim of a first-year pregnancy rate of 1.1 percent, but "partially ascribed" it "to the use of foam adjunctively by some of the subjects." He also said that in the second and third years, no additional pregnancies were "observed"—by whom, he didn't say.

Such claims naturally boosted Shield sales. Robins has said that in 1972 it sold 883,500 units—more than twice the number of Lippes Loops and five times the number of Saf-T-Coils. Yet by May of that year, Robins's Research Committee had received and was discussing reports that the nullip Shield was often difficult to insert and frequently unable to prevent pregnancy, contrary to advertising claims. Independent studies also raised troubling doubts. At the Kaiser-Permanente Medical Center in Sacramento, the pregnancy rate in 296 Shield-wearing nullips was 5.6 percent—four times higher than in wearers of two rival IUDs. At Beth Israel Hospital in Boston, the twelve-month rate in 258 Shield-wearers —one-third of them nullips—was 10.1 percent. In Dr. Mary Gabrielson's study, it will be recalled, all 1,209 participants—some as young as fourteen years old—were fitted with nullip Shields. In addition to the high 5.1-percent pregnancy rate, she reported a "high rate of removal for medical reasons," attributing about 80 percent of the removals to "pain and/or bleeding" and 15 percent to infection. Robins knew of these results but did not cite them in its eight-page "Progress Report" ad.

In August 1972, about a month before the ad's first appearance,

Robins began changing the labeling in the package to say that nullips fitted with Shields may have severe cramps for several days and may need medication for relief. In October, about two months before the ad's final appearance, Robins initiated a similar change in the "Answers to Your Patients' Questions" brochure.

The inadequacy of this change emerges clearly in the story of Mary Kornhauser, related in the Introduction to this book. As the reader may recall, Mary could end seven hellish years of pelvic infection only by undergoing drastic surgery that left her, at age twenty-five, forever unable to bear children. The beginning of her story is similar to that of the stories of many other young women who fell victim to the nullip Shield in the early 1970s.

After graduation from Winston Churchill Senior High School in Potomac, Maryland, Mary went to the University of Colorado in Boulder in August 1971. Eighteen years old and a virgin, she went to the student health service and said she was interested in birth control. She was given birth-control pills but, she told me, "I gained a lot of weight on them. My body became swollen, and I felt like an elephant." She decided, some time later, to go off the pills.

In February 1972, she returned to the health service and this time was given mimeographed information sheets and a pamphlet. She is uncertain whether these were health service or Robins materials. In any case, she said, "I recall walking away with the information in my head being very pro–Dalkon Shield, because it was being touted as the brand-new safe IUD for women who have never given birth before. I went back and asked for the Dalkon Shield, based on that information."

A health service physician inserted a Shield on February 16, 1972. For her, "the insertion was as easy as pie. I loved it. I decided it was the greatest thing, and I talked about it to friends —recommended it. I had no ill effects—or so I thought at the time. The tag line on the Shield was that it appeared to be maintenance-free, as opposed to inserting a diaphragm every time you had relations, or taking a pill every day. I recall this being discussed among my peers as a major asset for the Dalkon Shield."

Mary stayed in Boulder in the summer of 1972, working in a

dorm cafeteria but living off campus. "I started experiencing cramping and pain," she said. As instructed, she checked the string to be sure she had not expelled the device and that it had not shifted position in the womb. The string check revealed no problems, "but I still was in pain."

Since she wasn't enrolled as a summer student, she couldn't go to the health center, and so, after missing her menstrual period, she went to Planned Parenthood. Someone there checked the IUD, said it was fine, and, as was common at the time, gave her an injection of hormones to bring on her period. "They missed and hit my sciatic nerve," she said. "I had tremendous pain, and my left leg was paralyzed." She flew home to Maryland for a neurological exam and was pronounced fit. Her leg pain lessened and she was able to walk again.

Starting in August, when the fall term began, she went to classes and seemed to be healthy for about four weeks, until she caught a cold she couldn't shake. Meanwhile, the pain lingered, and it was sometimes quite sharp, particularly in the abdominal area. During this time she went to the health service several times.

"Each time I kept saying, 'Something's wrong. I have a pain, something's wrong.' They said, 'No, you have a little cold or a yeast infection—nothing serious.' They gave me medication, codeine for cough due to a cold, but even though codeine masks pain, it got worse." Later the health center took blood and urine samples and concluded that she had a bladder infection. There was no talk of the IUD or of taking it out.

The health center put her on Macrodantin, an antibacterial drug widely used in bladder infections, and Pyridium, a urinary-tract painkiller. But the pain worsened, and one day in early October 1972, Mary remembers, "I became blind with pain. I was hysterical. I kept saying, 'There's something wrong with me. I have this pain.' I phoned the assistant dean, who dispatched someone to drive me to the health center, and they put me in the infirmary. I had developed colitis from the stress of the situation, and they put me on phenobarbital. I woke up after a few days, really downed out because of the barbiturates, and after having tremendous nightmares."

She felt that she couldn't cope with school while suffering from problems that the health service "didn't take seriously." The university and her family agreed, and

> the decision was made to allow me to withdraw. I remember walking—limping—and I remember opening up the note from the health center saying that they recommended withdrawing because I was mentally unstable and having a nervous breakdown, something to that effect. Meaning that I had no idea whether I was crazy or not, at that point. I had no reality left. I was diagnosed as mentally unstable, as opposed to having PID [pelvic inflammatory disease]. At that time, I had a typical blind faith in a doctor's word as truth, so I believed him.
>
> My assumption is that if PID had been diagnosed at that time and treated properly, I would not only be in possession of a reproductive system and my own hormones, neither of which I have now, but I would be able to have children. If they had caught it at that time, I could have been cured, be normal, healthy, be able to have children, instead of having undergone seven years of pain, in and out of hospitals, and having a total hysterectomy and losing the ability to bear children at age twenty-five.

To all complaints about pain and efficacy, the response was finally the same. Claiborne Robins and William Zimmer, in a signed statement in the company's annual report for 1975, stated the position to which they have steadfastly adhered ever since: "The Shield, when properly used, is a safe and effective IUD." In January 1984, Robins swore that he was "not sure" why his company had ever sold the Shield in two sizes. At a deposition in February 1984, the chairman was unable to explain how he could continue to insist the Shield was safe when, as he admitted, he had no idea how many wearers had died, been treated in hospitals for infections, or had become infertile. He chose instead to find fault not with the Shield of either size, but with its users. But while a doctor might have used a Shield improperly—he might, for example, have inserted it improperly—it was not true that the expertise of the inserter was "the key" to Shield problems, as Robins swore.

How a woman—or a girl of fourteen—might have used the device improperly is not at all clear, but the Robins Company nevertheless continued to blame the people it misled—the doctors and the women—for the injuries caused by the device.

Executives of cigarette companies, when on public view, would rather be caught dead than not smoking. Cigarettes could scarcely be more visible, and IUDs could hardly be less so. While A. H. Robins was publicly hailing the Dalkon Shield as "the modern, superior IUD," how could anyone know if, say, the wives or daughters of company officers were wearing the Shield? In early 1984, plaintiffs' lawyers Michael V. Ciresi and Dale Larson tried to find out, and they developed some striking "do as I say, not as I do" deposition testimony: four officers and a woman employee —all having access to inside information on Shield hazards— didn't or wouldn't touch it.

Dr. Carl Lunsford, senior vice-president for research and development, testified that neither his wife nor any of his three daughters (aged thirty-five, thirty-two, and twenty-nine) had worn the Shield. Asked by Larson whether he knew "of any individual or person who's used the Dalkon Shield," Lunsford replied, "I do not."

Patricia A. Lashley, William Forrest's personal secretary and paralegal responsible for getting safety-related materials to the company's law department, testified that she had worn IUDs—but never the Shield. In organizing, filing, and reading the documents, she had undoubtedly become familiar with the sworn judgment of many medical experts that the Shield caused PID.

Ciresi asked Lashley, "I take it you never used the Dalkon Shield?" Robins counsel Thomas W. Kemp objected to this "invasion of her privacy," but Ciresi said his question was "highly relevant." If Lashley had not worn the IUD, he said, she may have abstained on the basis of information that was "in-house [and] was not distributed to other women who did use the Dalkon Shield. . . ."

Had Lashley worn an IUD "during the period 1970 through 1975?" Ciresi asked her on February 28. "Yes," she replied. "But it was not the Dalkon Shield?" Her reply was, "Correct." During the period the Shield was on sale, she added, she had "used several different kinds," yet had never asked her physician for a Shield. Three months after swearing that she had worn an IUD before 1975, Lashley swore that she had not worn one until *after* 1975. "When was the first time ever that you were inserted with an IUD?" Ciresi asked her on May 24. She answered that the first time she was fitted with an IUD was in 1976.

Dr. Frederick Clark, who had primary medical responsibilities for the Shield, received almost every one of the dozens of bad-news medical and scientific reports about the Shield's effectiveness as well as its safety. But in public—in appearances before the FDA and on Capitol Hill, and in sworn testimony in depositions and trials—he remained one of the Shield's most stalwart advocates and defenders.

Clark is the father of three daughters who, in 1984, ranged in age from twenty-six to thirty-four. In conversations with them, he said in reply to Ciresi's questions, he had learned that the eldest wears an IUD but that her sisters never have. He testified that he did not know if any of his daughters had used the Shield. "Never asked them?" Ciresi inquired. "Not that I am aware of," Clark replied.

Ellen Preston, who had dealt with questions and complaints about the Shield from the medical profession, gave testimony in which she did not dispute that while Robins was telling doctors and women in the population at large that removal of the Shield was advisable only in event of pregnancy, she was telling employees that removal was advisable even if they were *not* pregnant. On May 8, 1974, Robins had sent out a "Dear Doctor" letter that advised removal of the Shield from women with confirmed pregnancies while neither counseling removal from nonpregnant wearers nor suggesting any restraint on implanting new Shields.

Dr. Preston acknowledged to Ciresi that before the mailing, she "may have" advised Robins employees fitted with Shields to have them removed. He asked if it had not been her "general practice . . . to advise [inquiring] employees of the A. H. Robins Company . . . to remove the Dalkon Shield regardless of whether they were pregnant or not?" "I'm sorry, I just don't recall it," she said. "You just have no recollection of that?" "No, sir, I do not," she swore.

William Forrest, who signed all Shield promotional materials until June 1974, when Robins suspended domestic sales, testified that his wife had worn a Shield until it was surgically removed. She had also had a hysterectomy. Although IUD removals and hysterectomies were frequently connected and simultaneous events for many infected Shield wearers, Forrest steadfastly denied a connection in his wife's case and gave vague and widely differing dates for the two events. He and his wife, he explained, did not discuss such matters in detail. Indeed, Forrest gave a series of confusing accounts of his wife's hysterectomy and its possible relationship to the Shield she had worn. This exchange between Ciresi and Forrest is illustrative:

> Q: Did her doctor advise her that her hysterectomy was in any way related to the Dalkon Shield?
> A: Not that I know of, no, sir.
> Q: Did you ever ask her that?
> A: I don't recall. I may have asked her that. I don't recall the doctor telling her that. . . .
> Q: . . . Are you telling the ladies and gentlemen of the jury that you and your wife have never had a discussion concerning whether or not the Dalkon Shield played a part in her hysterectomy?
> A: Well, certainly, as I indicated to you, we had very general discussions. Now, if I asked her whether that played a part, I don't recall specifically if I did. If I did, to my knowledge, there was no indication that it did.

Why should it matter what Forrest asked or was told by his wife on this painful and intimate subject, from which one may sensibly want to turn away? Perhaps because Forrest did not show comparable sensitivity and deference to the very large numbers of other women who had worn Shields, were stricken by PID, and sued Robins. He readily conceded that these women had faced interrogation that was often relentless, irrelevant, and intimidating about their sex lives, even before marriage, and about their personal hygiene. Attorneys working for Forrest had asked these questions. But, he said, he had not asked his wife questions of this kind, and he didn't know if her gynecologist had.

Claiborne Robins, Sr., volunteered at a deposition in February 1984 that Claiborne Robins, Jr., had told him that his second wife, Mary Ellen, had worn a Shield. Under questioning, the father said he did not know when his son and Mary Ellen had married, how long she had worn the IUD, or whether she had worn it after 1974. He also said he did not know if either of his own two daughters had worn the Shield, and he was unable to name an employee, or a relative of an employee, who had worn a Shield after 1974.

On privacy grounds, by contrast, director and retired president William Zimmer and retired senior vice-president Roy Smith flatly refused to answer questions about the Shield as they may have pertained to members of their families. "It is none of your business, and it is none of the court's business," Zimmer said.

7

Dodging the FDA

Clear statutory authority for the FDA to prevent the
marketing of medical devices which have not had
adequate premarket testing could have prevented the
deaths and injuries associated with the use of IUDs like
the Shield.
—*Medical Device Amendments of 1976*, a report by the
Committee on Interstate and Foreign Commerce[1]

The first true food and drug legislation was introduced in Congress
in the 1880s. For a quarter-century thereafter, such bills were
defeated by a formidable coalition of quacks, scoundrels, and
vested interests, including venal legislators and newspaper pub-
lishers. Finally, in 1906, Congress enacted the Pure Food and
Drugs Act.[2] Dr. Harvey W. Wiley, who had led the battle for
passage of the act, said that patent medicines foisted on the public
constituted "the most wretched and disgraceful evil." He told of
"a weak solution of sulphuric and sulphurous acids, with an occa-
sional trace of hydrochloric and hydrobromic acids," that was
guaranteed to "cure"

asthma, abscess, anemia, bronchitis, blood poison, bowel
troubles, coughs, colds, consumption, contagious diseases,
cancer, catarrh, dysentery, diarrhea, dyspepsia, dandruff, ec-
zema, erysipelas, fevers, gallstones, goiter, gout, hay fever,
influenza, la grippe, leucorrhea, malaria, neuralgia, piles,
quinsy, rheumatism, scrofula, skin diseases, tuberculosis, tu-

mors, throat troubles, and ulcers—all arranged nicely in the advertisements in alphabetical form so that your particular ill could easily be located. . . .[3]

The 1906 law prohibited false *or* misleading advertising. In 1911, the Supreme Court eviscerated the prohibition by ruling that it applied to a product's identity but *not* to its claimed curative powers. In 1912, Congress, in a misguided effort to counter the ruling, amended the law to forbid false *and* fraudulent labeling. But this only made matters worse because false statements, to be illegal, had to be proved to have been made with *intent* to deceive. In 1913, however, Congress showed its concern for animals: it passed a law prohibiting the sale of worthless drugs and serums for treating cattle, hogs, and sheep.

In 1933, a Senate bill was introduced to overcome the weaknesses in the 1906 law. It was quickly attacked by the United Medicine Manufacturers of America. President Roosevelt made several pleas to congressional leaders to pass the bill, but he had little success. The Senate and House committee hearings, rich in news that mattered to people, were ignored by all major newspapers but the *St. Louis Post-Dispatch* and the *Christian Science Monitor.*

Then, in 1937, a chemist at the S. E. Massengill Company found that he could dissolve a formerly insoluble sulfa drug in a chemical relative of radiator antifreeze. This discovery created a marketing opportunity because doctors had long sought a liquid sulfa solution, and the Bristol, Tennessee, enterprise promptly seized upon it. Massengill began to sell "Elixir of Sulfanilamide" after checking it for appearance, flavor, and fragrance—but not safety. The first reports of deaths in consumers of Elixir reached the Food and Drug Administration in October 1937; the final death toll was 108, if one includes the suicide of the chemist.

Congress responded in 1938 by passing the Food, Drug, and Cosmetic Act. It required a manufacturer seeking to put a new drug on sale to test it for safety and report the results to the FDA. The new law also closed the gaping "false and fraudulent" loophole a quarter-century after Congress had created it. Still, Congress chose not to require medicines to be proved effective as well as safe in the uses for which manufacturers recommended them. Yet a potent drug that is ineffective is often unsafe because it can cause serious adverse reactions; moreover, resorting to a useless drug can delay more effective therapy and so be additionally hazardous.

The effectiveness issue did not disappear. In 1962, President Kennedy said that 20 percent of the new drug entities listed since 1956 had been found "incapable of sustaining one or more of their sponsor's claims," i.e., manufacturers were touting one out of five new drug compounds for at least one medical condition in which it was useless. But it was not until the thalidomide crisis, also in 1962, that Congress, responding to catastrophe with its customary better-late-than-never hindsight, enacted the Kefauver-Harris Amendments. These required drug manufacturers to provide, among other things, "substantial evidence"—defined as well-controlled clinical experiments done by specialists in the particular field—for claims of effectiveness.[4]

Finally, in 1976, Congress adopted the Medical Device Amendments. For this characteristically Pavlovian response, the bell-ringer was the excesses of the A. H. Robins Company, particularly its refusal to test the safety and effectiveness of a device before falsely and misleadingly advertising and promoting it.

The primary concern of the S. E. Massengill Company about its unregulated Elixir was its sales appeal, not its safety, and the primary concern of the A. H. Robins Company about its unregulated intrauterine device was—one-third of a century later—no different.

Six months before Robins began to sell the Shield, its executives wrote memos saying that it should be studied for safety and effectiveness in women and in laboratory animals. Their concern was practical, not moral: they believed Congress would soon enact a testing requirement for medical devices and that it was necessary to prepare to comply. "I would estimate that prolonged animal and human implantation studies would be required," Dr. Oscar Klioze, director of pharmaceutical research, wrote in June 1970, adding, "This is particularly true in view of the approximately two-year implantation time for the device in normal usage." Jack Freund, the most senior physician, also cited a need for "added studies to support the effectiveness and safety" of the Shield. Frederick

Clark, the medical director, agreed in a memo ten weeks later, on August 31, in which he said, "In light of extreme probability of device legislation in next twelve months it behooves us to commence indicated studies as soon as possible." As things turned out, Congress waited six years to enact such a requirement—until Robins had amply proved the need for it by drawing millions of women into a vast, uncontrolled experiment that caused injury to thousands.

The fact is that although Robins showed some concern that the Dalkon Shield would come under federal regulation, it never conducted the tests that would have been reasonably and minimally required. Instead, it tried to find and promote data that could be construed as supporting its claims for the safety and efficacy of the Shield. In this way, Robins hoped to circumvent expected device regulations.

Not only did the Robins Company fail to initiate its own testing; it actively turned down a series of proposals from outside the company for studies that had the potential to provide an early warning of the pelvic infections that would turn up in actual use. The proposals, which would have required only small sums of money for their implementation, came from members of the faculty of the Medical College of Virginia, which was close at hand in Richmond, and which had frequently been a source of consultants for Robins. First, Dr. John A. Board, an obstetrician-gynecologist and Robins consultant, whose wife, Anne, was a Robins physician, and whose research nurse was experienced in contraceptive studies, proposed to do a clinical evaluation of the Shield. A second proposal came from Dr. William T. Jolly, chairman of MCV's anatomy department; he wanted to study, under a powerful scanning electron microscope, the Shield's effects on uterine tissue.

Dr. Solon E. Davis, who was teaching at MCV at the time of the Board and Jolly proposals, said in an interview, "It is not clear that they [Robins officials] were interested in any significant . . . consultation arrangement." Indeed they weren't; Robins declined the MCV offers and also a third proposal, made by Dr. G. E. Weinberg of Cleveland, Ohio, for a clinical study. In a subsequent chronology, William Forrest said that Clark had written letters to Board and Weinberg indicating "that we are in the preparatory stage for marketing and are presently securing detailed information on previous studies initiated by the Dalkon Corporation—[we] will then assess needs for further study-type information." In fact, Dalkon had done no safety studies, and Clark was making transparent excuses.

Then, in December 1970—the month before Robins launched the Shield internationally, Dr. A. N. Chremos, director of clinical pharmacology, turned down a proposal by Thad Earl. Chremos, in a revealing letter, told Earl: "In view of the limited research budget for the Dalkon Shield, it will be difficult for us to find money in the future for research expenses incurred outside our specifically set up studies."

If good cause figured in the rejection of Earl, it was nowhere to be seen in the case of a request from the University of Kentucky Medical Center in Lexington. Physicians there had inserted Shields in about five hundred women and gathered follow-up data on a large proportion of them. On June 23, 1972, the center's Dr. Avis Erickson phoned Ellen Preston. In a memo five days later, Preston said:

> The data has been pulled together, coded, keypunched, and is in the process of being analyzed. This has taken a considerable amount of time, etc., including 200 hours of computer time. At least one person . . . will be working full time with the data until at least the end of July.
>
> They plan to publish, and the lady called . . . to request some financial assistance. She was unable to suggest an amount. I told her I would present the proposal to the proper people here. . . .
>
> I inquired as to what their experience had been with the Shield. She said they had pulled a random sample of 100 Dalkon Shield patients, and [a] preliminary look at this data *was not very favorable.* [Emphasis added.]

Preston sent the memo to her boss, Dr. Clark, and asked, "What do you suggest?" The medical director replied the same day, June 28:

Kitty—

My reaction, perhaps unduly and undesirably influenced by your last sentence, is to parry the query by the following:

1. Pursue the matter of amount requested—However—

2. Indicate that we are presently conducting a survey designed to gain information on some "high" and "low" pregnancy rates, to be followed by an attempt to explore the "whys" of each. Until we are further along in this, we are not in a position to make commitments to retrospective data evaluation, unless selected by the above process. . . .

Before Preston was able to write to Dr. Erickson, the Kentucky physician phoned on July 6 to ask if a decision had been reached. "She said they would accept anything and mentioned an amount of $500 to $1,000 . . . to pay two graduate students who were working on the data," Preston said in a memo on the call. Preston wrote that she had given Erickson an oral summary of Clark's advice and indicated that "I was not at all optimistic about obtaining approval for any assistance." In a subsequent letter to Erickson, Preston ascribed a false deliberative dignity to the rejection, saying that "our Dalkon Shield Study Committee" had turned her down because "they feel that we have no funds at the present time for this type of Dalkon Shield study." Her explanation was, almost verbatim, Clark's suggested "parry," and of course there was no "Dalkon Shield Study Committee." As Clark's memo makes clear, "this type of Dalkon Shield study" was the kind that might yield adverse results.

In March 1973, a request for a grant came to a Robins salesman from Drs. Clay Wells and Jesse Mendoza of Women and Infants Hospital in Providence, Rhode Island. Hospital physicians had inserted Shields in about one thousand women. Some of the women had developed problems, and the hospital wanted to know if money was available to review its data. Preston wrote to the salesman who had relayed the information: "As I indicated to you during our telephone conversation, I am not very amenable at this point to expending a great deal of money or personnel time to analyze Dalkon Shield data which is anticipated to be unfavorable."

Robins was so chilly to funding requests that it gave short shrift

to two more of its paid consultants, Hugh Davis and Donald Ostergard. "We can't afford the luxury of setting up a formal clinic study
with Davis," Robert Murphey, director of scientific development
and international research, said in a memo in February 1971. In
March 1973, Ostergard proposed a bacteriological study bearing
on IUD-related pelvic inflammatory disease. Preston turned him
down with a letter six months later, saying that "we just can't fit
the price tag [$20,000 to $30,000] into what we see as our needs
for the Shield over the next year or two. . . . I would still like to
be able to determine in some way a little more definitely what
relationship exists between the Dalkon Shield and PID. If you
have any ideas, a little less expensive ones, we would certainly like
to hear them."

By August 1973, when Robins was shipping Shields at an
estimated rate of 62,400 a month, Preston had become almost
zealous in her opposition to paying for research that might reflect
adversely on the Shield. On August 3, in a memo on a conversation
with Dr. Myron Moorehead of Columbus, Ohio, she said, "We
obviously were not interested in paying premium prices for unfavorable data. . . ." Twenty-four days later she wrote a "Clinical Project
Plan Proposal" suggesting "creative" ways of using Robins's ten-
investigator study. The following excerpt reveals a deliberate failure to acknowledge the consequences for anything but sales:

> In my opinion our number one priority, even obligation, is
> to make further use of the vast amount of data in our own
> [ten-investigator] prospective studies. . . . Although a number
> of very favorable reports on the Shield have been published,
> some highly unfavorable data has also been published. It is
> my understanding that within our own data there are single
> studies of very favorable data which could be used to coun-
> teract some of this already published material. . . . Certainly
> any initial report on AHR data must include all ten studies,
> but we could "break out" the individual studies to show this
> favorable data. . . .

Preston did not comment on the grave deficiencies in the study,
such as the staggering loss-to-follow-up rates and the work of one

investigator, Donald Ostergard, which her husband, Lester Preston, Robins's director of scientific information, had denounced eighteen months earlier as possibly "a clear-cut case of GIGO."

Another grave problem, involving seemingly favorable data, came to light much later. One of the clinics in the ten-investigator study, the Northwest Ohio Family Planning Agency (NOFPA) in Defiance, participated from August 1971, when Dr. Thad Earl was the clinic's medical director, to December 1973, after Dr. Paul E. Palmer had succeeded him. Robins's summaries of the results, prepared by Lester Preston from forms filled out by the investigators, showed that NOFPA had inserted Shields in 149 women, and that only one out of that number had developed pelvic inflammatory disease.

Dr. Robert E. Barnett, who had had no connection with the study, succeeded Palmer in 1980 as medical director of NOFPA. In the summer of 1984, a plaintiffs' lawyer asked him to search for the original raw data, which were in boxes in the clinic's basement. The reason given by the lawyer was that in Shield court cases, women who had been devastated by pelvic inflammatory disease were faced by Robins's repeated claims that the ten-investigator study, which it has called "the Cadillac of the IUD studies," had shown the Shield to be associated with PID at rates no higher than the rates for rival IUDs.

Barnett agreed to search for the raw data. He found medical charts on about five hundred women who had been fitted with Shields, and by cross-matching dates of insertion and other clues, he isolated the data for 120 of the 149 women who had been in the ten-investigator study. "I was astonished at what I found," Barnett reported in a letter to Robins on July 13, 1984:

> There are documented pelvic infections in *18* of these 120 patients in the study. This is quite disturbing since, according to A. H. Robins Co., summary data of this study indicates that only one infection was encountered among the [149] patients in the study.
>
> I am concerned about the implications of these findings and would like to know how the data was originally reviewed. . . . It is my understanding that a representative from A. H.

Robins actually invited the Family Planning Agency to retrieve the data but it is not clear whether this representative
actually reviewed the charts himself, or whether he received
the information from someone at the agency who had reviewed the charts [Barnett told me that Dr. Palmer had told
him he did not know who had retrieved the data].

In any case, it appears that the study design, including data
retrieval method (whatever that was) was apparently not adequate to determine product safety since the official report of
the study indicates an infection rate of 0.6 percent when the
actual infection rate was fifteen to twenty times higher than
that. I'm sure I don't need to tell you that this is a very
significant discrepancy, the implications of which are as astro-
nomical in proportion as they are long-reaching.

Barnett closed the letter by saying he would "very much like to
talk with A. H. Robins" about the situation. Two months later,
Fletcher Owen, Robins's assistant vice-president for medical services, phoned to acknowledge receipt of the letter and to promise
a reply. In a certified letter to Owen three months after that, on
December 26, 1984, Barnett told Owen that he had received no
reply.[5] Four months later, toward the end of March 1985, however, Owen made a surprising admission: the company had prepared and sent to Barnett an eleven-page summary of the NOFPA
data, and it suggested problems "which I think may well have led
to some discrepancies." Barnett told the *Richmond Times-Dispatch*,
and Owen acknowledged, that a question on the forms about the
presence of pelvic infections had in some cases not been answered,
and that the blank spaces on the forms simply were interpreted to
mean that there had been no PID.[6]

Of course, Ellen Preston could not have known about the shod-
diness of this particular study, but her determined quest for good
news inevitably led her far from standards of scientific objectivity.
Her August 1973 memo went on to say:

We have, prior to the maturity of our own studies, attempted to pick up some quick, favorable statistics by retro-
spectively analyzing data made available to us. Most attempts

at this have failed in that anticipated low (around 2 percent) pregnancy rates have been higher. To date none of these studies have been published. So at this time there continues to exist a need for additional data of a favorable nature for our utilization and publication. Obviously to meet this need, studies will have to be accepted on a very selected basis, i.e., those known in advance to be favorable (pregnancy rate of 2 percent or less).

In October 1973, two months after starting her crusade to hustle up favorable Shield data, Preston asked eight Robins officials to convene a meeting. What had motivated her? Plaintiffs' attorney Michael Ciresi asked her this question at a deposition in 1974. "We attempted to find favorable data . . . because we had a great deal of unfavorable data already," she answered.

The concern about Robins's lack of contraceptive research and development continued to agitate several officials of the company. In January 1972, Shield project coordinator Kenneth Moore wrote a memo in which he said, "The big unanswered question is how far is management willing to go with contraceptive research, specifically intrauterine device research. In other words, how many dollars are they willing to spend to improve the existing Dalkon Shield and to develop the Dalkon Shield of tomorrow?" Late that year, Moore was able to report that Robins was indeed participating in some studies of how Shield wearers had fared, and was looking at data from other retrospective studies that had been offered for analysis. Robins's primary purpose in participating was "to make available for publication extremely good Dalkon Shield results," Moore said in a memo on October 4, 1972. Five weeks later, he wrote in another memo that an interdisciplinary committee had recommended a program whose objectives included "foster[ing] publication of favorable Dalkon Shield data in major professional journals and the presentation of like data at major meetings. . . . It is recommended that we engage in at least ten retrospective studies in 1973 for the purpose of obtaining favorable Dalkon Shield data."

Animal studies normally precede clinical trials; what of them? In July 1971—a month in which an estimated 2,250 women were being fitted with Shields every day—Dr. Murphey affirmed in a memo that "we possess inadequate support data from animal studies as to long-term safety of the current Dalkon Shield." Two months later, Robins started a two-year study in baboons, which have reproductive tracts highly similar to women's. Among eight, one "perished," and among ten, three suffered perforation of the uterus, Dr. John W. Ward, director of toxicology and assistant director of scientific development, has testified. Robins has never revealed these results to the medical profession.

In the absence of federal regulation, Robins felt free to market a product untested for safety or efficacy. Its actions in response to even a hint of federal regulation were no more honorable. They concealed and distorted facts and engaged in a series of erratic, zigzag maneuvers.

As we have seen, there was copper in the Shield marketed by Robins, but not in the one originally tested by Hugh Davis. At Robins, two days before the purchase, W. Roy Smith, the director of product planning, told senior executives that he was deeply concerned about plans to market an IUD without disclosure to the physician that copper and copper sulfate were in the plastic from which the matrix was molded. For one thing, he warned in a memo on June 10, 1970, copper sulfate may have a "deleterious effect." For another, he said, Robins might be breaching an "implied warranty" by not forthrightly disclosing to physicians that the salt had been added to the matrix plastic "for the express purpose of getting an added 'drug effect,'" by which he meant chemical enhancement of the Shield's efficacy.

Smith's superiors decided to ignore his cautionary advice—and made a point of reassuring physicians about the safety and effectiveness of copper. On December 8, 1970—twenty-four days before the start of global Shield marketing—Ray B. Hanchey, who directed instruction and training of Robins's sales force, distributed to the salesmen a "Communiqué" on the "Scientific Background" of IUDs. This two-and-a-half-page paper—a source of disinformation for the physicians who would hear the salesmen's spiel—attributed to many unnamed researchers the belief that intrauterine-device contraception "approaches the ideal." Hanchey's "Communiqué" began:

SECOND GENERATION INTRAUTERINE DEVICES

Improved birth control methods are now featuring intrauterine devices which combine new designs with a trace of copper to offer effectiveness virtually equal to the pill and with few side effects. . . .

Many investigators feel that there is *no reason to anticipate adverse reactions to the copper.*

At Johns Hopkins, Dr. Davis is having similarly encouraging results with a shield-shaped device in which copper ions are blended with plastic as the device is manufactured. He reports that it has been inserted in nine hundred women since last October; none have become pregnant. [How did Davis know?]

The "Communiqué" was a zig. A memo only eight days later was a very sharp zag. R. W. Nickless, management coordinator for pharmaceutical products, told a half-dozen executives on December 16:

> The problem is this—Dr. Davis has overpublicized the copper content, and as a result, has put us in the position of acknowledging or defending the fact. It seems to me the copper content should be regarded as, 1. experimental. 2. confidential. . . .
>
> I would like to see the following action to head off questions, concerns and speculations arising from the publicized copper content:
>
> 1. Dr. Davis, et al, should be told to treat the contents of this product in as confidential a way as we treat other product formulas.
>
> 2. All sales representatives have had some exposure to the "copper story" and should be told to answer [physicians'] questions about the Shield's components as being a "confidential blending of ingredients to achieve engineering objectives" or some such statement.
>
> 3. All references to copper for "outsiders" should be reserved for investigational purposes.

The point, it seems to me, is that we can easily sell the advantages of the Shield on the basis of the design or anatomical engineering without more unproved speculations about copper—which seems to upset rather than convince and reassure buyers. I don't believe we need to go into the many reasons why the copper story can be damaging to us, and there is the matter of device legislation or other FDA control. . . .

I urge very strongly that we take protective action on this matter.

Nickless's "protective action" was too late for *Good Housekeeping* magazine, which had already locked into its January 1971 issue an article in which Hugh Davis put another zig in the copper story. "With the addition of copper the Shield device is virtually 100 percent effective in preventing pregnancies," he claimed.

March 1971 brought another zag. John Burke, the general sales manager, tried to direct the salesmen completely away from the copper component. In a memo, he told them to stress the Shield's "specific design features" in explaining its "overall superiority." If a doctor asks questions about the copper and copper salt, he said, tell him that they "are incorporated into a special plastic blend from which the Shield is molded. Then, if necessary, you can inform the doctor that the only known contributions of the copper additives relate to certain physical and mechanical properties, such as improved radio-opacity with less barium sulfate, and the more desirable 'flow-melt index.' "

Meanwhile, G. D. Searle & Company was seeking to market the Cu-7 IUD, contending that its copper content increased its efficacy. This compelled the slow-moving FDA to face the issue of whether to regulate IUDs, or at least some IUDs, as drugs. Its decision was that the Cu-7, because it contained a non-inert substance, was a new drug and, as such, subject to all of the premarket testing and other requirements of the drug law. Regulation being a fate that Robins wanted to avoid at all costs, Burke sent another memo to the salesmen on April 27. With a forcefulness and clarity lacking in the original, he said that the purpose of his March memo was to emphasize that the copper additives *had nothing* to do with the contraceptive effectiveness of the Shield, . . . it is essential that you avoid any suggestion or implication that the copper additives contribute to or enhance the contraceptive effectiveness of the Shield. . . .

A retrospective examination of available clinical data on the Shield indicates that *there is no difference in the pregnancy rates between Shields containing the copper additives and those which are free of copper.* [Emphasis added.]

This should be viewed as a highly fortunate situation because it is now obvious (based on rulings regarding Searle's "Cu-7") that any copper containing intrauterine device for which clinical data substantiates [*sic*] a contribution of the copper to the contraceptive effectiveness of that device, is considered by the FDA to be a *new drug*. . . .

On May 19, a Robins delegation led by Robert Murphey met with FDA officials to claim that the copper and copper salt in the Shield served only to improve physical or mechanical characteristics of the device. "The meeting was most cordial in every respect," Murphey said in a memo. Dr. Edwin M. Ortiz, director of the agency's Division of Metabolic and Endocrine Drug Products, "expressed appreciation for Robins' efforts in gathering the information for them. . . . On the basis of the data in hand at this time, it does not appear that the FDA people would be justified in classing the Dalkon Shield as a drug. . . . Our studies of all aspects of the Dalkon Shield are continuing in anticipation of eventual device legislation and to protect against any unexpected change in regulatory attitudes." At a deposition in 1984, plaintiffs' attorney Michael Ciresi recounted the story to Roger Tuttle, who had been a Robins attorney. "So Robins lied to the FDA, correct?" Ciresi asked. "It would certainly appear so," Tuttle replied.

Sixteen days after meeting with the Robins delegation, the FDA proposed a compromise regulation. As finally agreed upon in March 1973, the compromise would be that the agency would treat as a regulated "drug" an IUD that contained a "heavy" metal, such as copper, or any other substance that might be biologically "active" in the body; an IUD would be an unregulated device if fabricated entirely from inactive materials or if substances "added to improve the physical characteristics . . . [did] not contribute to contraception through chemical action on or within the body."

For a time, Robins considered making a copperless Shield as a protective action. Kenneth Moore favored this course; Dr. A. N. Chremos opposed it. Chremos "feels our defense of copper which was submitted to the FDA locks us in," Moore said in a memo on October 7, 1971. "In other words, removal would be an acknowledgement of guilt."

A month later, Robins officials met to discuss the Shield's inadequate radiopacity, which made X-ray detection difficult, and recommended removal of copper. "Some say that the copper (regardless of source) contributes to radiopacity," Moore said on November 12. "It is generally agreed that this is very questionable." He ignored what sales manager Burke, eight months earlier, had told the salesmen to tell doctors, i.e., that "the only known contributions of the copper additives relate to certain physical and mechanical properties, such as improved radio-opacity. . . ."

In February 1972, five Robins doctors and scientists met with Moore. He asked, "Does copper in Shield accomplish anything [?] No! [was the] general consensus." This meant that it was all for nothing that large numbers of women had been exposed to copper sulfate and that the medical profession and the FDA had been deceived. Jack Freund wrote a month later that "the presence of copper exposes the Shield to possible FDA action on the basis that it is a drug. Information about the Shield was submitted to the FDA on May 19, 1971. No further word has been received." Meanwhile, Freund recommended that Robins develop a copperless Shield but "continue marketing the present shield until a suitable replacement is developed." Robins ended up distributing a total of 2.8 million old-model Shields in the United States alone.

IV

Trouble

The product is manufactured in accordance with good manufacturing practices. Each component of, and the device itself, is quality assurance tested.

—A. H. Robins's senior vice-president Jack Freund, in testimony before a House Government Operations subcommittee, June 12, 1973

8

The String

The thread-sized "tail string" of any intrauterine device serves one purpose for the wearer and another for the doctor. The woman need only touch it to make sure she has not expelled the IUD; the physician who must remove the device may need only to tug or yank the string. An IUD string runs between the vagina, where bacteria are alway present, and the uterus, which is germ-free. It passes through the cervix, where cervical mucus is the body's natural defense against bacterial invasion of the uterus and result-ant pelvic inflammatory disease. The mucus almost always stops germs on the exterior of a tail string.

Starting in the 1960s, the strings on nearly all IUDs were impervious monofilaments, meaning that bacteria *on* them could not get *into* them. To the naked eye, the Dalkon Shield string—0.4 millimeter in diameter—was a monofilament as well. Actually, however, it was a cylindrical sheath encasing 200 to 450 round monofilaments separated by spaces. And although the string was knotted near both ends, neither end was actually sealed. Any bacteria that got into the spaces between the filaments would be insulated from the body's antibacterial action while being drawn into the womb by "wicking," a phenomenon similar to that by which a string draws the melting wax of a candle to the flame.

The open-ended, multifilament string was at the core of the Dalkon Shield catastrophe, being a major cause of pelvic inflamma-

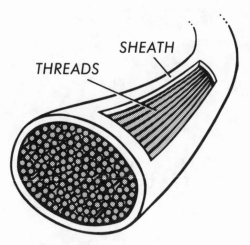

THREADS

SHEATH

A cross section of the Dalkon Shield tail string showing the hundreds of tiny threads within the sheath. Bacteria climb between these threads from the vagina into the uterus, causing infection.

tory disease and its dreadful consequences. Robins executives were repeatedly warned of the string's wicking properties, but they failed or refused to listen. Instead, they stonewalled, deceived, covered up, and covered up the cover-ups, and in doing so they inflicted on women an absolutely avoidable worldwide epidemic of pelvic infections. Even by April 1985 the company would not implicate the string, saying: "Robins believes that serious scientific questions exist about whether the Dalkon Shield poses a significantly different risk of infections [from that presented by] other IUDs."[1]

Irwin Lerner, the Shield's listed inventor, wanted a string that would not be stiff, but that would also not break under the stress of removing an IUD with eight or ten fins planted in the lining of the womb so as to provide the superior "retention" about which Robins bragged.[2] His search for the "right" string was quite casual; he turned to a Danish friend who steered him to Supramid, the trade name for a suture material made by a firm in West Germany.[3] Kenneth Moore said Lerner had told him that the specifications had been set by "a trial and error process based strictly on experience."

The medical literature since 1956 had warned that nylon would deteriorate in body cavities. The Shield sheath and filaments were made of Supramid, which was nylon 6, a variant of nylon that had never been used in an IUD string. Obviously, deterioration of the sheath or filaments would give easy access to bacteria. Nylon 6 also will degrade in the uterine environment, a paid company consultant, plastics chemist F. Murray Goodman of the University of California at San Diego, has sworn. Albert E. Martin, who led Robins's analytical research group, has testified that he had long known of nylon's potential for deterioration in the body. On learning that Robins was about to buy an IUD with a nylon string, he said he had passed this "basic information" to several Robins officials, including Jack Freund. Before Robins bought the Shield from the Dalkon Corporation in June 1970, Dr. Freund asked Oscar Klioze, director of pharmaceutical research and analytical services, to discuss its "technical aspects" with Irwin Lerner. On June 8—four days before the deal was signed—Dr. Klioze told Freund that no one knew how long the string would be chemically stable in the body *in vivo*. "The device has not been subjected to any formal stability testing," his memo said.

On June 29, 1970—seventeen days after Robins bought the Shield—R. W. Nickless warned about wicking in a confidential "Orientation Report" that contained the statement, "The string or 'tail' situation needs a careful review since the present 'tail' is reported (by Mr. Lerner) to have a 'wicking' tendency."

Nickless sent the report to thirty-nine executives, including Claiborne Robins, William Zimmer, Carl Lunsford, several vice-presidents, and senior scientists and physicians including Drs. Freund and Owen. No records I have seen show that any of the executives were moved to act on the information. In a 1983 deposition, Owen was asked, "And when you were advised of that, you understood that meant to wick bacteria, correct?" He replied, "Yes, sir." Kenneth Moore swore he hadn't heard of the report until four years after it was written.

In March 1971, twelve weeks after Robins began Shield sales worldwide, salesman Walter W. Schoenberger of Long Beach, California, sent to the medical department a query in which he asked: "What is our Dalkon 'string' made of? Competition (Ortho) is telling my doctors that: it will break, it will fray easily, and that it is 'multilayered' so that the inner core acts as a wick to induce infection into the uterus."

Owen referred the query to Ellen Preston, who had recently been made responsible for alerting doctors to possible hazards. She has sworn that Owen never told her to find out what the string was made of. Owen has sworn he had told her to do just that. In any case, Preston assigned Dr. Anne W. Board to reply to Schoenberger. Nearly a month later, Board wrote Schoenberger that she had been told by David A. Mefford, director of quality assurance, that "the string is composed of a multifilament surgical suture enclosed in a nylon sheath."

In October, Martin and Moore discussed their concerns about "physical changes that might take place in the Shield in utero" and "about how extensive [the] loss of the integrity of the string might be with time. . . ." Moore asked Martin to try to find out if the "intrauterine environment has had any effect" on the string. Robins finally hired its first polymer expert, Thomas C. Yu, in 1972 —nylon is a polymer plastic—but Moore requested no more than half of his time so as to leave the rest free for Robins's veterinary products.

In April 1972, John Autian of the University of Tennessee, an expert on plastics toxicology, discussed the Shield with Robins executives, at their invitation. Moore wrote later, "I was particularly impressed by [his] recommendation that we conduct a lot of acute toxicity testing." By then, Robins had distributed more than 1.4 million Shields and was shipping out about 2,000 a day.

In August 1972, Robins's representative in Tokyo reported a Japanese doctor's worry "about the possibility of infections entering into the uterus through that part of the tail extending into the vagina." But Dr. Chremos assured the representative that IUD strings do "not play a significant role as a conveyor of infection into the uterus."

"It is of utmost importance that we set up our testing program for used Dalkon Shields in the near future," Moore emphasized again on February 7, 1973. *"Considering that we have been marketing the device for going on three years,"* he wrote, *"it is about time that data are collected on the effect of the uterine environment. . . ."* [Emphasis added.] Later, Robins retrieved 303 used strings for examination by Thomas Yu. He found defects in all but

35. Albert Martin, Yu's boss, has sworn that Robins has no written records of the exams or of the results.

In September 1973, Robins's medical officer in England told home-office officials that a London gynecologist had implanted Shields in three hundred women, had seen severe pelvic infections develop in four to eight, and "is almost certain that such infection is caused by the string . . . acting as a wick. . . ." Preston replied that such wicking as may occur "is overcome entirely by having the filaments enclosed in the sheath." To be sure, she added, Dr. Chremos granted that "a problem might exist" if the Shield broke and destroyed the sheath's integrity. She said breakage "can happen" but speculated it was not "very frequent," based on Chremos's "hypothesis," for which, she said later, he had no experimental data.

In January 1975, Robert W. Tankersley, Jr., Robins's head of microbiological research, outlined four experiments to find out if any type of string wicked bacteria. He estimated they would take two and a half weeks, use four rabbits, and cost a total of $90. The experiments were not funded.

Robins never told physicians that the Shield string was multifilamented and had interstices among the filaments so that any deterioration could lead to life-threatening infections. That these facts *should* have been divulged by the company was not acknowledged by Ellen Preston. "Did it ever occur to you to ask physicians whether they would like to know that the Dalkon Shield tail string presented an additional avenue by which bacteria could get from the vagina into the uterus?" plaintiffs' attorney Michael Ciresi asked Preston at a deposition in 1984. "I've never discussed that with any physician, and in my opinion it was not a necessary fact to provide," she replied. "Doctor, would you, as a physician who was going to insert an intrauterine device, want to know whether that [IUD] created an additional avenue by which bacteria could get from the vagina into the uterus?" Ciresi asked. "I just don't agree with the assumption," Preston said. "I wouldn't want to know."

Yet by the time of Preston's deposition, the facts were in. Robert E. Manchester, a plaintiffs' lawyer in Burlington, Vermont, had retained three academic experts to do diverse string studies. He reported their conclusion to the Food and Drug Administration in 1983: the deterioration of a Shield string is "insidious and unknown either to the woman wearer or her physician during performance of an external examination."

At the University of Lowell in Massachusetts, plastics engineer Aldo Crugnola had studied three hundred used Shields for tears or abrasions in the sheaths, through which bacteria could reach the spaces between the filaments and ascend to the uterus. His "very conservative" estimates were that "obvious ruptures" had exposed filaments of 42 percent of the IUDs that had been in place for up to six months "and in 67 percent of those *in situ* twenty-four or more months." Many breaks were "at the point where the string is attached," he said. "Encrustations" had broken off in layers and chunks, taking with them pieces of embrittled, "tenaciously bonded" sheath, he added.

At the University of Vermont, microbiologist Paula Fives-Taylor had coated Shield strings with saliva, which in some ways is similar to vaginal fluids. Her major findings—which may explain why most Shield pelvic infections occurred only after long-term use— were as follows:

- Bacteria could seep directly into the uterus via sheath holes at or in the double knot, and could nestle and grow on the outer surface.
- The numbers of bacteria adhering to strings—particularly to their top and middle portions—increased 40 percent when *in situ* for twenty-five to thirty-six months, but three-fold (200 percent) after thirty-seven to forty-eight months.
- String that was three to four years old had ten times as many bacteria between the filaments as did new strings. The string of a rival IUD that had been implanted for four years had no increase in bacterial adhesion.

At the University of Texas in Houston, biostatistician Tom Downs compared the risks of PID as linked to various IUDs, using data from the federally funded Women's Health Study. It involved 662 women who had been treated in sixteen hospitals for pelvic infections, and 2,369 controls. He found that a woman wearing a Shield for thirty-six months was 9.2 times more likely to suffer PID than a woman using no contraception, while a woman fitted with any of several other IUDs ran a risk only 1.2 times greater. The U.S. Centers for Disease Control reached similar conclusions.

"You don't know to this day whether or not the Dalkon Shield tail string deteriorates *in situ,* do you?" Michael Ciresi asked Ellen Preston in 1984. She replied, "I think I have a pretty good idea that it does not." Based on what evidence? "I think there are documents around, but I don't know where they are," she said.

The Dalkon Corporation had recognized that Shield components could deteriorate with time, and had made a conscientious recommendation to doctors: "At the end of two years, replacement with a fresh Dalkon Shield is recommended." It is after a Shield is worn for three years that the frequency of bacterial invasions of the uterus soars, as shown by Paula Fives-Taylor. Dalkon's cautionary advice had the potential for averting infection in countless women, but of course it could also hurt sales. The latter troubled Robins executives after they acquired the Shield; Kenneth Moore, for one, noted that the Shield's leading competitor's prescribing instructions, or labeling, did not urge removal and replacement after two years. "It [is] generally acknowledged that we are losing sales because of this," he said in November 1971. To even up the competition, Moore counseled dropping the two-year replacement advice from the Shield labeling. Under oath afterward, he also emphasized that many physicians had protested that they—not a manufacturer—should choose the time for removal and replacement.

Contrary advice was offered on April 18, 1972, by John Autian, the plastics toxicologist. At his meeting with Robins executives, he was asked "about establishing time periods beyond which the Dalkon Shield should no longer be used," Moore wrote to Dr. Freund and W. Roy Smith the same day. "Dr. Autian indicated that we should be thinking in terms of establishing definite limitations. . . . [He] feels that we have a definite problem with this [nylon string] because historically it has been shown that nylon does deteriorate *in situ* over a period of time."

Nevertheless, in July 1972, Robins dropped the two-year recommendation. The new instruction said, "The need for removal and/or replacement of the Dalkon Shield is dictated largely by patient tolerance." Two months later, Robins armed its salesmen with a new competitive tool by telling them to note "that we no longer recommend replacement of the Dalkon Shield every two years." Robins did not tell them—and they were consequently unable to tell the physicians on whom they called—of the deterioration of nylon, of string defects, or of possible resultant hazards. For eight years, Robins did not rescind or amend its advice. Instead, it persisted in claiming that a nonpregnant woman could continue to use a Shield safely unless and until symptoms of infection appeared.

E. Wayne Crowder, the quality-control supervisor at Chap Stick, identified problems of quality and safety early in the production of the Shield. His actions, and Robins's response to them, clearly demonstrate Robins's interlocked refusals to make the health of women a concern and to heed warnings from its own employees.

To hold down production costs, as has been noted, Robins decided to make Shields at its Chap Stick plant in Lynchburg, Virginia, rather than at its headquarters in Richmond. One day in mid-March 1971, Crowder saw two women employees tying string to a piece of plastic. "I thought it was a fishing lure," he testified at a deposition. "I had no previous knowledge of the device." It was, of course, a Shield, and the women were attaching the string, with a double knot, to the plastic matrix. "Were any quality-control procedures in effect at the time?" he was asked. "No," he said.[4]

Quality-control problems accumulated from the start. Daniel E. French, president of Chap Stick, called Supramid "quite unsatisfactory because of stiffness and a tendency to break during the tying operation. . . ."[5] David Mefford, Robins's quality-assurance director, found Supramid's strength "not uniform from reel to reel" and rated the specifications "too low."[6] Kenneth Moore said that Robins "should be very concerned" by a report showing "that after a period of seventeen months in situ an 80-percent loss of strength of nylon cord was experienced."[7]

Predictably, rupturing and tearing of the string occurred frequently during the assembly process. In June 1971, Charles H. Leys, vice-president for operations at Chap Stick, told Mefford that the sheaths on "several thousand" Shields had been "stripped slightly or been mashed in tying." The IUDs with mashed string "can be used," Mefford answered. In March 1973, Wayne Crowder told Chap Stick officials that he had conducted an examination of 64,000 Shields that had passed inspection and were awaiting shipment. His report said 9.94 percent had defects, and 52 percent of the defects—more than 3,300—were "broken string sheaths."

Independent confirmation came later from Dr. Howard J. Tatum, a leading gynecological researcher who is now at Emory University. In 239 new Shields that had been inspected, packaged, and actually shipped, he found that 9 percent (twenty-one) had sheath breaks, most of them in the portion of the string that would be in the womb.[8]

In 1973, tests showed that string samples arriving early in the year broke only under a force averaging more than 11 pounds; samples arriving in July and August had an average breaking strength of 7.5 pounds.

In view of all of this, it could not have come as a surprise that doctors trying to remove Shields began to complain that the strings broke and that they had to resort to surgery. As early as October 1972, for example, a Robins salesman reported that Dr. Walter E. Fox of Beverly Hills, California, had told him that "large numbers are *breaking.*"

Once bacteria had passed through sheath breaks and found refuge in the tiny between-the-filaments spaces, they could rise to the attachment double knot in the uterus. Most of the holes—or cracks or strains that could become holes—found by Tatum, Moore, and Crowder were immediately below the knot.

In late March 1971, less than two weeks after Wayne Crowder had learned of the Shield's existence, he demonstrated one easy, inexpensive solution to the wicking problem: use heat to seal the open string ends. The demonstration occurred at the Dalkon plant in Stamford, Connecticut. Crowder, who had gone there to learn more about producing Shields, was talking with Irwin Lerner, Dalkon's president. Lerner claimed that the sheath would keep the filaments dry and that the attachment double knot and the single "locator" knot—an aid to the physician in putting the IUD in its proper position—would prevent bacterial wicking. Skeptical,

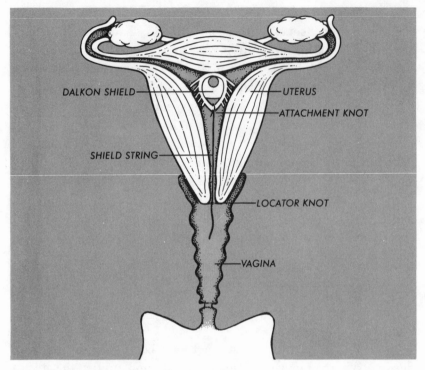

The Dalkon Shield in place, showing tail string.

Crowder applied the flame of a cigarette lighter to the open end of a piece of string and saw it shrivel into a small, solid bead. "I suggested that that might be a more positive means of sealing than the knots," Crowder testified. "He just said he would think about it."

Crowder repeated the heat-sealing demonstration twice, first for Julian W. Ross, his immediate superior and Chap Stick's research director, and then for Chap Stick's president, Daniel French. Crowder said he speculated to French about septic abortions, saying string-caused infection would be "extremely serious if a pregnancy should occur." Crowder has testified that French termed his concern about string-caused infection "reasonable" while predicting that "Robins wouldn't go for" heat-sealing. "He said that they had too much time and money invested in the present configuration," Crowder testified. "He also made reference to the cost," which he estimated at five to ten cents per Shield, and ended the conversation with a "joke" that "maybe I could get some of the girls in the factory to help me with the testing."

Crowder had also spotted the "small holes in the sheathing immediately below the attachment knot." Fearing that the holes, like the open string ends, would cause pelvic infections, he spoke to Ross in early April 1971. "His response was that the device wasn't my responsibility and to leave it alone," Crowder testified. Later he took it upon himself to do a microscopic examination of about half of a lot of 10,000 to 12,000 strings that had been approved and attached to Shields, and found holes in many of them. "Very much concerned," he rejected the entire batch of IUDs. But it was rumored that his rejection would be overruled and the batch shipped to buyers.

In June, while awaiting a decision, Crowder did two scientifically primitive but critically important wicking experiments. In one, he clipped off a piece of string below the attachment double knot and suspended the lower portion in a beaker of water. Several hours later he removed and dried the submerged portion and then " 'milked' . . . a small drop of water . . . from within the string." In the second test, he again clipped strings below the attachment knots. This time, however, he submerged the lower ends for a few days to find out if water would pass through the locator knots. He established that water seeped above the knots in every case.

Crowder reported his results to Ross, hoping to make him see the hazard and lead him to take remedial action. Instead, Ross "became quite angry and reminded me as before that it wasn't my responsibility," Crowder testified. He added, "I told him that I couldn't, in good conscience, not say something about something that I felt could cause infections. And he said that my conscience didn't pay my salary. . . . He referred to my persistent 'insubordination' [and said that] if I valued my job I would do as I was told."[9]

Meanwhile, Robins requested information from Chap Stick about the stiffness of the string, because of complaints that during intercourse it caused discomfort to men. Crowder saw the request as an opportunity to write a memo revealing his experimental evidence that the open string ends were a potential source of infection. He knew that the Chap Stick bureaucracy would have to buck the memo up to the Robins bureaucracy. "The sheath does contribute very heavily to stiffness," he wrote. Then, proceeding to his real concern, he said that Lerner had told him its purpose was to keep the filaments dry and germ-free. But he pointed out that water and, by implication, bacteria can be shown to enter and exit the string via its open ends, and implied that the sheath was worthless.

The date on Crowder's memo was July 28, 1971. Shield project manager Moore claimed under oath not to have seen it until "a few months" later. On October 11, Moore said, Lerner told him that he had done a wicking experiment with "another liquid" and that the locator knot had blocked its ascent. Lerner had chosen the liquid, and it was India ink. In a deposition, he made a qualified claim for the knot's blocking power, saying the India ink had come up to it "in some of the experiment." He admitted he had not tested the string for what mattered: wicking of bacteria. Moore had not asked company scientists an obvious question: did the particles in viscous India ink and the bacteria in vaginal fluid have comparable potentials to wick? Under questioning by Douglas E. Bragg, a Denver plaintiffs' lawyer, it emerged that he had not tried to duplicate the test or told Robins physicians about it. He said he had not written memos on either the ink test or the visit to Lerner.

Crowder sent his memo to Ross, who, he said, "appeared to be furious because I had [included] the statements concerning the string problems. . . . He was very agitated, yelling. . . ." In this and subsequent encounters in which he approved "the use or shipment or sale of some product that I regarded as possibly dangerous," Ross renewed his threats "to my employment" and repeated "that my conscience didn't pay my salary."

Still, French shared Crowder's desire to make changes, so he phoned and wrote to Ellen Preston to try to win the crucial support of the parent company's medical department. On August 9 she told her boss, Frederick Clark: "Mr. French says that the reason given for the sheath is that it provides protection against bacterial invasion. He points out, however, that both ends of the string are cut and left open. It seems to him if this is so that the ends will wick body fluids containing bacteria."

David Mefford, the quality-assurance director, had resisted making changes in the Shield or its components. By early September 1971, however, he had come to "believe the time to make changes is rapidly approaching." But he said in a revealing memo to Oscar

Klioze, his superior: "I don't intend to initiate any of these changes because for the most part they are medical or marketing decisions. . . . Most changes would have slowed down production and with the supply so critical, this would have been unwise." Heat-sealing, for example, would create a "production problem." The effort to improve the string failed. Although discussions in Robins's Research Committee "make it obvious that there are a number of suggested changes which should receive serious consideration," Klioze told French on September 7, it was "the consensus" of the committee and C. E. Morton, vice-president and general manager, that "the Shield continue to be manufactured according to present specifications until management directs otherwise." The message to Chap Stick was to lay off, and French heard it clearly, as shown by his memorable team-player reply to Klioze on September 9, 1971:

> As I indicated in our telephone conversation, it is not the intention of the Chap Stick Company to attempt any unauthorized improvements in the Dalkon Shield. My only interest in the Dalkon Shield is to produce it at the lowest possible price, and, therefore, increase Robins' gross profit level. We will certainly await complete instructions and authorization from Robins prior to instituting any changes.

No changes were formally required, and certainly none were instituted, even though it became more and more evident that Crowder had been right to sound the alarm. The Population Council's Howard Tatum suspected that the Shield string was causing PID. In 1974, he and Dr. Maclyn McCarty began a series of tests. The results confirmed Crowder's fears, implicating the string in PID in both pregnant and nonpregnant wearers. In one study, bacteria "cultured" from thirty-one of thirty-six used strings were infectious; bacteria from six monofilaments were not. In examinations with a scanning electron microscope they saw "innumerable bacteria" among the filaments of eight out of ten used string segments cut from atop the attachment knot in the uterus. The Shield is "defective" and "unreasonably dangerous," Tatum charged in a deposition.[10]

Tatum offered to brief Robins on the experiments, and in mid-August 1974, Tankersley, the microbiological-research chief, and Mefford—neither one a physician—spent about two hours with him and McCarty. He testified they did not fault his methods, dispute his results, or suggest more tests—and sent a "note thanking us for our hospitality. . . ." A day later, Tankersley began a test of new strings from sterile packages. It showed wicking. He said he called Frederick Clark, who "indicated to me that they had considered the wicking possibilities and found them negligible and of no concern."

Later in 1974, Tankersley designed a study with a high potential to elicit key data. Biskind Laboratories in San Francisco would wash off external bacteria from used strings, mince the strings, and analyze the puree. He has sworn Biskind never finished the test, saying it had submitted "lab slips," not "results." Yet he also testified that the slips "revealed the results": Biskind found bacteria in the minced strings. Robins termed the findings "confidential."[11]

Still later, in November 1974, Dr. J. Stewart Templeton, Robins's representative in Horsham, England, suggested an alternative to more "drastic remedies for the string problem": "It might be more simple to heat-seal the ends of the present string." Obviously unaware of Crowder's on-the-spot experiment, he said he was uncertain whether heat-sealing could be done, but added, "I've no doubt that there is someone in Richmond who knows the answer to that question."

Ellen Preston commented to Frederick Clark that she wished Robins had taken Crowder's advice. "It is too late to 'heat seal' now," she said. "Heat sealing would have been a good thing to have done four years ago." She wrote the memo nearly five months after the halt in U.S. Shield sales. Clark testified in 1977 that he continued to believe the string would wick fluids only as far as the locator knot.

Klioze swore in 1976 "that the very reason for the sheath" was to prevent wicking. He swore in 1983: "I'm not sure exactly that I ever understood the exact function of the sheath." He swore in 1976 that destruction of the sheath's integrity would frustrate its purpose: preventing bacterial migration. He swore in 1983: "I don't know what would happen if the sheath deteriorated."

Wayne Crowder got no reward for being right. His experience was similar to that of many straight-arrow employees of large organizations, governmental or private. They assume that if they blow the whistle on a serious problem, their leaders will straighten things out—only to discover that they become pariahs while the problems continue to fester and be covered up. Initially, Crowder told me, the company's reactions to his warnings led him into "confusion and bewilderment—I didn't know what was going on." As time went on, "I felt a great sense of disappointment, maybe betrayal, frustration." How did it happen that Robins physicians and scientists didn't share his perception of imminent hazard, not to mention the personal integrity that led him to act? He said that he did not assume that going to medical school or getting a doctoral degree in a scientific discipline necessarily enhanced characteristics such as common sense. After all, he said, referring to the dangers of an open-ended, multifilament string: "no exceptional genius was required to understand the hazards of that design."[12]

Wayne Crowder's story is a simple one: he did what he believed to be morally right, and what he did could have prevented PID in thousands of women. In 1978, when he was forty-one years old and earning $13,500 a year, he was forced out of Chap Stick, where he had worked for fifteen years, and given six months' severance pay. In a lawsuit in 1980, he accused Robins of an improper retaliatory discharge. He was too late, a judge ruled in 1984: Virginia state law requires such a complaint to be filed within a year after discharge; he had filed his two years afterwards. Since leaving Robins he has had only odd jobs, and was still unable to find regular employment as of April 1985. He and his wife, a medical technician, have two children.

Yet, even as A. H. Robins officials ignored Crowder's warnings, they searched for a new string—secretly and "desperately," in the word of Kenneth Moore. They have sworn that the search was unrelated to the possibility that the original open-ended, multifilament string caused PID. "It was the contrary," Allen Polon, Moore's successor, testified. Tankersley, the microbiological research director, testified that "there was no safety reason behind my search."

In August 1971, only eight months after Robins had begun to sell Shields worldwide, Chap Stick president Daniel French, citing production problems, urged that a substitute be found. Moore and others said repeatedly that the problems were aggravated by having a remote foreign supplier. An important juncture was reached on March 2, 1972, when senior vice-president Freund implied that Robins's scientific group had found the Shield string unsuitable. "Continue marketing the present Shield until a suitable replacement is developed," he recommended in a report to the Management Committee.[13]

Moore urged an "all out" search in the hope of coming up with "one or more suitable replacements within eight to ten weeks." By August the effort seemed to be succeeding, thanks to consultant John Autian's suggestion of Gore-Tex, a form of Teflon.

Initially, Robins officials were enthusiastic: Gore-Tex would not wick, and was soft, strong, and nearly indestructible. But it was also so slick that doctors might need a special forceps for Shield removals, and this, said product planning chief Roy Smith, could give competitors "a field day." And there was a safety factor: to the naked eye, Gore-Tex was smooth; under a microscope, it had saucerlike recesses in which germs could lodge. Such an "orange peel" surface led Tankersley to imagine some horrible consequences: If a string with an orange-peel surface were on the Dalkon Shield now, he wrote in a memo on October 22, 1974, "I imagine there would be drying corporate gonads hanging from every telephone pole between here and D.C."

Somehow, Gore-Tex remained an option for two and a half years. Moore testified to his "understanding" that Gore-Tex was finally rejected because of "the results of clinical trials." But Robins admitted in a court paper in November 1982 that there had been no "clinical tests in which Dalkon Shields tied with Gore-Tex string were inserted in humans." None were inserted in animals, either, Dr. Fletcher Owen admitted. The truth lay elsewhere.

The estimated cost of a Gore-Tex string was 6.1 cents, compared with Supramid's 0.63 cents. For one million Shields, which Robins sold for as much as $4.35 each, Gore-Tex would have cost about $61,000, or approximately $54,000 more than Supramid. Robins decided to forego Gore-Tex in 1975, when its average net earnings were nearly $70,000 a day. Moore said Robins had pursued possible use of Gore-Tex "despite its increased cost." Wayne Crowder said, "The final objection that I was aware of . . . had to do with it costing some ten times as much."

One might assume that the Shield project coordinator would not find it necessary to ask, in 1975, "what material is presently being used for the string on other marketed IUDs?" Polon did ask the question in a memo. The word came back that some IUD makers were using Prolene Suture (polypropylene) "and therefore it may be unwise for [Robins] to enter an already sensitive and emotional market with such an exotic material as Gore-Tex."

Polon then took a series of simple steps that could have been taken four and a half years earlier, when Nickless sounded the first wicking alarm. He obtained some other IUDs and asked Thomas Yu, the polymer chemist, to analyze the string. In a matter of days, Polon was thanking Yu for giving the company "the confidence we needed in pursuing polypropylene. . . ." But Ethicon, Inc., the source of Prolene Suture, was owned by Johnson & Johnson, which also owned Ortho Pharmaceutical Corporation—and Ortho sold the rival Lippes Loop. Ethicon, Polon quickly found, didn't care to sell polypropylene to Robins. Within three weeks, however, he had gotten some from Ethicon, U.K., in Britain, which was prepared to supply Robins, and had Wayne Crowder's assurance that it was "the most suitable" of all of the possible alternative strings he had tested.

Nothing came of it all. In January 1975, the FDA formally cited Supramid as hazardous, "a factor that may have contributed to the . . . 219 infected pregnancies and 11 deaths reported to date." In its periodic *Drug Bulletin* for physicians, the FDA stated, "Robins will replace the multifilament string with a monofilament string similar to those used in other IUDs."

Eight months later, however, Robins announced in a press release that it would not resume Shield sales. It cited adverse publicity and other factors that "would make the successful re-entry of the Dalkon Shield difficult if not impossible." The release ignored the *Drug Bulletin,* said nothing of the possible hazard of the multifilament string or of wicking, and claimed that the Shield, "when properly used, is a safe and effective IUD."

In 1982, Claiborne Robins, Jr., was asked by plaintiffs' lawyer Bradley Post: "When did you first become aware that there might be problems with the tail string of the Dalkon Shield?" "I'm not familiar with the fact that there is a problem with the Dalkon Shield," Robins swore. By the end of 1981, his company, according to its annual report, "had disposed of approximately 4,200 cases and claims alleging injuries arising from use of the Dalkon Shield." The massive litigation arose mainly from PID blamed on wicking. Later, in September 1983, Robins acknowledged that wicking had been "brought to my attention over the last thirteen years," but swore he didn't "know what it meant."

Under oath in 1984, Carl Lunsford, the senior vice-president for research and development, told Dale Larson that he was "not personally aware" that the material used in the string might degrade in the body. He was "not aware" of any effort to test string materials in women. He "never asked"—and does not recall "wondering"—how the string held up. Lunsford was also "not aware" that the Shield string had hundreds of filaments.

In January 1984, Claiborne Robins was asked if he knew the string was multifilamented. "I am not aware of the nature of the string," he swore.

9

Insidious Infections, Insidious Cover-ups

On June 23, 1972, a Midwestern physician sent an alarming letter to A. H. Robins. Six women in whom he had implanted the Dalkon Shield had become pregnant while it was in place, and five of them had gone on to suffer life-threatening spontaneous infected abortions. His report was not the first to link the Shield to infected pregnancies. Rather, it was their sheer number in a single physician's experience that made the report ominous. Yet another aspect made the warning unique, and that was its source: Thad Earl—the Ohio general practitioner who was one of the very first physicians to insert the Shield and who, even then, as a $30,000-a-year consultant to Robins, was busily promoting it. Earl's warning had the potential, in the judgment of Bradley Post, to save "most of the women who have been killed and maimed by this device."

Had Robins not neglected Earl's warning, Carie M. Palmer of Elkhart, Kansas, almost certainly would not have become a Shield victim, and she would then not have won the largest award of punitive damages against a pharmaceutical manufacturer made up to that time.

Mrs. Palmer was fitted with a Shield in January 1973, six months after Earl's warning reached Richmond. She became pregnant in August, when she was twenty-four. Three months later she became violently ill, went into shock, suffered a near-fatal pelvic infection, and lost her unborn child. She has had recurring health problems ever since. She sued Robins, and her case went to trial in Denver in 1979. After hearing evidence for nearly two months, a jury awarded her $600,000 to compensate for her injuries, and $6.2 million to punish Robins.[1] The company asked Judge Robert P. Fullerton to set the awards aside. He refused, in an opinion citing the Earl warning.

"The evidence showed that once the company was made specifically aware of the numerous dangerous side effects of the device . . . it suppressed that information . . . made additional false claims, and then resorted to an effort to cover up the facts," Fullerton wrote in June 1980. Although the Colorado Supreme Court sat on Robins's appeal for five years, it finally upheld both awards, three to two, in June 1984. Notably, Robins did not appeal to the United States Supreme Court.

In his letter, Earl told Robins that he was "advising physicians that the device should be removed as soon as a diagnosis of pregnancy is made" because to leave it in place was "hazardous." He pointed out that in the six pregnancies, only the one woman whose Shield he removed "carried full term, the rest all aborted and became septic" at three and a half to five months. He urged Robins to investigate the problem: "I realize that this is a small statistic but I feel we should correlate this data with other investigators across the country, because most [Shield prescribers] are experiencing the same problem."

Earl did not accord to the warning the urgency it merited. It was the third paragraph of the third page of a five-page, single-spaced letter to the general sales manager, John Burke, to whom he reported. Indeed, Robins said Earl "buried" the warning, and Ellen Preston, by then Robins's Shield physician monitor for fifteen months, has testified that he never followed it up with her. But Earl did send copies to Fletcher Owen, A. N. Chremos, and Kenneth Moore. Moore, in turn, sent copies to ten more executives along with a four-page memo in which he took up "the points as they are listed in the letter." For unexplained reasons, spontaneous septic abortions did not make Moore's list. His addressees in the medical department were Frederick Clark and Ellen Preston.

For a report of an adverse reaction to a Robins medical product, Preston has said, the letter had unusually wide internal distribution. But that did not inhibit Robins's aggressive global marketing of the Shield. In September—more than two months after the receipt of Earl's letter—Robins began to run its eight-page Shield advertisement, "A Progress Report," the costliest ad in company history. The ad, which ran through December, cited Earl's incredible claim of a 0.5-percent pregnancy rate—but not his somber warning.[2]

The extensive circulation of Earl's warning makes it all the more striking that no one admits to having mentioned it to William Zimmer III, Robins's chief executive officer and president. "The first time I had heard about this problem of spontaneous abortion was in the summer of 1973," Zimmer told me. It was in June 1973 that a Robins delegation went before a House Government Operations subcommittee, acclaimed the Shield's safety, and said nothing of the letter. In 1984, Claiborne Robins was asked whether he had been aware at the time of the hazard that Earl had mentioned. "I am not aware that there was a hazard," he swore. By mid-1974, the Food and Drug Administration was concerned enough about spontaneous septic abortions to ask Robins to suspend Shield sales, and the company did so on June 28; but not until four months later did it get around to telling the FDA of the Earl letter.

The medical department answered letters from doctors routinely and usually swiftly. Frequently this was done by Preston, a pediatrician who, as we have seen, never treated a patient with a pelvic infection or inserted or removed an IUD. She testified in 1984 that she had received a copy of Earl's letter. "I didn't read the letter, it went to the files, and did not come directly to my attention till months or even a year or so later," she told plaintiffs' lawyer Michael Ciresi. "That does not excuse my not reading it, but at least it is the reason I think that I didn't say something to somebody," Preston said.

Earl has sworn he had no response from anyone at Robins. Yet a three-page, single-spaced reply was prepared, at Burke's direction. It was dated August 22, 1972—two months after Earl wrote to Burke—and was signed by Moore. "Are you aware . . . that Dr. Earl did not receive this letter?" a plaintiffs' lawyer asked Moore in September 1982. "Obviously I've been told fairly recently that he did not, which comes as a great deal of surprise to me," Moore testified. "I can't believe it, to be quite honest with you."

The reply dealt mostly with technical matters about which Moore, a pharmacist with no medical training, claimed no expertise. In writing it, had he sought advice from any of the doctors or executives who had seen Earl's letter? His testimony at a trial in mid-1979 was that he did not recall having done so. His sworn answer in a deposition three years later was, "Considering my background, state of knowledge at that time, I can't imagine that I composed this letter . . . without consulting with somebody." Also under oath, Dr. Clark was asked if Earl's letter had been "buried." "I would not subscribe to the possible connotation of the word 'buried,' " Clark said. "To the best of my knowledge, this letter was not consciously, positively, calculatedly hidden." If numerous doctors in addition to Earl had been finding spontaneous septic abortions, could this "affect sales of the Dalkon Shield?" Clark replied, "It would be one of the things that certainly would have, true." In the month in which Earl wrote the letter, Robins has estimated, it shipped 82,000 Shields.

Earl's warning was scarcely an isolated one; several other physicians, both before and after his letter, provided sometimes dramatic alerts to Robins about PID and spontaneous septic abortions in Shield users.

One of the earliest tremors was caused by Solon E. Davis, the Medical College of Virginia OB-GYN who had been retained briefly by the company when it bought the Shield in 1970. He recalled in testimony and interviews that his wife had worn a Shield without trouble, and that he and about six other MCV doctors were inserting it in their patients. In the predawn hours of March 30, 1971, Davis said, the MCV Hospital in Richmond summoned him to give emergency treatment to a woman who had a septic abortion so severe that she "clearly should have died," on the basis of what he had been taught in medical school only a decade before. He said she had to be hospitalized and suffered "all sorts of dreadful complications."

At the time, Davis said, he made an ominous prediction to his MCV colleagues: "a syndrome" of spontaneous septic abortion in women who had the Shield in place would emerge in the early second trimester, when the uterus has expanded to the point that it tends to pull into it a tail string that may be contaminated. He said he did not expect that a direct report from him on a single case would influence the company, and he did not make one. But he said he did mention the case and repeat the prediction to Thad Earl in the spring of 1972, at an OB-GYN meeting in Chicago where Earl was pushing the Shield. At the same time, Davis said, Earl revealed to him that spontaneous septic abortions had developed in his own patients.

Nearly four months before Earl's letter, Dr. Andrew F. Latteier, an OB-GYN instructor at the University of Utah, made a bitter complaint to a Robins salesman, who reported to the company on March 1, 1972, that "five girls in a row developed a pelvic infection, three of [whom] had to be hospitalized. He said if he had his way it would be removed from the market. He was so angry it was impossible to discuss the problem with him."

On June 5, another Robins salesman told Ellen Preston of a woman in Dayton, Ohio, who conceived nine months after having a Shield inserted, became very ill with PID, went to a hospital, "and became progressively worse until May third when she aborted." The fetus was malformed.

Dr. Frank W. George, an osteopathic general practitioner in Dayton who had inserted the Shield, wanted to know what knowledge Robins may have about Shield-related PID and fetal malformations. Preston wrote him that "no case of malformation of fetus or infant associated with the Dalkon Shield has been reported to us."

She routinely advised Dr. Owen, the director of medical services, and Clark, her boss, of communications from physicians, and they, in turn, circulated her reports to other executives. Had she made a point of calling this first malformation to their attention? "I don't recall," she testified.

On June 20, 1972, seven days before Earl's letter was time-stamped at the company, Lindsay R. Curtis, one of six OB-GYNs who staffed the Ogden Woman's Clinic in Ogden, Utah, dropped by the company's offices. He had inserted about fifty Shields and had written what he calls "patient education material" to promote other Robins products. He and his companion, a medical student, were guests of Dale Taylor, vice-president for market planning and development. The visitors had a casual, unplanned meeting with Taylor and four other officials, including Drs. Clark, Preston, and Chremos, during which Dr. Curtis said he had seen three cases of severe PID in wearers, and that he and his colleagues had stopped using the device. He went on to tell a gripping story. A twenty-five-year-old woman was fitted with a Shield soon after the birth of her second child and became pregnant a month or so later. In mid-trimester she became severely infected, ran a fever as high as 105 degrees, and entered George Washington University Hospital in Washington. Excellent treatment saved her life, but she gave birth to a premature, stillborn baby. The woman was Curtis's daughter. The visiting medical student was her husband.

Preston wrote to Curtis a few days later, saying she was "disappointed to hear that your [Shield] experience had not been altogether favorable. . . ." She said that other cases of PID had come in but had been "very infrequent."

On October 6, about four months after Preston saw Earl's letter, Preston heard from Dr. Gilles A. Marchand, an OB-GYN in New London, Connecticut. He reported " 'four cases of very severe infection' " in several patients who had conceived while wearing Shields, she wrote in a memo to her files. "Recently he almost lost one patient due to infection during pregnancy." She said she told Marchand that "infections of this sort had not been a big problem."

On November 1, salesman Philip J. Schmid in Madison, Wisconsin, told Preston that four OB-GYNs had "some patients who became pregnant and then developed severe PID, all with the Dalkon Shield in place." One nearly died.

In a second letter on March 6, 1973, Schmid told Preston that a single unnamed OB-GYN had four cases and had recently stopped inserting Shields "because of severe complications" following pregnancy. All four women had no complications until they had been pregnant for twenty weeks, Schmid wrote. Then—"almost to the exact day"—each ran a 105-degree temperature, suffered severe pain, developed an infection, and aborted.

Six weeks later, on April 16, a particularly strong alert came to Preston in a memo from her colleague in the medical department, Dr. Anne Board:

Dr. Leo Dunn and others at MCV have inquired . . . about the problem of septic abortion associated with the Dalkon Shield.

As well as I can determine, there is a feeling or rumor *(based upon the fact that several individuals have each experienced one case)* that if a patient becomes pregnant while having a Dalkon Shield in place, therapeutic abortion should be carried out post-haste. [Emphasis added.]

The reason for this is that patients with Dalkon Shields are more likely to experience septic abortion than either (1) patients using other IUDs or (2) patients without IUDs who happen to experience spontaneous abortions.

On June 15, Dr. Leland L. Fellows of Alamogordo, New Mexico, reported on two women who had near-fatal spontaneous septic abortions and asked, "Are there other such reports around the country?" There were indeed. But Robins's scorekeeping on infected pregnancies was, to say the least, bizarre. Consider the prompt reply that Preston made to Dr. Marchand in New London on October 12, and the chronology of reported spontaneous septic abortions that Clark submitted to the FDA in June 1974.

Until October 1972, Preston said she told Marchand, "we did know of two other cases of rather severe infection during pregnancy." Up to the same time, similarly, Clark's chronology also listed only two cases: the Ohio woman whose fetus was malformed, and Dr. Curtis's daughter. Setting aside Thad Earl's five cases, they seemed to have forgotten that in a face-to-face meeting, Curtis had told them of two more cases in his clinic in Ogden, Utah, as Preston herself had reported in a memo. Then, after Marchand's four cases, came salesman Schmid's report of the four Wisconsin OB-GYNs who had "some" cases in Wisconsin. After *that* came Schmid's report of the one OB-GYN with four cases. The point is not the befuddling numbers, but Preston's remarkably deflationary memory. Writing to Schmid eleven days after this single salesman had told her of four plus "some" cases, she told him, "So far as I know we have had two or three instances reported to us of severe septicemia similar to the cases you described."[3]

Like the limbo to which the Earl letter had been consigned,

Robins's non-investigation of reports such as those from the MCV and Drs. Marchand and Fellows made it easy to continue to claim that there was no proof of a cause-and-effect relationship between the Shield and a high rate of septic abortions. On September 12, 1973, however, Robins did get a jolt. Robins salesman M. Briggs Hamilton disclosed that the U.S. Centers for Disease Control was asking hospitals for data on IUDs and pelvic infections. He had learned this at the Medical Center Hospital of Vermont in Burlington, where, he wrote, the entire OB-GYN department had become convinced of a connection between PID and IUDs. He enclosed a copy of a report by Dr. Philip B. Mead of the University of Vermont. In the six-month period ending June 26, Mead told the CDC, seven women—the youngest sixteen years of age, the oldest thirty-six—had been admitted to the hospital with life-threatening infections, including three spontaneous septic abortions. All had been wearing Shields "primarily because that is all they are using in this area," Hamilton said. All seven had recovered. A month later, Preston circulated the report with a note calling it "disturbing" to have seven such cases in six months at a single hospital, but "difficult to understand in view of our own prospective studies and others [which found] essentially no problem with PID." She sent Mead seven written questions so as to help "define the dimensions" of the PID problem. She did that on November 13—two months after receiving Hamilton's letter.

Dr. C. Donald Christian, head of OB-GYN at the University of Arizona Medical Center in Tucson, played a key role in discovering and in alerting the world to Shield-related fatal spontaneous septic abortions. On October 8, 1972, another physician in his department inserted a Shield in a thirty-one-year-old Arizona woman. Several weeks later she learned she was pregnant. Her doctor left the IUD in place, a common practice at the time. On March 27, 1973, she complained of a sense of fullness in her abdomen and of what Christian termed a "flu-like syndrome." But her two children had flu, so there seemed to be no cause for alarm.

During the night of March 28–29, however, she was beset by uncontrollable chills and a 103-degree fever and was taken to a hospital. The next day, it became manifest that she had a grave pelvic infection. Within seventy-two hours after the flu diagnosis, she was dead, and her nineteen-week-old fetus aborted.

The death troubled and perplexed Christian. Later—probably in early 1973—a neighbor asked him to phone a Texas physician on an unrelated subject. The immediate matter having been disposed of, the Texan said, "While I have you on the phone . . ." and proceeded to tell him he was troubled because two of his patients had suffered spontaneous septic abortions, each with a Shield in place.

One, a twenty-four-year-old mother of two children who had been fitted with a Shield in January 1972, conceived three and a half months later, in April. On August 18 she developed symptoms suggesting some sort of flu: sore throat, painful right ear, fever, nausea, vomiting. On August 20 she entered a hospital. On August 21 she aborted. On August 22 she died. Hers was the first known fatal spontaneous septic abortion in a U.S. Shield wearer.

The similarity of the two fatal cases struck Christian forcibly. "The greatest concern is the rather insidious yet rapid manner in which these patients become ill. . . . The first symptoms, which were disarmingly innocuous in and of themselves, occurred within thirty-one and seventy-two hours of death." By the time the true nature of the infection is clear, he emphasized, "the margin of safety that time ordinarily provides in treating such infections is not present."[4]

In his travels in several states, Christian asked the physicians he met if they had been having problems with IUDs. Many of them said they had, and that nearly always the IUD involved was the Shield. In the spring of 1973, as a result, he contacted Robins, trying but failing to reach William Zimmer, and also the Centers for Disease Control and the FDA. The FDA "kept telling me to go away, in essence," he told me in interviews. At about the same time, his University of Arizona OB-GYN colleague, Dr. Duncan Reid, notified Robins of a fatal spontaneous septic abortion.

The follow-up was left to Fletcher Owen, the medical services director. In a memo on June 8, he told Preston, "Ask to call back Dr. Donald Christian, head of department." Somehow, Preston became confused. "So far as I knew," she said in a memo on November 21, "information supplied to us in the spring came from Dr. Duncan Reid of his [Christian's] department and involved only one death associated with the Dalkon Shield." A year after Owen's memo, on June 11, 1974, Frederick Clark gave a panel of FDA advisers a list of cases of spontaneous septic abortions that "came to our attention." For the first six months of 1973, the period covering Reid's report of a fatality, he listed "0 fatalities."

While Christian was awaiting a response from Robins in the latter half of 1973, the House Government Operations subcommittee held its hearing on IUDs. Jack Freund testified that the company knew of four hundred complaints about the Shield. "How many *individuals?*" asked subcommittee chairman L. H. Fountain. Freund said he would find out. Afterward, he filed a summary that divided complaints into ten classes; none was spontaneous septic abortion. Buried in the footnotes, however, was a response to Fountain. Contrary to his request and Freund's assent to it, footnote number 6 listed eight *reports*—not individual cases. Years later, Frederick Clark testified that Robins had known at the time of eleven cases. This was a small concession, considering the numerous cases it excluded, among them Thad Earl's five cases and the "several" at MCV.

Not until footnote number 13 did Robins's summary reveal that one of the reported cases was fatal: "Subsequent to May 31, 1973, A. H. Robins received indirectly a report on a death associated with the Dalkon Shield in [Arizona], which was allegedly due to septic abortion. The medical department is currently investigating this case." The investigating of fatal septic abortions was sluggish at best, which was no hindrance to sales.

In October, Robins decided to add a warning to the Shield labeling for American physicians: "Severe sepsis with fatal outcome, most often associated with spontaneous abortion following pregnancy with the Dalkon Shield *in situ*. . . ." Previous labeling mentioned pelvic inflammatory disease in neither the "Warnings" nor the "Precautions" section. Instead, in the "Adverse Effects" section that followed, Robins concluded a five-line, small-type listing with the word "Infection." Robins said nothing about what kind of infection it had in mind.

In November—more than five months after Christian and Reid had made their separate calls to Robins—Ellen Preston had a talk

with Dr. Wayne Heine, a member of Christian's OB-GYN department. He suggested that she talk to the chairman. She did so on
November 21, when, according to her memo, she phoned

> to determine what the facts were in a report we received from
> several sources over the past ten days to two weeks having
> to do with several deaths associated with the Dalkon Shield. It
> was alleged that these deaths were reported by him to a group
> called the Travel Club at a gathering at Acapulco. . . .
>
> During the course of [the] ten to fifteen minute conversa-
> tion, Dr. Christian made the following points:
>
> 1. This information had been supplied to the president of our
>   company way back in the spring of 1973.
> 2. The company had done nothing about the information and
>   had assumed a very "unstatesmanlike" attitude toward
>   this very serious problem of sepsis and septic abortion
>   associated with the Dalkon Shield.
> 3. Our salesmen continued to pooh-pooh and dismiss any
>   information indicating that there was any problem with the
>   Dalkon Shield. . . .
>
> My replies to Dr. Christian point by point were as follows:
>
> 1. . . . [Owen's] note does not convey to me the idea that we
>   should have gotten in touch with . . . Christian perhaps
>   instead of . . . Reid. Perhaps this is why Dr. Christian was
>   so hostile.
> 2. I indicated to Dr. Christian that this information about the
>   death Dr. Reid had reported had been passed on to the
>   FDA. Furthermore, revised labeling pointed out the prob-
>   lem of septic abortion and recommended consideration be
>   given to removing the Shield if pregnancy was diagnosed,
>   etc.
> 3. For our salesmen we attempted to keep problems as-
>   sociated with our products . . . in proper perspective as best
>   we could on the basis of available information. . . . I
>   inquired as to whether the three deaths he had collected

were all associated with pregnancy. He replied that was the whole point. I suppose that was intended to mean that I had asked a dumb question. . . .

Dr. Christian indicated that he would be glad to go over these cases with us and give us the facts if somebody wanted to come to Tucson to visit. . . . I told him I would get in touch with him later.

"I had been desperately trying to get Robins's attention, and I was happy to have her come out here and look at my materials," Christian told me. Nineteen days later, on December 10, Preston visited him in Tucson to tell him, as she put it in a memo on the meeting, "that we wanted to do what was right about it and we needed his help." She wrote that he strongly suspected the Shield was a uniquely hazardous IUD and suggested that Robins warn doctors to be alert to spontaneous septic abortions in Shield wearers. Once again, she said, he criticized Robins's "poor policy in having our salesmen deny any problems," saying they had done this at the OB-GYN convention in Miami in May. But he "conceded at once that perhaps at that point . . . we actually did not have any information," she said. "I emphasized that we did not." In fact, as has been pointed out, she had detailed information in hand or available on a substantial number of spontaneous septic abortions, exclusive of Thad Earl's five.

Christian put Preston on notice of his intent to publish an article, saying, according to her memo, "that he could call the editors of several journals and get it published in the next issue with a black border, etc., and that would be the end of the Dalkon Shield." With that "offer," Christian told me, "I think I got her attention, finally." Eleven days later, Robins made a report to the FDA. It listed four fatal spontaneous septic abortions in Shield wearers, as compared with one in users of other IUDs. As for nonfatal cases, the company report listed nineteen, still not counting Earl's.

Christian's draft article reached the *American Journal of Obstetrics and Gynecology* on December 24, and, he said, because of the article's importance, the journal doubled its normal publication pace. Even so, mainly because of the time needed for peer review of journal articles, the final version would not see print until the issue of June 15, 1974. The article renewed a point Christian had made in his meeting with Preston when he referred to the survey in which the CDC had sent a questionnaire to almost all physicians likely to be involved with intrauterine contraception. Taking aim at the performance of the FDA, but momentarily confusing it with the CDC, he said, "Certainly, if there were five botulism deaths from one type of mushroom soup, the Food and Drug Administration would do more than put out a questionnaire."

On January 4, 1974, Robins offered to present its data on spontaneous septic abortions (but not on pelvic infections in non-pregnant Shield wearers) to an expert OB-GYN advisory committee of the FDA's Bureau of Medical Devices and Diagnostic Products (BMDDP). Bureau officials Joseph M. Mamana and Harry E. Butts wanted to accept the offer. While it was pending, however, Robins implemented a new stratagem. It scheduled its own day-long "Conference on Septic Spontaneous Abortion" for February 15 and named twelve OB-GYNs as conferees. Although Christian was one of them, five others were paid members of the Robins Advisory Panel on Family Planning and Birth Control—essentially a Shield speakers' bureau. They had been chosen by the company from among OB-GYNs who had reported "good results" with the Shield. Shield developer Hugh Davis attended and spoke.

The invisible man—because he was not invited—was Robins's highest-paid consultant, Thad Earl. The invisible cases—ignored in the ostensibly complete packet of materials provided to the panelists and never mentioned by participating Robins officials, including Drs. Clark, Preston, and Chremos—were mainly Earl's. Preston, asked later if she had withheld information about Earl's cases, testified that "it was not deliberately withheld." Nor were the panelists told that R. W. Nickless had alerted thirty-nine other executives to wicking—and therefore to the risk of infection caused by the multifilament string—three and a half years earlier. "In my opinion," Preston has testified, "it was not a necessary fact to provide."

Christian posed the bottom-line question: "Do the physicians here believe there is an increased risk of serious sepsis [infection] in pregnancy patients with Dalkon Shields as compared to those patients with other devices in the U.S.?" Robins's "confidential" unsigned minutes say that five conferees voted "no," five voted "yes," and two abstained. How the paid advisers voted could not be ascertained.

Christian remains angry that Robins officials "sat on their data, not sharing it with us in a supposedly open forum." Another participant, Dr. Howard Tatum, then a senior scientist at Rockefeller University and the nonprofit Population Council, called Robins "irresponsible," for the same reason. One of the paid advisers, Dr. Robert A. Hatcher of Emory University, told me, "I think they did a very great disservice to physicians in withholding information which their company undoubtedly had at its disposal."[5]

W. Roy Smith, a Robins vice-president at the time of the conference, did not attend it, but has testified that if he—as a former independent pharmaceutical maker—had to decide the fate of a product on the basis of an evenly divided vote of ten medical experts, "I would certainly want to go to the most conservative case." Meaning "taking the product off the market . . . ?" asked plaintiffs' lawyer Michael Ciresi. "Yes, sir," Smith replied.

Robins did no such thing. Instead, as it interpreted the conference outcome to the medical profession, the panelists had concluded that the Shield was no more likely than other IUDs to cause spontaneous septic abortions—the claim the company makes to the present day.

By mid-April, Robins had prepared a draft of a proposed "Dear Doctor" letter. It said that in addition to the known five fatal spontaneous septic abortions suffered by IUD users, four of whom had been fitted with Shields, the company knew of nonfatal episodes in thirty-six additional IUD wearers, thirty-two of whom had worn the Shield. In addition, the letter advised removal of the Shield on confirmation of pregnancy (as had Thad Earl twenty months earlier) and cautioned about potential severe complications following initial flu-like symptoms (as had Dr. Christian). It said prospective users should be told that an accidental pregnancy could make therapeutic abortion desirable.

The letter did not advise removal of the Shield from nonpregnant women who showed signs of pelvic infection (and the company would not give such advice until 1980). Yet Dr. Clark, who signed the letter, testified in 1984 that he believed at the time it was mailed that the IUD should be removed in those cases as well. Moreover, the letter said nothing of wicking, understated the number of reported spontaneous septic abortions, particularly by excluding Earl's five, and asserted that the significance of these events "for the Dalkon Shield, specifically, is still uncertain. . . ."

At the time, Roger Tuttle, the former Shield defense attorney, was warning Robins that the volume of Shield litigation was soaring and was "going to hit you like a ton of bricks." But "nobody in management wanted to look around and say, 'You are the rascal who put me in this hole,' " he told me. "Everybody was heading for his own tree." Certainly, however, Robins's officers had the presence of mind to see that a "Dear Doctor" letter would help the defense against lawsuits by enabling the company to argue that it had a good-faith concern with women's safety. Obviously, the letter would be an even better defense if approved by the FDA staff. On April 16, Robins officials brought the draft to the FDA devices unit, hoping that bureau officials Joseph Mamana and Harry Butts would bless it. They not only refused, but said they regarded the letter as an inadequate way to tell physicians about the problem. Ten days later, Mamana urged the FDA to get a court order enjoining Robins to halt distribution and recall all Shields in supply pipelines.[6]

Undeterred, Robins sent the "Dear Doctor" letter, dated May 8, 1974, to a reported 120,000 U.S. and Canadian physicians. Was one purpose "to get a jump on Dr. Christian's article?" Preston was asked. "Well, that might have been a factor that was discussed," she testified.

Both before and after the letter, Preston testified, she had recommended removal to some women who phoned her. Had she also told Robins employees—pregnant or not—to remove the Shield, Ciresi asked. "I may have," she replied. "I—I don't recall right now."

The letter was, of course, mum about the tail string. Tuttle testified in 1984 that Owen and Clark's "party line" to him had consistently been that the string did not cause pelvic infections. But with the "Dear Doctor" letter, he testified, they admitted to him—privately—that the string could cause the infections but insisted that they didn't know the incidence to be statistically significant.

On May 22, two weeks after the letter went out, three BMDDP officials—Dr. Robert A. Skufca, head of the Medical Review Group, and Butts and Mamana—asked the company to halt distribution until the bureau's OB-GYN advisory committee could take up the matter at a two-day meeting in early June. The company declined. Its reasons are illuminated by a May 24 memo, brought to light by later litigation, which reported that Tuttle had expressed the opinion

> that if this product is taken off the market it will be a "confession of liability" and Robins would lose many of the pending lawsuits. At this time there are forty-seven suits pending for a total amount in excess of $25 million. . . . Also the point was made that whether this product were taken off the market or allowed to die slowly, there would still be lawsuits "in process" for as long as ten years in the future.

On May 29, the Planned Parenthood Federation of America, which had accidentally learned of the Robins letter, prepared to warn Shield-wearing patients in its clinics that they faced "a serious risk" if they became pregnant.

On May 30, the CDC told the FDA of the results of the questionnaire it had mailed in 1973 to 35,544 medical and osteopathic physicians. The survey yielded reports on 3,502 women who were hospitalized with IUD-related disease and injury in the first six months of 1973. The key findings, not made public for several weeks, were dismaying for Shield wearers.

Among all of these hospitalized women, "the ratio of complicated pregnancies to other diagnoses is twice as high for Dalkon Shield wearers as it is for all other (including unknown) types of IUDs," the survey found. Moreover, among the hospitalized women who had never borne a child and were fitted with small-size IUDs, more than 73 percent had worn Shields. The incidence of pregnancy with complications was 61.6 percent among Shield wearers, compared with 29.6 percent for the Lippes Loop and 6.9

percent for the Saf-T-Coil. For pelvic infection: Shield, 49.8 percent; Loop, 32.6 percent; Saf-T-Coil, 7.7 percent. For "other infection": Shield, 50.8 percent; Loop, 30.2 percent; Saf-T-Coil, 9.5 percent.

Five of the women died. Two had worn the Loop, two the Saf-T-Coil, and one the Shield. Notably, however, the survey did not pick up four of the five fatal spontaneous septic abortions uncovered by Dr. Christian, because they had occurred in a time period not covered by the survey.

The FDA had two separate groups of OB-GYN advisers: the BMDDP's device panel and a Bureau of Drugs committee. For a meeting of the device panel on June 10–11 and a separate meeting of the drug committee on June 13–14, the FDA asked Robins to supply information on the Shield's construction and physical characteristics. By that time, as has been noted, Robins had for nearly four years been accumulating—and suppressing—information on the tendency of the string to wick. General counsel William Forrest was asked in 1984 if Robins had provided for this or later FDA hearings any document "which bore upon the wicking hazard." He replied, "Not to my knowledge."

Dr. Clark, testifying at the device panel hearing on June 11, five weeks after the "Dear Doctor" letter was dated, defended the Shield's efficacy and safety. But the panel, despite being denied the vital information about wicking, was not persuaded, mostly because of the difficulty of reconciling the defense with a constantly rising toll of spontaneous septic abortions.

The device advisers concluded that in preventing pregnancy, the small-size Shield "is less effective than other IUDs," while the standard-size Shield "is no more effective and possibly less effective." They also concluded, 5 to 0, with two abstentions, "that the risk of septic abortion and septicemia is greater than with other IUDs." Furthermore, they judged, 4 to 2, that the Shield carries a comparatively greater risk of death. Finally, by the closest possible vote—4 to 3—they recommended withdrawal of the Shield from the market "for a lack of demonstrated safety." As of that time, according to Clark's testimony, Robins knew of six fatal and seventy nonfatal spontaneous septic abortions in American Shield users.

The drug committee then met and evaluated the same body of information. Without spelling out its reasons, it voted, 4 to 2, simply to recommend withdrawal of the Shield from the market. Its chairman was Dr. Theodore M. King, OB-GYN department chairman at the Johns Hopkins School of Medicine and a colleague of Shield developer Hugh Davis since 1971.

Neither the panel nor the committee decided the key issue: *how* the FDA was to accomplish withdrawal. Specifically, neither group of outside advisers said explicitly whether it wanted withdrawal to be compulsory, under a law empowering the FDA to get a court injunction to halt interstate shipments of adulterated and misbranded products.

On June 24, BMDDP officials urged FDA Commissioner Alexander M. Schmidt to take a forceful action: ask Robins to cease distribution of Shields and "recall all stocks of the device which have not been implanted." If Robins refused, Dr. Schmidt would designate the Shield a "health hazard" and order a "Class 1 Recall." This would enable the agency to get a court injunction.

Larry R. Pilot, the BMDDP's compliance chief, initialed the recommendation, but top-level FDA officials rejected it. At a large meeting, Pilot told me, they concluded that "the inability of the advisory committees to come out with something more forceful" left the agency unable "to support the charge that the device was a hazard to health." Schmidt told me he does not remember whether he ever saw the memo and emphasized the lack of hard scientific data available to the agency at the time.

Meanwhile, Robins, accepting the inevitability of *some* kind of agency move, sought the weakest possible regulatory action, a legally voluntary suspension of sales, because it would inflict the least damage on the company's defense against Shield lawsuits and on its reputation. Moreover, the company would be free to resume sales of the Shield if it could develop a safer model.

On June 26—after the reported toll of fatal spontaneous septic abortions had risen to 7 and of nonfatal cases to 103—Commissioner Schmidt accepted Robins's proposal to suspend sales, pending a hearing by the two FDA advisory bodies. The FDA and Robins announced the action two days later.

Inside the company, Claiborne Robins was jubilant. Understandably so. In a sense, he had once again managed to dodge regulation and get the FDA to do precisely what he wished. He sent an exultant memo to eight senior executives and six lesser company officials. Albeit inadvertently, the memo hinted at how a regulatory staff trying to protect the public can be blindsided by corporate legions with access to agency bosses. Here are excerpts from the memo, entitled "Dalkon Shield Activity, May–June 1974" and dated July 2:

> I would like to congratulate you . . . for the outstanding job you have all done. . . .
>
> The task force of Medical, the Law Department and Public Affairs performed a seemingly impossible task, which I think was finalized with the appearance of Commissioner Alexander M. Schmidt, M.D., on the Walter Cronkite news program (CBS) Friday night. We had all felt that the decision would be political, and to have Dr. Schmidt announce his action— taken against the vote of the panels—was indicative of the input of our team which had been working constantly with the FDA during the period leading up to the announcement. Dr. Fred Clark is to be especially commended for his leadership of the medical group.
>
> The group of Medical, Law and PA representatives who went to the FDA Thursday worked out a joint release, which helped reinforce our image as an ethical pharmaceutical company, which places the safety and efficacy of our products in a primary position.

So far as anyone knew, the sales halt was temporary: the Shield was eligible to return to the market. But in agreeing to the suspension, Schmidt said that the safety issue had yet to be resolved and that the two advisory groups would be reconvened to confront it. In July, the FDA announced that the device and drug advisers, sitting as an ad hoc committee, would hold a hearing on August 21–22.[7] The agency's stated purpose: "to consider the safety issues related to the Dalkon Shield and other IUDs. The hearing *will particularly consider whether there are any differences in safety between the Dalkon Shield and other IUDs.*" [Emphasis added.] On

August 15, six days before the meeting, William Zimmer sent an extraordinary directive to seventeen executives, including Clark, Preston, and Owen. His exclusive focus was precisely on the component of the Shield that accounted for "any differences in safety" between the Shield and other devices:

> You are requested to immediately search your pertinent files for *any* letters, memos or notes or written communications relating in any way to the thread utilized for the tail for the Dalkon Shield and send them to Ken Moore. To the extent that you have had any oral communications with third parties on this subject which are not memorialized in writing, please submit a memo on any such communications to Mr. Moore.
>
> This project is of utmost importance, and should be completed by Friday, August 16 [the next day].

It is undisputed that the directive produced a large volume of paper, but not a scrap of it was ever seen by the FDA advisers. By the time they met, the toll of reported fatal spontaneous septic abortions stood at eleven and the nonfatal cases at 209, but Robins had made it difficult for them to find out exactly why the toll was high and rising.

At the two-day hearing, in which Dr. Christian participated, the most important testimony came from the Population Council's Dr. Howard Tatum, and in fact it involved the Shield string. As reported in the preceding chapter, Tatum in 1974 had begun a series of studies designed to determine whether bacteria in the vagina, after a Shield had been in place for a period of months, could get into the spaces between the filaments and use them as pathways into the uterus. By summer, his preliminary results indicated that this could happen, and he promptly alerted Robins. At the FDA hearing, he disclosed these troubling results; later studies were even more incriminating.

Robins, it will be recalled, had done no such studies, and had effectively buried the experiments done by Wayne Crowder more than three years earlier. At the hearing, nevertheless, Clark disparaged Tatum's work and claimed that the wicking theory "has only recently been formulated." In doing so, he ignored not only

Crowder, but also Nickless's warning about wicking, which had gone to the thirty-nine executives on June 29, 1970—more than four years earlier. General counsel Forrest, who helped to prepare Clark's presentation, has said that he had learned of that warning at some point before doing so.

Clark claimed to the advisers that assertions that the Shield was unusually hazardous "cannot be justified." Christian disagreed. While spontaneous septic abortions in the fourth to sixth months of pregnancy had been almost unknown in the past, he emphasized, nearly all known cases in Shield wearers had occurred during exactly that time.

The ad hoc committee recommended continuing the moratorium on sales until such time as a controlled scientific study demonstrated the safety of the existing Shield or a redesigned model. It also recommended creation of a "specially appointed subcommittee" of eight advisers led by Theodore King, chairman of the drug committee, and Dr. Horace E. Thompson, chairman of the device panel, to weigh Robins's defenses against the troubling evidence, particularly the still-rising infection toll and the findings of Dr. Christian and the Centers for Disease Control.

Particularly because the ad hoc committee did not urge a recall, Claiborne Robins was exultant once again. "Against a very tough 'jury,' we have presented our case in such a manner that the very real threat of dire and precipitous action was avoided," he said in a memo to nine of his top executives. "It appears that we are in a stronger position now than prior to this hearing," he added. His assessment of the situation was to be confirmed in a roller-coaster sequel, in which the agency's advisers went one way and then another—but Commissioner Schmidt went Robins's way.

The specially appointed subcommittee met on August 31 and September 1, the Labor Day weekend. Family commitments prevented the attendance of two members who had taken a relatively hard line against the Shield. The subcommittee's draft report somehow managed to give no credence either to the CDC findings or to Dr. Christian's article. It failed to explain the increasing numbers of Shield-related infected pregnancies, and bought Robins's position almost in full. "It is recognized that the Dalkon Shield is different in physical structure from all other intrauterine devices," the report said, and went on to comment that "it is not apparent from the available information that the safety and efficacy of the Dalkon Shield is significantly different from the other IUDs." The report also saw nothing troubling in the Shield's unique string. It went to the full ad hoc committee, which, in a poll conducted by telephone, approved it, 12 to 6.

Along with some outside experts, the dissenters on the ad hoc committee asked the FDA to reject the report. One of them, Dr. Richard P. Dickey of Louisiana State University, a member of the device panel, made some calculations about the relative safety of IUDs. Imputing a uniform 3-percent pregnancy rate to each of the three leading makes—the Shield, the Lippes Loop, and the Saf-T-Coil—he calculated from the sales figures the expected number of fatal septic abortions. He found that for the Shield, the expected deaths were 5.4, but 11 had been reported; for the Loop, 7.9 were expected, but only 4 had been reported, and for the Saf-T-Coil, 3.3 were expected, and none had been reported. Comparisons based on sales figures raised problems, however. The IUD manufacturers had supplied the sales figures to the FDA in confidence, and the agency, in turn, treated the figures as trade secrets under the law; it gave them to its outside advisers with that understanding.

Refining his analysis, Dickey calculated the relative risk of a fatal septic pregnancy for each of the IUDs, and the result was stark: a Shield fatality rate three times the Loop's and four times the Saf-T-Coil's. But some of the FDA's advisers, including Dr. King, were skeptical, contending that only data on actual IUD *insertions* could yield reliable results. Precise insertion figures were unavailable, but it was not unreasonable to assume that the ratio of sales to insertions was roughly similar for all three makes. If this ratio was uncertain, it would have been sensible for the FDA to inquire of the manufacturers if the assumption was true or false.

Essentially, Dickey posed a challenge: using sales figures, he found positive evidence of an unusual hazard in the Shield, and was willing to invoke this evidence to protect women. King and others, for want of *irrefutable* evidence, preferred to give the benefit of the doubt to the manufacturer.

Subsequently, Dickey told the FDA he had taped a television interview in which he disclosed merely the comparative death rates

—*not* the sales figures from which he had derived them. The FDA cautioned him that he "may have released information . . . which is not disclosable to the general public."

Ultimately, the number of American Shield wearers reported to have had fatal septic abortions was fifteen, compared with five for all other makes of IUDs combined. That was a vindication of Dickey's approach, but a terribly unhappy one.

In October, Robins told the FDA of the spontaneous septic abortion cases that Thad Earl had disclosed to the company twenty-seven months earlier. On October 29 and 30, following Dr. Tatum's submissions of more troubling test data on the Shield string, the ad hoc committee met to prepare a final report.

In that document, the panel stood fast on the Shield's efficacy, saying that it appeared to be about the same as that of other IUDs. But even with the wicking papers still hidden from it, it made a sharp switch on safety. It said that the available data "suggest that the Dalkon Shield may have potentially hazardous characteristics," and "its safety remains in question." Although it still recommended that the Shield not be removed from asymptomatic non-pregnant patients, it recommended "that the moratorium on commercial distribution . . . remain in effect pending accumulation of definitive data."

Dr. Schmidt then set off a furor. In an announcement on December 20, he said that Robins had agreed to a new approach in the event that it was to put the Shield back on the market: it would distribute the device only to physicians who would agree to register new patients with the company at the time of insertion and keep detailed records on the women so long as they wore the IUD. And, Schmidt said, Robins had indicated that the Shield it would put on sale would have a *monofilament* string.

At the time, and at a hearing held by Senator Edward Kennedy a few weeks later, in January 1975, some of the FDA's advisers expressed considerable anger at the commissioner's action; they viewed it as a repudiation of their recommendations—particularly the one for continuing the sales moratorium until definitive data were in hand. One adviser, Dr. Emanuel A. Friedman of Boston, resigned, charging that Schmidt had "emasculated" the advisory panels and had taken a "nonscientific" approach to data-gathering.

He finally rescinded his resignation, though to this day he characterizes the performance of senior FDA officials as "protective of the pharmaceutical industry and not of the women at risk."

In January 1975, Robins directed its salesmen to retrieve Shields in United States supply channels, including physicians' offices, hospitals, and nearly 1,500 family-planning clinics. The retrieval was one of several hints that the company had already abandoned plans to remarket the Shield. The formal announcement came finally in August 1975. A company press release cited the marketing hiatus combined with adverse publicity and uncertainty as to when the FDA would finish designing the patient-registry system.

The decision to stop sales, Dr. Owen emphasized in later testimony, "was based upon economic considerations rather than any real concern regarding the safety and/or efficacy of the Dalkon Shield." He had it wrong: the abandonment was based upon economic considerations, to be sure; but the economic considerations, rather than being divorced from any real concern about safety, were rooted in it. It was simply that the concern had to be concealed.

The involvement of the FDA and its outside advisers sent a message about government regulation, which at best is no panacea. The content of the message is that a corporation willing to use concealment, deception, and distortion in matters affecting public safety and health can manipulate and defeat regulatory mechanisms, converting them into a governmental cover story for corporate cover-ups.

V

Toughing It Out

You have taken the bottom line as your guiding beacon
and the low road as your route. This is corporate
irresponsibility at its meanest.

—Judge Miles W. Lord to three senior officers of the
A. H. Robins Company, February 29, 1984

10

Witnesses for the Defense

A. H. Robins retained a number of academics—Ph.D.'s as well as OB-GYNs—as expert witnesses or consultants for the company's defense. The company paid them well, not only in recognition of their services but for the borrowed glory of their great universities. The following are of particular interest.

Hugh J. Davis, the developer of the Shield, was an associate professor at the Johns Hopkins School of Medicine in Baltimore, when he left that institution in 1982. For his share of the Dalkon Corporation's rights to the Shield, Robins paid him $242,850 in cash. It also agreed to pay royalties to the secretary-treasurer of Dalkon, who distributed them to three owners, of whom Davis was one. Davis's share from this direct stake in sales volume would total $382,527. Finally, Robins retained him as a consultant at $20,000 annually for three years, with an option to renew for two more. All of these terms were secret.

In 1972, Roger Tuttle, then a company in-house attorney, asked Davis to be a defense witness. Tuttle has testified that when Davis balked, Tuttle told him of his "obligation" as a paid consultant to testify. Tuttle told me he overcame Davis's reluctance with a sweetener: an extra $500 (later $550) a day, plus expenses. "Every time I had any contact with Hugh Davis," Tuttle said, "the first topic Davis wanted to talk about was 'What am I going to get paid?' "

At the time, Tuttle was defending the first wave of lawsuits, in which women who had suffered perforation of the uterus blamed the Shield. Tuttle, guided by the medical department, blamed the doctors who had inserted it. Once Davis agreed to testify, Tuttle made an offer to a few plaintiffs' lawyers: drop Robins from their cases and Davis would testify against the physician defendants.

Davis did testify in February 1974, at a deposition for two consolidated cases, and also at a trial. At the deposition, Davis said he had been "offered," but had declined, stock in Dalkon. "I felt there would be a conflict of interest," he testified. "I did not feel I should be in a position of testing and evaluating a device in which, on one side, I was functioning as an evaluator and on the other side I was in a capacity to, as a private individual, profit from participating in the corporation." Asked more pointedly if he had ever owned stock in Dalkon, he said he did not know. Pressed harder, he said he had "never received any stock certificates."

Davis also swore that he had "never received any royalty from the Dalkon Corporation," Davis's attorney, Joseph G. Finnerty, Jr., told me. "You do have to look very carefully at the words he said. . . . He's very precise." Tuttle has testified that not until several months afterward did he learn of Davis's stake in the Shield, having been kept in ignorance of the arrangements by his boss, William Forrest. Davis "did not tell the truth, either to me or under oath," Tuttle charged in a deposition.[1]

Over a twenty-month period following the deposition, plaintiffs' lawyer Bradley Post gathered up the documents and evidence about Davis's secret financial arrangements and presented them at a second deposition. This time, Davis, though "very precise" with words, could find none to save himself.

In 1974 he denied having stock certificates; in 1976 he could not deny his signature on a document citing his 35-percent interest in Dalkon as of April 1970. In 1974 he swore he had not become a Dalkon owner because he would have a conflict of interest were he to acquire stock while he was testing and evaluating the Shield; now he admitted—again under oath—that it was "correct" that while in a position to profit from the Shield, he had tested and evaluated it. In 1974 he denied having received royalties from Dalkon; now he owned up to having received more than $300,000 in royalties—via Dalkon's secretary-treasurer. In 1974 he would have a jury believe he had no financial interest at all in the Shield; now he admitted that by the time he testified, Robins had paid him approximately $725,000.

Roger Tuttle used blunt language to characterize Davis's 1974 testimony about his ownership of Dalkon. Davis "flat-out perjured himself," Tuttle testified. E. Claiborne Robins had a different view. "I don't have any knowledge of anything that would question his integrity," he testified in 1984.

Davis gave the second deposition in November 1976. The cover story of that month's issue of *Mother Jones* magazine was on the Shield, and it recalled Davis's appearance before a Senate subcommittee in January 1970, long after he had become a hidden owner of Dalkon. Was he telling the Senate that he had "no particular commercial interest in any of the intrauterine devices?" he was asked. "That is correct," he said. "Davis had committed perjury," *Mother Jones* said.[2] Accompanying the text of the article was a half-page box headlined "How Much They Made"; the total given for Davis was $712,500.

During a Western fund-raising trip, Dr. Steven Muller, president of Johns Hopkins University, picked up the magazine in the office of a prospective benefactor and was jolted to read an article disclosing that a long-time Hopkins faculty member was a principal target of a muckraking exposé, partly for collecting an estimated $350,000 in Shield royalties.

Estelle A. Fishbein, Johns Hopkins's general counsel, is also its sole spokesman in the Davis episode.[3] Shortly, she told me, Dr. Richard S. Ross, the medical dean, conducted an inquiry. In a statement that raises as many questions as it answers, she said, "A review of Dr. Davis's published reports and the transcript of his Senate testimony in January 1970 did not yield evidence that he misrepresented the facts as they were known at that time." Ross's "conclusions, reached in December 1976–January 1977, were based on *information available to him at that time*, which, of course, did not include deposition testimony," Fishbein said. When I interviewed her in April 1983, she said, "We had no knowledge of Dr. Davis's testimony under oath in 1974 and 1976. . . ." She provided only sketchy information about the inquiry, not saying, for example, whether it dealt with the propriety of a faculty member having made a concealed royalty arrangement that had yielded hundreds of thousands of dollars in fees. "The dean personally interviewed Dr. Davis, and Dr. Davis provided the dean with a summary of his consultative activities and associated financial arrangements," she said in a letter in July. "The dean did not make a written report on the matter." Fishbein provided no details of the inquiry, while noting that the university lacks subpoena powers.

But former medical dean David M. Rogers, who left Johns Hopkins at the end of 1971 to become president of the Robert Wood Johnson Foundation, said in an interview: "If the facts are as presented, in my judgment [Davis's conduct] was the sort of thing that would lead to swift investigation and probable dismissal from the faculty." Instead, Davis remained at Hopkins until June 30, 1982. "His research productivity took a nosedive in 1974," his department chairman, Dr. Theodore King, has testified. "Because of that, primarily, he was not promoted, and so he was provided with essentially what amounts to a term of contract . . . at the end of two years, you're finished."[4]

Louis G. Keith, professor at Northwestern University Medical School, was the medical director of the Illinois Family Planning Council from 1972 to 1978. By April 1985, Keith had been paid $277,092. By then, too, an FBI investigation of possible perjury had begun. The investigation grew out of litigation in which Keith testified for the defense against Linda Harre of Tampa, Florida. She had suffered pelvic inflammatory disease, was left unable to bear a child, and blamed the Shield, calling it defective and unreasonably dangerous. In 1981, she sued Robins in U.S. District Court in Tampa.

The central issue was whether the Shield tail string had wicked bacteria into her womb and caused PID. Testifying for Harre in 1983, Dr. Howard Tatum said that his laboratory experiments at Rockefeller University a decade earlier had demonstrated that the string did wick bacteria. Dr. Harvey J. Bank of the Medical University of South Carolina said that his own recent tests also showed wicking.

Robins's sole expert witness on the subject was Keith, who testified on March 14 and 15, 1983, the final days of the jury trial.

He had this exchange with Charles Osthimer III, who, with Thomas H. Sloan, Jr., his partner in Bronson, Bronson & McKinnon in San Francisco, represented Robins:

Q: Now, Doctor, have you done or are you doing any studies under your direction on the Dalkon Shield tail string itself?

A: Yes, studies are being done under my direction.

Keith went on to testify that the general purpose of the studies was "to gain information on the allegation that had been made by some individuals that the string wicked bacteria." Could he "draw a diagram . . . of the way in which you conducted these experiments?" He could; he drew illustrations and explained how they were done. Then:

Q: Now, Dr. Keith, in conducting these experiments, did you have somebody working with you who was a microbiologist?

A: I did.

Q: And did you have someone working with you who was an expert in the use of radioactive labeling of bacteria?

A: Yes. These people were experts.

Keith concluded that, in his opinion, the Shield had not contributed to Linda Harre's PID, the Shield string did not wick bacteria, and the Shield was not unreasonably dangerous. In their closing argument, defense counsel asserted that "the best test" had been done "under the auspices of Dr. Keith," that this test more accurately reproduced *in vivo* conditions than Tatum's, and that it demolished claims of wicking. The jury believed Keith, and Linda Harre lost her case.

About eight months later, on November 1, 1983, Keith testified at a deposition, this time as a prospective witness for Robins in a Shield trial in Superior Court in San Francisco. With Bronson, Bronson & McKinnon still representing the company, plaintiffs' lawyer Dennis B. Conklin had this exchange with Keith:

Q: Have you done any experimental work on new Dalkon Shield tail strings?

A: No, other than to look at one under the microscope.

Q: You haven't done any wicking experiments?

A: I haven't.

Q: Has somebody under your supervision done some?

A: Not under my supervision. I didn't supervise anybody.

Q: Has somebody at your request done wicking experiments?

A: I have knowledge of somebody who has done some, but—

Q: Is that—?

A: Dr. Eric Brown.

Q: Who is Dr. Eric Brown?

A: Professor of Microbiology at Chicago Medical School.

Q: When did he do these?

A: Within the last six months.

Q: Are those the same ones that you testified about in Florida?

A: Yes.

In Tampa, Keith swore that Shield string studies "are being done *under my direction*"; in San Francisco he swore that *no* wicking experiments were done *"under my supervision."* In Tampa he was asked to, and did, diagram "the way in which *you conducted* these experiments"; in San Francisco he testified that he hadn't done experimental work on Shield strings. In Tampa he was asked whether a microbiologist had worked with him *"in conducting these experiments,"* and he swore that one had; in San Francisco he swore he had done no experiments. Since he had done none, obviously no microbiologist could have worked with him.

Keith testified in San Francisco that Dr. Brown's studies had been conducted within six months of November 1, meaning May 1 or later; yet he identified Brown's studies as the ones he had referred to in Tampa *in mid-March.* In Tampa he diagrammed the studies; in San Francisco he said he had not observed the studies and that what he knew about them came from Brown and from looking at Brown's lab books.

Harre's lawyer, Sidney L. Matthew, charged that "a fraud was committed" on the federal court in Florida and asked the judge,

William J. Castagna, to order a new trial. Castagna refused. "At most," Matthew had "revealed a series of minor inconsistencies in Dr. Keith's testimony," he ruled in January 1984. Matthew appealed to the Eleventh U.S. Circuit Court of Appeals, and a year later, on January 21, 1985, a unanimous three-judge panel reversed Castagna and sent the case back for a new trial. What Castagna had rated as "minor inconsistencies," they called "intractable conflicts." They wrote an opinion which concluded that Keith had given "false testimony" in Tampa, with "complicity of counsel," and that Castagna's district court had "abused its discretion" in denying Harre's motion for a new trial.

By April, Keith was under investigation for perjury. John M. Fitzgibbons, deputy chief of the Criminal Division in the office of the United States Attorney in Tampa, told me, "We're well aware of the Eleventh Circuit's rather extraordinary opinion, but it is our policy not to confirm or deny the existence of an investigation." A spokesman for the FBI, which undertakes investigations at the request of United States Attorneys, said, "We are conducting an investigation."

Keith's attorney, much like Hugh Davis's, staked his case on precision of language. The judges' opinion, said Matthew F. Kennelly, "does not take into account the nuances of language used by lawyers and Dr. Keith."[5] Papers seeking to undo the ruling were filed by Robins, which said that Keith "did not lie," as well as by attorneys Osthimer and Sloan, and by Keith himself.[6]

Keith also played another role in his association with Robins. In 1974, he was one of the five paid members of the Robins Advisory Panel on Family Planning and Birth Control who participated in the company's Conference on Septic Spontaneous Abortion. A year later, Franklin M. Tatum III, a leading Shield defense attorney in McGuire, Woods & Battle, the Robins law firm, was Keith's host at a dinner. Keith has testified he had never met Tatum and had "no idea" beforehand why Tatum had invited him. But, he said, Tatum told him he was interested in the possibility of commissioning a review of the medical literature on the safety of IUDs and of a report on the findings. Keith said he recommended two professors at the University of North Carolina in Chapel Hill:

Gary S. Berger, an OB-GYN and co-owner of Berger, Keith & Associates, a medical consulting corporation for drug companies, and *David A. Edelman,* a biostatistician who was research director of the International Fertility Research Program (now the International Family Research Program), Research Triangle Park, North Carolina. They were friends of Keith—Berger since 1971, Edelman since 1974.

In 1976 or 1977, according to a synthesis of the trio's deposition testimony, they set up Medical Research Consultants (MRC) in Edelman's home in Chapel Hill. The owners were Edelman, Berger, and their wives; Keith said he was an original partner and consultant. Keith testified in 1984 that he did not know who funded MRC. A few weeks later, however, Berger swore at a trial that MRC got large sums from Robins, and that he himself had been paid approximately $50,000 for MRC's Shield-related studies: "That is money that I received for work that I had done for Robins." Edelman has testified that MRC has done "a fair amount of ghost-writing," mainly of OB-GYN articles. In the spring of 1977, Tatum met with Berger and Edelman and hired them to do the medical literature review and report, focusing on the relationship of IUDs to pelvic inflammatory disease and ectopic pregnancies. Berger said the project took "some months" or "a year"; yet, although Robins had been billed at $300 a day, he recalled having been paid only about $1,500.

Also in 1977, McGuire, Woods retained Berger and Edelman as Shield consultants and witnesses in behalf of Robins; by April 1985, Berger had been paid $307,291 and Edelman $152,481. For Edelman, Berger, and Keith, the grand total was $736,864. In the same year, the three experts began discussing a larger undertaking: a book built on the Berger-Edelman report for Robins, but involving Keith as the third coauthor.

The book, *Intrauterine Devices and Their Complications,* was published in the spring of 1979. According to the law firm, it paid Keith no fee until more than a year later, in October 1980. The book does not hint at a connection of any sort between the three authors and either Robins or McGuire, Woods. At the same time, the book views the Shield most favorably—amid the rising tide of litigation in 1979, five years after Robins had halted domestic sales.[7] The book and Keith also figured in a civil fraud action filed by the Illinois attorney general.[8]

In an interview with Keith and Berger in 1983, Keith said, "I have no connection with A. H. Robins." Berger also denied any such connection. I expressed surprise because Roscoe E. Puckett, Jr., Robins's manager of public information, had told me earlier in the day that both were expert witnesses for Robins. They protested that Puckett was unknown to them and then grudgingly conceded that McGuire, Woods retained them.

In June 1984, when plaintiffs' lawyer Aaron M. Levine questioned him at a deposition, Keith was still insisting on the distinction between Robins and the law firm it hired. Berger, Keith & Associates had been retained by Robins's attorneys, he said, but "we had had no dealings with Robins." Puckett had called Berger and Keith practicing OB-GYNs, and this drew an objection in my phone interview; the description "misrepresented us," Keith said, because "we are both considered scholars."

The men's book would be particularly welcome to Robins and its experts. They were facing formidable difficulties from a closely controlled clinical investigation—the largest of its kind. For almost two years, starting in October 1976, the federally funded Women's Health Study gathered data in interviews with 622 women who had entered sixteen hospitals after being afflicted by PID for the first time, and with 2,369 "controls"—hospitalized women who said they had never had PID. The results, published in 1981, showed that the risk of PID in women who wore IUDs was 1.6 times higher than in women who used no contraceptive at all. The results clashed with the conclusion that Edelman, Berger, and Keith had reached in *Intrauterine Devices* two years earlier, namely that "an objective overview of the research to date" did not permit a conclusion that IUDs generally cause PID.

Because the Women's Health Study was the first survey of sufficient size to allow a determination of the risk of IUD-caused PID on a brand-by-brand basis, the Centers for Disease Control then proceeded to break down the data. The analysis found a PID risk *five to nearly ten times higher in women who wore the Shield than in women who wore other IUDs.* This finding began to be widely known in the fall of 1982, although the CDC did not release its final report until May 1983.

This finding, too, clashed with *Intrauterine Devices,* which relied heavily on a statistical table guilty of many sins. First of all, the table bunched together five of the Shield's competitors, including two that had been discredited and were no longer sold. This made a one-to-one comparison with the Shield impossible. More important, the table used *unpublished* data from Robins's so-called ten-investigator study, in which Shields were inserted in 2,391 women. But no other IUD maker was asked if it would provide unpublished data, Berger has conceded.

In Shield-wearers, according to the table, the PID rate thirteen to twenty-four months after insertion was 2.5 per 100 woman-years —a statistically insignificant 0.3 percent higher than the average for five other IUDs. But a claim for this rate was made possible only by the application of a double standard to the number of women who had been lost to follow-up during the studies. For the competitor IUDs, the loss to follow-up did not exceed 15 percent. For the Shield, however, Robins's records from its own ten-investigator study showed that follow-up losses were more than twice as high—34.5 percent on the average. At one clinic, the loss was 91 percent.

The late Dr. Christopher J. Tietze, an expert on birth-control studies, said of the nondisclosure of the double standard, "I don't think it's proper, ethically." Irving Sivin, the Population Council's IUD data specialist, told me that it was "bad science." Keith disagreed. Is the comparison of the five rival IUDs to the Shield "intellectually honest?" he was asked in a deposition. "I think it is," he said. Similarly, Berger swore that the book's purpose "was to present an accurate assessment of what the literature showed [and not] a defense of the Dalkon Shield." Edelman, in an interview in 1985, said that the research in the book "can be verified, based on the scientific information available at that time."

Learning of the not-yet-published CDC finding about the high risk of PID in Shield users, Keith, Berger, and Edelman launched a preemptive strike. They published a sixty-two-page, heavily footnoted, issue-length monograph in *Current Problems in Obstetrics and Gynecology,* a little-known, for-profit publication with a three-member editorial board. One member is Keith. They claimed to have "additional evidence" showing "that there are no differences in the risk of PID to different IUD users." More plainly, as they made clear in the 1983 interview, they were saying—while the litigation tide was running much more strongly than it had in 1979 —that the Shield caused no more PID than did other IUDs.

The reader could not check the "additional evidence" because its source was "unpublished data." In fact, these statistics had been gathered by Robert Snowden, a British sociologist. Warning that his results were still tentative and not ripe for publication, Snowden disclosed them at a gathering of Shield defense experts at the Pointe Resort in Phoenix, Arizona, in May 1982. No one had told Snowden that the data would show up in *Current Problems,* where, he has testified, he discovered them only because he chanced to subscribe to it. Did he authorize publication of the data? "No, I didn't," he testified.

Moreover, Snowden said, he had told Franklin Tatum, the defense attorney, that a table in the article based on his data listed an erroneously low PID rate for the Shield and erroneously high rates for rival IUDs. "I certainly [told Tatum] that those rates were incorrect as they appeared in that table," Snowden testified. "And I expressed my dislike of the fact that this had been used and that the new draft I was producing would not be exactly the same."

Attila Toth was, in 1981, an assistant professor at Cornell University Medical College. At that time he told Dr. Fletcher B. Owen, Jr., Robins's director of medical services, that he was upset by "headlines" about Shield lawsuits filed by women who had PID. He proposed to do a two-part study that "would be of paramount importance in explaining the IUD-related [PID] and at the same time relieve some of the blame from drug companies. . . ." In "our current litigation-conscious society," he told Owen in a letter, "every drug company entangled in IUD-related [PID] cases could use this type of work for its own defense."

What Toth held out was a startling switch in the focus of responsibility for PID: from the devices themselves to the sex partners of women who wore them—specifically, to men who were infertile or who had had genital-tract infections. "Firstly," Toth wrote, "we would like to show that infertile males and males with a past history of genital tract infection have many more bacteria in their seminal fluid than men in a monogamous marriage situation and those who easily reproduce."

In his subsequent research proposal, Toth went further, saying that one of his aims was "to alert the public that it is probably not the IUD per se that causes the pelvic infection, but bacteria derived from the seminal fluid of asymptomatic male carriers in conjunction with the IUD." He said the second part of the study would try to show that seminal fluid could carry the same germs quickly through the hostile environment of the cervical mucus, and would look into "what other diseases can be associated with men who walk around with a lot of sperms and bacteria."

Toth's proposal meshed neatly with Robins's strategy for defending against Shield lawsuits, for two reasons: It would not distinguish the Shield from monofilament-string IUDs—all IUDs, in Robins's view, were basically the same, insofar as PID was concerned—and it would tend to divert blame for Shield-induced infections to "risk factors" in the plaintiffs and their sex partners, such as the nature and frequency of sexual activity.

Shortly, as Toth had requested, Robins sent $97,516 (in two equal checks) for Cornell's McLeod Laboratory for Infertility, which Toth had helped to set up. This was an achievement of sorts: Toth became the only medical expert to be hired and paid directly by Robins in connection with its Shield problems. The bills for the others, who were retained by McGuire, Woods, went to Aetna Life & Casualty Company, which was the Shield insurer, and which retained McGuire, Woods as its Virginia counsel. Toth has testified that $5,000 of the payment went to him as a salary increase.

Toth completed the first part of the study in October 1982, and was elated. As he had foreseen, he told Robins, it showed "without doubt that it is not the intrauterine device per se but the infected seminal fluid that causes [PID] in women who use this type of birth control method."

In an interview in 1985, Toth deplored the CDC study, claiming that adverse publicity about the Shield had frightened doctors into needlessly hospitalizing women with PID, further skewing comparisons with other IUDs. He also said that Robins's funding of his research had no effect on its outcome, partly because of a little secret he revealed over the phone, namely that the research was already well along before he asked for the money, and when he got it, he used it mostly for secretarial and other staffing.

But claims such as Toth's were in for a battering. One came from a plaintiffs' expert, medical statistician Tom Downs of the University of Texas in Houston, who reviewed data gathered by the Women's Health Study. In a key analysis of PID in IUD wearers, he found that in women who wore the Shield for at least thirty-six months, the risk was not increased when adjusted for the number of sex partners; it changed negligibly when adjusted for gonorrhea. But the claims weren't helped either by two of Robins's own OB-GYN academic consultants, who were cross-examined at a Shield trial in St. Paul in 1983.

The Robins consultants were Karlis Adamsons, chairman of OB-GYN at the University of Puerto Rico, and Gerald I. Zatuchni of Northwestern University. (Adamsons's fees total at least $137,545, and Zatuchni's at least $64,810.) Plaintiffs' attorney Roger P. Brosnahan asked them about whether the risk factors "associated" with PID *caused* it in IUD wearers. " 'Associated' and 'caused' are [separated by] very big differences," Dr. Adamsons testified. Dr. Zatuchni was asked whether sexual intercourse caused PID. "Absolutely not," he said. "Multiple sex partners doesn't cause PID?" The reply was again, "Absolutely not."

If Robins believed that particular sexual or hygienic behavior caused PID in Shield wearers, it was obligated to warn physicians and women. Ernest Bender was asked in 1984 if management committees had had "any discussion of limiting sales to women based upon the frequency with which they have sex?" He answered, "I have no recollection of any such discussions."

A final point about Attila Toth: he, like Keith and Berger, tried to dissociate himself from Robins, while he was listed as a prospective defense witness. On January 20, 1983, seventeen months after Robins—not the law firm—issued a check for $48,758 for the first part of his study, he testified at a deposition in St. Paul.

Michael Cerisi asked him whether Robins had "retained" him to render any opinions in other Shield cases. "Have I been retained?" Toth responded. "What does that exactly mean?" Told he was simply being asked if he had been hired and would be paid by Robins for an opinion, he swore, "No, I have not." Ciresi persisted: "Not at all?" "No," Toth replied. A defense attorney then spoke up. Toth *"has had no contact with"* the company but "he's working for the lawyers," the attorney said (emphasis added). "We told him we represented the A. H. Robins Company." Franklin Tatum, the McGuire, Woods attorney, said later that the "no contact" statement was an error and that it was corrected the next day. Robins did not call Toth to testify in the trial.

Donald R. Ostergard, the OB-GYN at the University of California at Los Angeles who is also head physician in OB-GYN at Los Angeles County Harbor General Hospital, was in the Robins delegation that appeared at the House Government Operations subcommittee's hearing on IUDs in June 1973; he is so listed in the printed transcript of the hearing. "I am not a consultant to Robins at the present time, nor have I ever been," Ostergard told Representative L. H. Fountain, the chairman. "Robins is paying my expenses, of course, to come to this particular hearing."

Actually, Robins disclosed subsequently, it had, up to that time, paid $38,688 in fees and expenses for the assistant professor's participation in its ten-investigator study. The next day, Ostergard billed Robins for expenses of $358.97—plus "fees" of $1,500. He got a check for $1,858.97 and a letter from Dr. Ellen Preston, the pediatrician who was in charge of Shield post-marketing surveillance. The check was for "your expenses and fees in connection with 'our' testimony," she wrote. Under oath about three and a half years later, Frederick Clark testified that "Robins did retain Dr. Ostergard as a consultant for that day." By February 1975, Robins had paid $82,955 for Ostergard's services.

In an interview in 1985, Ostergard said that he never considered himself to be a Robins consultant because he "was presenting information to the subcommittee but not to the A. H. Robins Company," and because the "fees" for going to Capitol Hill were for "my time away from the office." As for the rest of the money, he said, "I think they misaddressed one or two of the checks," but every penny went to Harbor General Hospital's Professional Staff Association. "I derived no personal dollars into my bank account from that," he said.

Max Elstein, a British OB-GYN, was asked by Robins to be an expert witness at a trial in St. Paul in 1983. By then, Robins had paid him $119,222 in consulting and witness fees, in addition to a grant of $100,000 to fund his research in 1976–1978 at the University of Southampton. He is expected, the company said,

> to express the opinion that any transcervical appendage [tail string] can produce a wicking effect and further that in his opinion the tail string of the Dalkon Shield is not significantly different in this respect from the transcervical appendage of other intrauterine devices.

More plainly, Elstein was to attest under oath to this proposition: that the probability of bacterial invasion of the germ-free womb via a Shield string, consisting of hundreds of filaments with spaces between them that germs *can* enter, is about the same as via a monofilament, the interior of which germs *cannot* enter. In a deposition in 1981, he rested his claim mainly on one clinical study that concluded there was "no statistically significant difference" between the Shield and other IUDs. His chance to tell a jury about the study—which Keith, Berger, and Edelman cited in their sixty-two-page monograph—came in United States District Court in St. Paul on May 2, 1983.

The study was unusual: twenty-two women who were going to have hysterectomies, and who did not have PID, agreed to be fitted in advance of surgery with IUDs, some with strings, some without. The total number in whom Shields with multifilament strings was implanted was *three*—and two of the three would wear the devices *less than six months.* As if the tiny number and the brief duration weren't startling enough, cross-examination by Michael Ciresi elicited more facts that surely would make any independent scientist question the value of such a study.

Elstein had visited Robins in 1975, when, he testified, he knew that the Shield string had been publicly implicated in PID. The protocol for his study—"developed while I was there"—was clearly questionable. At least some of the hysterectomies were done immediately after menses, which flushes out the cervical mucus that attacks and kills bacteria. The study design for counting bacteria did not differentiate between those on the outside and those on the inside of Shield strings. In order to make the counts, in addition, the strings were sliced into cylindrical sections. The cutting instrument was a scalpel. A cold one would have let most of the bacteria survive for the counting; a hot one tends to kill germs. "Did you use a cold scalpel?" Ciresi asked. "Sterile scalpel," Elstein replied.

The jury, unconvinced by the science of Max Elstein (and other defense experts), awarded the plaintiffs, Brenda and Robert Strempke, damages of $1.75 million, all but $250,000 of it punitive. Elstein told me in 1985, by which time he was at the University of Manchester, that he did consider the study involving three Shield users to be "inadequate [and] incomplete" and conceded that statistically significant conclusions "obviously can't be drawn" from it.

Robert Snowden, the British sociologist, is director of the Institute of Population Studies at the University of Exeter. In 1984 testimony, William Forrest, Jr., said that because of their confidence in the medical department, neither Claiborne Robins nor any other executive had proposed to hire any outside leading medical experts to review medical records for evidence of whether the Shield string had caused pelvic infections. By that time, control over Shield matters had been in Forrest's hands for a decade. Why, Ciresi asked him, had he not directed the medical department to hire one, two, or more "renowned experts"? Forrest replied that Robins had indeed "experts independent of the . . . company." Who? Robert Snowden, said Forrest. But he was a sociologist, not a medical scientist, Ciresi reminded him. Moreover, he pointed out, Snowden himself had testified (at two trials) that he was unqualified to testify on the cause of PID. Forrest said, "In my opinion he is qualified."

In 1973 Snowden became a Robins consultant; by mid-1983, Robins or its law firm had paid him fees of $4,052 and had made "grants and payments" of $41,588 to his Institute.

Starting in 1971, Snowden had been asking United Kingdom physicians to fill out forms on their experience with IUDs, starting with insertion. In an interview in 1985, he said that he had accumulated 90,000 filled-out forms and stored them, unanalyzed, in "tea chests in the basement." He mentioned this to David Edelman, the North Carolina biostatistician, and Edelman told him, " 'I know some people who would be very interested in that.' " Shortly he heard from Franklin Tatum, the McGuire, Woods attorney, who commissioned an analysis.

On May 26, 1984, the respected *British Medical Journal* published an article in which Snowden and Bernard Pearson, a lecturer in economics and social statistics, said that they had analyzed data on nearly eight thousand women who had been fitted with the United Kingdom's four most popular IUDs—two models of the Lippes Loop, the Gravigard (Copper 7) and the Shield. The devices were inserted at a network of family-planning clinics. None of the women had ever worn an IUD before; all were followed up for examination for infection—though how closely is unclear.

Snowden and Pearson—neither one a physician—acknowledged that "the difficulty in diagnosing [PID] is well known." They concluded, however, that "fears that the Dalkon Shield may be associated with a higher incidence of pelvic infection than other intrauterine devices may have been unjustified."

At a deposition in 1984, William Zimmer acclaimed the report as "the most comprehensive study that has ever been made in this world." Ciresi flatly rejected the claim, charging that the true incidence of Shield-related PID had been diluted by the study's inclusion of women "who had absolutely no illness [in] any way related to pelvic inflammatory disease."

Snowden told me, "We honestly did our best." Yet he himself raised some doubts about whether his study exonerated the Shield. He said that PID in Shield users seemed to be an "American problem, in the sense that we have not seen it in this country"; but when I asked if a contaminated string would be less hazardous in a British womb than in an American one, he acknowledged that the matter was perplexing. He also said that IUD usage in the United Kingdom has been relatively small, and that this somehow may have skewed the results.

Snowden's article also oddly balanced studies that "condemned" the Shield against studies that found it to be "the victim of unjustified claims." His example of the former was the large, carefully controlled, intensely reviewed, and federally funded CDC study; his example of the latter was the monograph done by Keith, Berger, and Edelman, who received more than $700,000 from the manufacturer and whose citation of his own work he had faulted.

Snowden and Pearson closed the article with thank-yous for help. One went to Robins for partial funding "for the subsequent more detailed analysis" of data. Snowden told me the company grant was "about $30,000 over four years."

Theodore M. King, the Johns Hopkins vice-president for medical affairs and former top outside adviser to the FDA on the Shield, has testified that Robins consulted him in four Shield cases (Estelle Fishbein, Johns Hopkins's general counsel, said the number was two) and that he spent one and a half days at the meeting of IUD experts convened by Robins attorneys at the Pointe Resort in May 1982. Fishbein resisted disclosing how much Robins had paid King, but finally said it "did not exceed $3,000," for expenses and an "honorarium" for attending the Arizona meeting. Terming the $3,000 a "paltry sum," she emphasized that Robins did not pay King for consulting and that he had never become a witness, although the company had listed him as a prospective witness.

In early 1983, King testified in a deposition that the Shield string was no more likely than a monofilament to cause PID. By then, as was noted, the unpublished but nearly final results of the CDC study—coauthored by an associate professor of OB-GYN at Johns Hopkins, Ronald T. Burkman—were widely known. In fact, the Edelman, Berger, and Keith monograph cited the "unpublished analyses" showing "that users of the Dalkon Shield had a significantly higher risk of PID requiring hospitalization. . . ."

The CDC announced its official, final summary on May 5, 1983, about three months after King testified, and shortly after his elevation to a vice-presidency. Following the announcement, King conceded through attorney Fishbein that the results showed a greater risk of PID in Shield users than in other IUD wearers. He said he had not read the study before giving the deposition.

For an entire decade the FDA had done almost nothing to protect Shield wearers. Now it was moved by the CDC data to warn every woman who might still be wearing a Shield—but no other make of IUD—to have it removed. Even in 1984, however, Robins executives continued to insist under oath that the PID risk was the same for the Shield as for other IUDs.

Plaintiffs' lawyer Dale Larson asked Claiborne Robins if he had read the CDC study; he replied that he had neither requested nor been offered a copy. Still, he testified that his company had not warned physicians and women of a higher Shield infection risk found by the government "because there is evidence that this is not correct," and "because our medical people and advisory people don't feel that that is a true statement." Could he identify anyone in his medical department—or *any* doctor—who had told him that the CDC and the FDA had erred? He named no one, but alluded to the then-unpublished Snowden study.

Ciresi asked Ellen Preston, who, as physician monitor, had persistently assured practicing physicians of the safety of the Shield, if she had read the CDC study. "No, I have not," she said.

11

Dirty Questions,
Dirty Tricks,
and the Secret Life
of Aetna Life

No one disputes that certain sexual activities or unhygienic habits can enhance the environment for pelvic inflammatory disease, even if they do not *cause* PID. This is why A. H. Robins had a right to make inquiries into highly private aspects of the lives of women who filed lawsuits blaming the Dalkon Shield for PID-related injuries. But it did not have a right to make *unreasonable and irrelevant* inquiries.

The record shows that Robins attorneys took depositions from Shield victims in which they asked not only intimate, but also demeaning and even intimidating questions. Although certain judges required defense counsel to show a connection between the questions and women's injuries, others did not do so and allowed Robins to ask at public trials what plaintiffs' lawyers call "dirty questions."

The following case is from the Shield suit of an Iowa mother of two children who had suffered PID and the consequent loss of her ovaries and womb. Robins's counsel took depositions from her and her husband, each in the presence of the other. To her, the company attorney put queries about her sexual relations before their marriage in 1963, *ten years before she was fitted with a Shield, and fifteen years before she was stricken with PID*. Her lawyer, Kenneth W. Green of Minneapolis, objected, calling such questions "disgusting as well as irrelevant."

Robins then submitted written questions, to her and also to her husband. These, Green said in an affidavit, were "even worse," partly because they returned to the premarital period. Two written questions to the wife were: "Prior to your marriage in 1963, did you have sexual relations with anybody else other than [your husband]?" and "Who were these sexual partners?"

Green's own daughter had worn a Shield and suffered two episodes of PID, one of which almost killed her. But knowing of the invasions of privacy, he advised her not to sue Robins, and she didn't.

Pantyhose can't cause PID; not even defense experts suggested they could. But in a case involving another Shield litigant, a Robins attorney made pantyhose an issue. Among his questions was whether she wore them and what fabric was used in the crotch. To the latter query she replied, "I'll answer that, but this sounds more like an obscene phone call than anything else."

During a deposition in Minnesota in May 1982, lawyers for a Boston woman directed her not to answer questions by Robins counsel about which way she wiped, and whether, and how often, she engaged in oral and anal intercourse and used so-called marital aids. Five months later, however, a judge compelled her to return to the Twin Cities to answer the questions. As late as January 1984, a Midwestern woman was asked if before she was fitted with a Shield she had had any sexual partners in addition to her husband. By then the couple had adopted two children, her ability to bear a child of her own having been ruined by Shield-related PID.

What could be *less* surprising than that among millions of Shield wearers—in all socioeconomic categories and in eighty countries —there would be some who had multiple sex partners or engaged in anal or oral sex, and some, too, whose personal hygiene would not live up to the standards that Robins's legal advisers prescribed?

Indeed, Dr. Ellen Preston has testified that such hygienic and sexual behavior "certainly was foreseeable." Similarly, Frederick Clark testified that a wide range of sexual and hygienic practices had been within the Shield's "expected environment of use." This may explain why Robins, in the Shield information that it provided to the medical profession and women, offered no cautionary advice whatsoever as to specific hygienic practices or particular sexual activity. To the contrary, its brochures for women were full of reassurances. One leaflet emphasized "Convenient Protection," "Medically Safe Protection," "Prolonged Protection," and contained this question-and-answer sequence:

> *Will the Dalkon Shield change my sexual desires or "nature"?*
>
> No. The convenience of the IUD helps make sex more natural.
>
> *May I take douches and use tampons if I am wearing the Dalkon Shield?*
>
> Yes. The device is higher up (inside the uterus) where it cannot be disturbed by douches or tampons, and in no way interferes with normal feminine hygiene practices.

The emphasis was on nature and "normal" feminine hygienic practices. Preston was asked whether Shield literature had advised the user to have only one sexual partner. "Why would it do that?" she responded. Similarly, Clark testified that cautions about sexual behavior and hygiene were "not considered and were not included in the product labeling."

Yet Robins used exactly those issues as the basis for its defense, to deter women from filing lawsuits, and to divert attention from the Shield itself if they did.

Brenda Strempke of Little Falls, Minnesota, suffered PID and impaired fertility. She and her husband, Robert, who were childless, sued and were put through an embarrassing pretrial invasion-of-privacy ordeal. Yet Robins produced not a single medical opinion or study to support the claim that her pelvic infection was caused by what she had done in her private life.

The couple was willing to settle for $195,000. Robins offered

$15,000 and wouldn't budge. Knowing that Robins would try to humiliate them at a trial, the Strempkes nonetheless insisted on exercising their legal rights as victims. Their jury trial began in February 1983 in United States District Court in St. Paul and lasted three and a half months.

As noted in the last chapter, the jury awarded the Strempkes $1.5 million in punitive damages plus $250,000 for Brenda's injuries, a total 177 times the $15,000 offer. The couple's law firm, Robins, Zelle, Larson & Kaplan, has said that trying the case cost it and the Strempkes more than $1 million. The company, in posttrial proceedings, did not deny having spent at least as much.

Robins, Zelle, an outstanding large law firm, mustered a team of highly talented lawyers and large resources, risked a lot of money, and hung in to the bitter end. Robins knew, however, that many small law firms and lawyers in solo practice could not possibly play in the same league and made every effort to force them and their Shield clients to settle out of court for small sums, by threatening them with prohibitive legal expenses and long, drawn-out trials.

Another tactic Robins has used to silence lawyers and plaintiffs is to offer settlements that contain conditions which prohibit lawyers from using their special knowledge and experience to represent other Shield victims. Yet the Code of Professional Responsibility provides that "in connection with the settlement of a controversy or suit, a lawyer shall not enter into an agreement that restricts his right to practice law."

In August 1983, according to Dale Larson, Clifford W. Perrin, Jr., a partner in Mays, Valentine, Davenport & Moore—a Richmond firm—made a settlement offer containing "an absolute condition," i.e., that Robins, Zelle "would not accept any additional Dalkon Shield cases." Larson said he rejected the offer, telling Perrin the condition violated the code. Three months later, he said, Mays, Valentine partner William R. Cogar "restated that same nonnegotiable condition," calling it a " 'deal breaker.' "

On June 29, 1984, Kenneth Green said in an affidavit that James Fitzmaurice, an attorney for Robins in Minneapolis, had made a similar settlement proposal to him, making it conditional on Green's "not taking over the trial of any of [five remaining] cases."

On July 2, plaintiffs' lawyer Rodney A. Klein in Sacramento,

California, said that he had let a Robins settlement offer seal his lips. "I am prevented from accepting representation of any additional plaintiff injured by the DS [Dalkon Shield]," Klein said in a telegram to Larson and his partner Michael Ciresi. "I must also refuse to provide you with results of experiments conducted on DS string by Department of Chemical Engineering and Microbiology at Stanford University by agreement with AHR [Robins]."

Klein's cryptic reference to string experiments at Stanford provided a glimpse into yet another Robins strategy: secret, large-scale testing for wicking. For its defense, Robins had to know everything possible about the string, because the string was a prime plaintiffs' target. But if the plaintiffs were to find out that Robins had commissioned string tests, which hardly could have been expected to exonerate the string, the case for the defense would be weakened to the plaintiffs' benefit. So Robins went to great lengths to conceal their existence. Secrecy may have been in order at first, but what if the tests were to demonstrate a hazard? Would Robins recognize an obligation to disclose the danger to the very large numbers of women still wearing Shields?

For the answer, one must go back to November 1983, eight months before Klein's telegram. Jonathan Lebedoff, a state district judge in Minneapolis, ordered Robins to disclose whatever information it had "about any published *or unpublished* scientific or medical data concerning tests, studies, or experiments run on or concerning the tail string of the Dalkon Shield." [Emphasis added.] Robins fought the order, but in February 1984, Judge Lebedoff signed a new order telling the company to disclose "fully and completely." Robins filed a paper asking him to reconsider; he refused. Finally, in late March, the revelation came: in the period 1976–83, Robins and its Shield insurer, Aetna Casualty & Surety Company, had commissioned university scientists—in secret—to do eight separate tests relating to wicking.

In Tallahassee, meanwhile, trial lawyers Sidney L. Matthew and S. Lindsey Gorman had been fighting for release of the studies. They saw a pattern of Robins settling cases or taking other actions to avoid producing the records. In a court brief, Gorman cited three examples. On June 12, 1984, in Charleston, South Carolina, U.S. District Judge C. Weston Houck ordered Robins to produce all of the documents within fifteen days; it settled the case immediately without producing any. On July 6 in Pensacola, in Matthew and Gorman's case, Senior U.S. District Judge Winston E. Arnow issued a similar order. Robins responded with legal delays for four months: a motion for Arnow to reconsider the order, then a motion for him to stay it, and finally a petition for a stay to the Eleventh U.S. Circuit Court of Appeals. In another Florida case, U.S. District Judge Maurice M. Paul ordered Robins on September 19 to produce the documents by October 5; the company settled the day before the deadline, again without producing the papers. In Matthew and Gorman's case, on September 20, Judge Arnow ordered Robins to produce the documents by November 5, threatening to strike its defenses should it disobey. At this, Robins yielded and, in December, began to turn over some records. Among them was a 1978 report by Dr. Ronald S. Gibbs of the University of Texas at San Antonio saying that bacterial migration, both inside and outside the multifilament Shield string, was "clearly more extensive" than with any tested monofilament from rival IUDs.

A ninth study, an extraordinarily important one, would also have remained secret if Dr. William M. O'Leary, professor and chairman of microbiology at Cornell University Medical College, had not insisted on publishing the results.

Because an IUD is inserted (and removed) via the vagina and the cervix, the normal insertion process is likely to inject bacteria into the germ-free uterus. The uniqueness of the study in question was that it circumvented the normal insertion process. The study was done in baboons, which, after chimpanzees, have a reproductive system most similar to the human female's. At New York University's primate center, veterinarian C. James Mahoney invented surgical techniques to bypass the vagina and cervix in implanting and removing an IUD. Thus it would be bacteria-free on insertion—and would be contaminated while in place only if the attached string were to import microorganisms into the womb.

On completion of the sixteen-month experiment, NYU sent the IUD strings to O'Leary for analysis. He found "a striking association" between multifilamented Shield strings and bacterial contamination of the uterus. The American Fertility Society published a report in *Fertility and Sterility* in February 1982.

For two years thereafter, Robins and Aetna used secrecy to disassociate themselves from the unwelcome results, though there were suggestions they had been involved with the study—particularly its financing. Had Robins paid for it? Aetna? Both? Had either or both paid NYU through a conduit? Was the conduit Harris W. Wagenseil, a lawyer with a San Francisco law firm that listed Aetna and Robins as its principal clients, and that worked with McGuire, Woods & Battle, their law firm in Richmond?

Plaintiffs' lawyers tried to get the answers from Robins's general counsel, William Forrest. "Robins did not fund that study," he testified at a deposition in June 1982. Was Wagenseil the pass-through? His counsel told him not to answer, on grounds of "the attorney work-product doctrine, and the attorney-client privilege."

For six months, NYU refused to tell me the source of funding, and John Brademas, the president of the university, did not acknowledge two written and several telephone queries.[1] By contrast, Cornell Medical Dean Thomas Meikle said in an interview that O'Leary had told him "it was his understanding that A. H. Robins had funded Mahoney." Dr. Meikle also said O'Leary had told him that at least once, attorney Wagenseil had asked for—and O'Leary had given him—interim results of the string analyses. O'Leary declined to be interviewed directly.

At last, in a February 1984 deposition, Forrest revealed that McGuire, Woods had indeed initiated the study and that "our insurer did as a part of the expenses of litigation probably pay for the study." An Aetna spokesman confirmed Forrest's account. Forrest said he did not know how much the study cost, and Aetna declined to say. Wagenseil refused to be interviewed, but testified later that he had "involvement" in the study, had made reports on it to McGuire, Woods, and believed Aetna had paid for it.

Aetna played two major roles in the Shield story, one out in the open and one behind the scenes. For more than seven years after Robins bought the Shield in June 1970, Aetna routinely provided product-liability insurance. But with the rising tide of claims and lawsuits, Aetna began to work actively backstage with Robins to conceal the menace that the Shield posed to public health. Yet this collaboration brought the two companies into a sharp and bitter conflict in which each had a stake of many tens of millions of dollars. Out of the conflict, perhaps ironically, came a new form of cooperation that suited Aetna's and Robins's interests—but rendered a severe disservice to women.

Probably no serious dispute would have arisen if Aetna's coverage had been permanent: in that case, it would have had to pick up the tabs regardless. But the policy was renewable—or *not* renewable—annually, and this gave Aetna the opportunity to exit from a steadily worsening situation. Alarmed by the constant increases in the volume of awards to victims and by the seemingly endless filing of new lawsuits, Aetna finally notified Robins that it would not insure the Shield after February 1978. This was an attempt by Aetna to put a lid on its liability. The core issue then became, at what point did Aetna's liability for an award to an injured Shield wearer begin? When the IUD was inserted, or when injury became manifest? To be sure, if liability began with *insertion*, the carrier would still be liable for *all* awards made even after the cut-off date, simply because the 2.2 million Shields worn by American women had been inserted by mid-1974. But if Aetna's liability began instead with *injury*, the insurer would be off the hook for the vast number of injuries that were likely to occur after February 28, 1978.

Each company, naturally, argued the position that favored its own interests. Robins contended that Aetna's liability began with insertion; Aetna contended it did not.

Finally, Robins sued Aetna in Circuit Court in Richmond. Roger Tuttle, the former Robins defense attorney, described the suit as "Armageddon." In an interim armistice, reached on March 9, 1977, the companies signed a cost-sharing pact intended "to resolve all disputes relative to insurance coverage for the Dalkon Shield cases," pending a ruling.[2]

The pact had some astonishing provisions. Aetna, waiving its customary immunities from liability, pledged to pay all so-called compensatory awards to Shield wearers—even awards arising from "expected or *intended* bodily injuries," and even awards made *"on account of Robins' failure to disclose important relevant information and the supplying of false and misleading information."* [Emphasis added.] Robins, in turn, agreed to continue to pay all punitive awards.[3] These terms continued even though Robins began, in 1978, to set aside funds to insure itself, after failing to find a new carrier.

Robins, Zelle obtained a copy of the agreement in pretrial discovery in the winter of 1983–84, and the law firm's Dale Larson scathingly denounced it in a court paper in January 1984. The pact, he said, was

> additional evidence that the hazard of the Dalkon Shield was so well known to *both* Aetna and A. H. Robins prior to 1977 that Robins could not acquire additional coverage after 1978 —yet both Aetna and A. H. Robins have persistently failed to warn, recall or otherwise sound the alarm to women users. . . .
>
> The agreement dramatically reveals that Aetna has evidence that A. H. Robins was intentionally causing injury by its product and its conduct way back in the mid-1970s. As part of the agreement, Aetna gave up its right to deny coverage on these grounds—but in so doing Aetna acknowledges both its secret knowledge and evidence of that conduct. . . .

In Hartford, Connecticut, Aetna said in a statement that it had made "a thorough investigation of each claim" and tried to resolve it fairly. But Aetna said it could not divulge its role fully, mainly because

> we are prevented by law from publicly discussing or otherwise disclosing any information provided to us in confidence by our clients. . . . Confidentiality is not only paramount to an insurer's relationships with its clients; it is also our business and legal principle without which it might not be possible for insurance companies to provide products [*sic*] liability insurance in any form.

Robins, in a reply brief, labeled Larson's charges "distempered, vitriolic and untrue . . . scandalous . . . bombast." Claiborne Robins testified in 1984 that he had no knowledge of the Aetna pact, although the subject had come up at the company's board meeting a few weeks after the agreement was signed. Shown the pertinent part of the meeting minutes, he testified, "My recollection is not as good as I would like. I don't recall."

On November 1, 1984, two days before the Aetna-Robins suit was to go to trial in Richmond, a settlement was announced. The deal was that Aetna agreed to put $70 million, and no more, into a defense fund. Robins had the full burden when that fund was exhausted. The agreement thus sidestepped the issue of when liability to Shield victims began.

How much Robins had paid from its own till in connection with Shield cases was uncertain. Claiborne Robins, Jr., in a deposition on September 20, 1983, raised the surprising possibility that the net cost to his company was *zero* as of that day—i.e., that the whole bill had been footed by Aetna. "I am aware of court judgments both for and against the A. H. Robins Company," he testified. "To the best of my knowledge, I don't think that the company has paid any monies." Has it "paid out any dollars in settlements or defense costs related to the Dalkon Shield litigation?" Dale Larson asked. "I don't know one way or the other," the CEO replied.[4]

It was not only in the Aetna case that Robins officials claimed ignorance as a defense. As Michael Ciresi said in 1984: "The defense strategy has been to insulate Robins's officials from the information gathered by the defense [legal] team, so as to enable them to testify that they have no medical or technical evidence that the Dalkon Shield causes injury to a degree different [from that caused by] other IUDs." It is clear that defense strategists cultivated ignorance. Consider the 1984 deposition of Jack Freund, the retired senior vice-president for research and development and highest-ranking Robins physician. In 595 pages, many devoted to lawyers' disputes in which Freund was silent, he responded to questions with 160 "I don't recall" types of answers.[5]

At about the same time, Patrick J. McNulty, a United States Magistrate presiding over a deposition by Forrest, was exasperated by a similar performance by the general counsel. Forrest, he said, was without any independent recall whatsoever of any knowledge he might ever have had of almost everything pertaining to the Dalkon Shield. Even questions regarding events, reports or other revelations which were so important one would expect them to be . . . indelibly engraved in a lawyer's memory are met with a request to see a document or memo to refresh the witness's recollection; if such document is produced, it is met with evasiveness, digression and unresponsiveness. A straightforward answer to the simplest question is obtained only by patient and laborious repetition.

Another stunning example of the ignorance strategy involved pelvic inflammatory disease and its hazards. The flood of litigation brought huge quantities of information about PID into the law department, such as reports and studies by plaintiffs' experts. Meanwhile, increasing numbers of doctors were reporting PID-related problems to the medical department, which was responsible for monitoring the safety of the Shield. Yet communications between the lawyers and doctors were severely and strangely constricted, as was revealed in a series of depositions in February 1984. Ciresi asked Frederick Clark, "Was there a rule or a directive or a regulation or a standard in effect in the Robins Company from 1970 through 1982 which stated that the medical department should not obtain information from the legal department?" Dr. Clark's answer was "Yes."

Clark went on to say that he himself had "authored [a] 'standard operating procedure,' under which complaints and adverse-reaction reports reaching the law department would not be treated as such because they had not been investigated to the degree that the FDA would have required."[6] In addition, he said that he "did not" ever ask Forrest or other Robins lawyers to provide him with the medical records on the women who had sued the company.

More head-in-the-sand testimony came from Dr. Fletcher Owen. Dr. Owen has testified repeatedly that Shield adverse-reaction reports were too few to achieve statistical significance. But under cross-examination, Owen admitted to Ciresi that his statistical base excluded letters or reports from certain physicians—those whose patients were suing the company for injuries attributed to the Shield. "So you don't consider those 'adverse reaction reports'?" Ciresi asked. "No, sir," Owen replied.

But perhaps Clark was overstating the case. Six days after he testified, Ciresi raised the subject with Forrest, who said, "If we received information, medical information, regarding our products, I think we customarily would provide that information to the medical department . . . because they are the appropriate people to evaluate" it. He maintained this position under questioning:

Q: . . . right up to today, do you consider it the legal department's responsibility to provide that [medical] information to the medical department?
A: I think we do consider it our responsibility to provide medical information that comes [into] our possession.
Q: And that would be true regardless of whether it arises in a litigation context or whether someone just sent you a letter, correct?
A: Yes, I think we would pass on medical information . . . to the medical department.

Later, Forrest hedged. He had passed on such information "perhaps from time to time . . . if I felt there was a reason to do so." He didn't "recall" having ever relayed doctors' opinions or reports that the string was causing pelvic infections. Had he relayed the similar opinions of plaintiffs' experts? "I did not have reason to do so," he said. "Did the medical department tell you they didn't want to see [such materials]?" Ciresi asked. "No," Forrest replied.

Forrest wasn't helped by the testimony of Patricia Lashley, who, in 1975, became the law department's liaison with the medical department and organized, filed, and controlled all of the law department's Shield documents. In that same year, Robins retained McGuire, Woods to coordinate its legal defenses, and the law firm became the central repository of medical information about the Shield, including information generated by plaintiffs' lawyers. In 1984, Ciresi and Lashley had this exchange:

Q: From the time you've been employed [1974] up to the present time, have you forwarded any reports from McGuire, Woods & Battle to your medical department?

A: No.

Q: Never?

A: Not that I recall.

Robins's other Shield law firm in Richmond—Mays, Valentine, Davenport & Moore—was retained partly to handle settlements of pelvic-infection claims that were not in the courts. Mays, Valentine filed reports with Forrest. Had any information from the firm on Shield-related PID gone to the medical department? Lashley did not recall that any had.

But the flow of information from the doctors to the lawyers was also peculiarly obstructed. Forrest admitted to Ciresi that when the doctors got reports on wicking, they did not send them to the lawyers. Still, the truth of the matter is that after domestic Shield sales ended and lawsuits began to pile up, Forrest and McGuire, Woods, which was coordinating the Shield defenses of as many as 150 other law firms around the country, were influencing if not controlling the decisions on medical questions. Thus, McGuire, Woods commissioned and received the reports of secret string tests, as did Forrest; the medical department did not.[7]

Even more striking, it was Robins's attorneys who originated and shaped a "Dear Doctor" letter that, although cited innumerable times as evidence of Robins's good-faith efforts to prevent PID in Shield wearers, was in fact a ploy. The attorneys' apparent purpose was to limit the ultimate number of Shield lawsuits and to put a cap on the payouts to victims—but to do these things without a hint of culpability on the company's part. To accomplish this purpose, the letter did "the right thing" (counseling physicians to remove Shields from women still wearing them) for the wrong reason (an obscure type of infection unrelated to the actual problem, PID). And to further the attorneys' goal, the letter said that the wearer of the device, not its maker, would have to bear the costs of removing it, even in cases requiring surgery. Thus did the letter minimize the potential for removals that would protect women, in order to maximize the money that Robins would save by not having to bear the cost of those removals.

Twice in 1977, plaintiffs' lawyer Bradley Post urged Robins to send a "Dear Doctor" letter recommending immediate removal of Dalkon Shields from any women still wearing them; neither of his written pleas was so much as acknowledged. Later in the same year, Aaron M. Levine, a plaintiffs' lawyer in Washington, D.C., and a consumer adviser to the FDA, had asked permission for Post and himself to go before the agency's Obstetrical and Gynecological Device Panel to argue that it should ask the FDA itself to send a "Dear Doctor" letter advising removal of the Shield. Dr. Lillian Yin, director of the Division of OB-GYN and Radiology Devices, let them make an unscheduled ten-minute presentation on December 5, 1977. At the time, Levine estimated, 800,000 American women were still wearing the Shield. The lawyers' effort failed, mainly because some FDA advisers doubted the wisdom of removing the IUDs from nonpregnant women who had no symptoms of infection or other problems.

In 1980, the pace of Shield lawsuits quickened: 992 were filed, three times the number in 1977, and the payout to victims was $23.7 million, almost four times the 1977 total. In addition, "60 Minutes" was preparing a highly unfavorable segment on the Shield for presentation in the spring of 1981 to a television audience of tens of millions.

It was in this climate of adverse publicity and litigation—three years after Post's appeals—that Robins finally decided to send a "Dear Doctor" letter. The letter would base its recommendation for removal of the Shield on the suspension of domestic sales six years earlier—not on the near certainty that by that time virtually every implanted Shield string had rotted into a dangerous reservoir of bacteria. But it was a diluted, weak, and odd recommendation.

The first draft said that "most authorities agree that the relative risk of PID is somewhat greater among IUD users. . . ." The second draft changed "most" to "many." The final version mentioned PID but acknowledged no "firm relationship between the duration of use of inert IUDs and an increased risk of pelvic infection generally." Unmentioned at all were wicking, string deterioration, and false and misleading Shield claims.

The letter, dated September 25, 1980, was signed by Fletcher

Owen. The tone was casual, as Janet Nowak of Westport, Connecticut, found out when she inquired as to why she and not Robins should have to pay for "recalling a defective and potentially life-threatening product." Removal, Owen told Nowak in reply,

> is not an urgent matter, and we anticipate that most of these removals will be done during a regularly scheduled gynecological visit. Under these circumstances, the cost of removal and/or replacement with another IUD should be borne by the patient. . . . I should like to underscore the fact that the A. H. Robins Company is not "recalling" a defective and potentially life-threatening product, as you have alleged. We are merely altering our recommendation pertaining to the period of time that an inert intrauterine contraceptive device can be used. . . .

By September 23, the eve of the mailing, the letter was a *fait accompli.* But Robins, as a maker of products regulated by the FDA, had taken care to preserve its relationships with the agency by having Owen call on the FDA's Dr. Yin. They talked for three hours; he called the meeting "friendly but [with] obvious difference of opinions." Most important, Yin didn't buy Robins's rationale for the letter. As stated in the letter, the company's reason for writing was to alert women that "a relationship has been suggested by recent literature" between long-term use of all makes of inert IUDs and infections caused by organisms called *Actinomyces israeli,* and that replacement of the devices at three-year intervals might minimize the problem. Owen's notes on the meeting said that Yin thought the "Dear Doctor" letter was "devious" and that its unadmitted "real purpose" was to have all Shields removed. His handwritten summary of Yin's response to the letter also reported:

> · She said we were attempting to drag other products (involve them) by implication & we had no right to do this.
> · She felt that there was no good scientific-medical reason to removal all D.S. . . . [but]
> · Said we should just say "We've had enough" & recommend all removal.

- Said we would be admitting guilt & get more suits.
- Is familiar [with] the 60 minutes plan & says this would look bad there. . . .

Yin missed only one of Robins's specious tactics. As lawyers Larson and Ciresi brought out in depositions, *Actinomyces* was so profoundly different from other pelvic infections as to be no justification at all for the letter. It was so rare that only thirty-one cases had been reported in a half-century. Robins had had only *five* reports of it in Shield users, compared with thousands of reports of other PID. Obviously, *Actinomyces* was no more than an alibi for suggesting Shield removal. As an alibi, it was splendid. It made the company appear to be almost noble, and it eased its litigation plight while reducing somewhat the number of users.

Where had the idea of harnessing *Actinomyces* originated? Not with Carl D. Lunsford, the research director—he testified that he had not been "aware" that there were only five cases. Instead, Lunsford pointed to William Forrest, but said the general counsel had not divulged *his* source of expertise on *Actinomyces.*

Lunsford also testified that Forrest and attorneys from McGuire, Woods had participated in the half-dozen meetings that led to the letter. Had anyone attending the meetings inquired whether *Actinomyces* victims were asked questions about their personal hygiene or sexual preferences? No one had, Lunsford testified. Had any of Robins's outside medical experts urged the "Dear Doctor" letter? None had, he conceded. Had Robins sent the letter to doctors in the seventy-nine other countries where it sold the Shield? Of course not.

Forrest, as might be expected, testified vaguely that the inspiration for the "Dear Doctor" letter had come from the medical department. Of course, his mission was not to protect women, but to prevent Shield cases from being filed, to win cases that were filed, and to pay as little as possible to dispose of cases Robins settled or lost. And no one could accuse Forrest of less than total dedication.

12

The Vanishing Documents

Thousands of documents sought by lawyers for victims of the Dalkon Shield sank from sight in suspicious circumstances. A few were hidden for a decade in a home basement in Tulsa, Oklahoma. Other records were destroyed, some admittedly in a city dump in Columbus, Indiana, and some allegedly in an A. H. Robins furnace. And despite court orders, the company did not produce truckloads of documents for judicial rulings on whether the women's lawyers could see the papers.

In late June 1974, the steadily rising toll of spontaneous septic abortions in Shield users led Robins to halt domestic sales of the device. The Food and Drug Administration then set August 21 and 22 for a hearing by a special committee of outside advisers on the safety and efficacy of IUDs, and asked Robins for documents bearing on the disproportionate share of IUD-related pelvic infections in Shield wearers. "The hearing will particularly consider whether there are any differences in safety between the Dalkon Shield and other IUDs," the agency announced on July 15.

Six days before the hearing, William Zimmer, as we have seen, directed more than a dozen executives "to immediately search your pertinent files for *any* letters, memos, or notes on oral or written communications relating in any way" to the string, and termed references to wicking "of particular interest." He said he wanted the documents delivered to Kenneth Moore by the next day, August 16, because the document search was "of utmost importance."

Not one document relating to the string or to wicking went to the FDA for the hearing, where Robins testified that existing evidence did not justify viewing the Shield as more hazardous than other IUDs. Nor did so much as a scrap of paper produced by the search surface in the following decade. In 1984, Shield victims' lawyers tried to solve the mystery by taking testimony from Zimmer and Moore and from William Forrest, who had received a copy of the 1974 directive.

Moore said he had collected the documents, but, under oath, he, Zimmer, and Forrest each disclaimed knowledge of the papers' whereabouts at any time thereafter. Zimmer said he had asked Moore what had happened to them and Moore had told him he didn't know. Moore said he didn't "recall" Zimmer asking him. Forrest said he had made no inquiries but had "no reason to believe" the documents were destroyed.

While Moore was collecting the documents in 1974, Roger Tuttle was preparing to try an early Shield lawsuit in Wichita, Kansas. He had custody of numerous boxes of files. In one of them, unknown to him, was an extraordinarily sensitive memo written by Frederick Clark on a meeting with Hugh Davis. The memo contained the bombshell disclosure about the low 1.1-percent pregnancy rate that Davis was claiming—namely that on June 8, 1970, four days before Robins bought the Shield, Davis already had new data showing a failure rate well above 1.1 percent. Yet Robins went ahead to make 1.1 percent what Tuttle calls "the foundation stone" of its sales and promotional campaigns.

During the pretrial period, a document-discovery session was held in Robins's medical department. Bradley Post, the plaintiff's lawyer in the Wichita case, and Tuttle attended. By Tuttle's account, someone suddenly said, " 'We have one more file,' " and "unceremoniously dumped" it on a table. "I was sitting next to Post," Tuttle said, "and he turned up the memo, and before I could do anything about it, he'd seen it." Tuttle said that he "hit the ceiling" because the medical department had not made him aware of the memo. Later, he testified, he discovered that keeping its own lawyer in the dark had become a company habit. The medical department was "forever pulling rabbits out of the hat that I didn't think existed," he testified.[1]

In the thirteen-week trial, the memo proved to be "devastating" to his defense, Tuttle testified. On February 7, 1975, the jury not only returned a verdict for Connie Deemer, Post's client, but made the first award of punitive damages to a Shield victim. For Robins, the importance of the exemplary award was not the sum of money, a relatively trivial $75,000, but its ominous message, which was that the first jury to try a Shield case to completion on the merits had decided to punish Robins—and had done so in awareness of only a small part of what is now known to be the whole truth about its conduct. Robins's fears were well founded. In the decade following the Deemer verdict, more than 14,000 American women filed Shield lawsuits. By the end of September 1984, nearly 1,200 of them, according to the company, were seeking punitive damages exceeding $12 *billion;* more than 2,100 others were litigating for exemplary awards in unspecified amounts.

The exposure of the Clark memo spelled trouble for Tuttle. He told about it years later, in a startling four-day deposition in July and August 1984 in Minneapolis. Three or four days before the Deemer verdict, Tuttle testified, general counsel Forrest, his boss, called him in and blamed him for not having been aware of the memo. Forrest said "that if I had done the kind of job that I was being paid for, the [paper] would never have been produced," Tuttle testified. His "comments were . . . to the effect that he didn't ever want that to happen again, and that the only way it wouldn't happen again would be if documents were no longer in existence. . . . And I said I couldn't be aware of that which had been withheld from me."

Then, Tuttle swore, Forrest ordered him to arrange the destruction of hundreds of "troublesome" Shield documents. Tuttle said he had relayed the order to others at Robins and has "every reason to believe that the people who reported back to me that it had been done did it." Tuttle named them as Kenneth Moore, Allen Polon, who succeeded Moore as Shield project coordinator, and Patricia Lashley, Forrest's paralegal.

The company immediately denounced Tuttle's charges as

"false" and "absurd." Forrest has sworn that he had "absolutely not" ordered Tuttle to destroy documents. At the same time, he testified, "I have no reason to believe that while he was in my employ he was not an honest man."

To implement the order, Tuttle said, Forrest arranged for a search of executive files. "I am bound to believe they [the executives] knew the reason," Tuttle said. Leading the list of those he named were E. Claiborne Robins, Sr., William Zimmer, and E. Claiborne Robins, Jr. He also named six men who were or would become senior vice-presidents: Ernest Bender, Jack Freund, C. E. Morton, Robert Murphey, W. Roy Smith, and George Thomas. Zimmer and Thomas are now directors of Robins; Freund and Smith are retired.

Tuttle identified six persons who brought him the papers to be destroyed: project directors Moore and Polon, paralegal Lashley, Arthur R. Cummings (Thomas's executive assistant and confidential secretary—now a vice-president), and the executive secretary to Ernest Bender. "Robins had a forced-draft furnace designed to destroy contaminated products," Tuttle testified, and Moore, Polon, and Lashley told him that the documents—probably "hundreds" of them—had been "burned in that furnace." The cleansed files were returned to their owners, he said.

A few weeks after Tuttle's deposition, Moore, Polon, and Lashley denied his charges under oath. Moore called them "absolutely not true." What became of the ten or twelve boxes of documents that had been collected? "I have no idea," Moore replied. "I turned them over to Mr. Tuttle or his secretary, and that's the last I saw of them." Moore became a Robins vice-president in January 1982. Polon denied that he had so much as searched for the papers, but remembered Tuttle as "a fine gentleman, a fine lawyer." Lashley testified, "I don't know that [documents] were destroyed."[2]

At the meeting with Forrest, Michael Ciresi asked Tuttle, did they talk about "the women who still had this device within their bodies"? About giving the information to the FDA, to a team of independent physician-evaluators, or even to the board and management of the company? To each such question Tuttle's answer was "No." Forrest, he said, "simply wanted them destroyed and destroyed quickly." "What was Mr. Forrest's response to your concerns?" Ciresi asked. " 'Do it,' " Tuttle replied. "And I saluted and resisted where I could."

Had they discussed the possible "criminal implications" of destroying documents? "I raised some questions," Tuttle replied. He said Forrest's response was that "it was not for me to worry about it, it was for me to follow orders." At the time, he pointed out, no court had yet issued a sweeping order for production of Shield documents. But as an attorney, he said, he was deeply concerned from that day on that the papers "were evidence in cases." He said he told Forrest that destruction would be legally as well as "morally wrong," but admitted that he "personally lacked the courage to throw down the gauntlet at that point in time."

What about resigning? asked Thomas Sloan, a Robins attorney from San Francisco. "I had that choice," Tuttle said. But "with a wife and two young children, I'll have to confess to you that I lacked the courage to do then what I know today was the right thing."

Why hadn't he done the destruction himself? Sloan asked. Having others do it was a "sop to my conscience," Tuttle said. "I didn't have the heart to do it . . . but the responsibility is mine, and I have to bear it."

Tuttle had yet another stunning disclosure in store. It involved the tensions he perceived between the duty he believed he owed his client, the higher duty he felt he owed the courts and the public —in this case, the women who "were or might become wearers of this device"—and the moral implications that "disturbed me as a Christian." The result was that "I selected out the most damaging of the documents," he said. "I saved them in the balancing . . . of the situation."

Tuttle said he had hidden the documents in the basement of his home in Tulsa and never told anyone but his wife of his secret until he revealed the entire destruction episode at the deposition. His assessment of the importance of the documents is undisputed. One, for example, was the Nickless memo in which almost forty Robins executives were told—seventeen days after the Shield was purchased—of the string's wicking properties. Copies of this and other papers in Tuttle's file had been so widely scattered that some survived in one or another file and had been obtained and used by plaintiffs' lawyers. But Tuttle had saved one highly important document that had never surfaced elsewhere. It was the memo in which Roy Smith, three days before Robins bought the Shield, raised explicit ethical reservations, particularly about selling an IUD that would leach copper into a woman's body, while not disclosing to doctors that the metal was in the plastic.

After Robins's defeat in Wichita, Forrest transferred responsibility for Shield litigation from Tuttle to McGuire, Woods & Battle. One of Virginia's largest law firms, it is also counsel in that state for Aetna.[3]

As part of his separation from Shield litigation, Tuttle testified in an exchange with Sloan, the defense attorney, he had met with two McGuire, Woods partners, Alexander H. Slaughter and Rosewell Page III—"just the three of us"—in March or April of 1975.

"I told Alex and Rosie that there had been a search, I told them who had done the searching, whose files had been searched, and that as a consequence there were considerable quantities of documents that—that had been burned," Tuttle swore. He said he had described the documents as "legally damaging where Robins's defense was concerned in respect of knowledge by top officers of the company and the lack of testing and the imperfect labeling." Had either Slaughter or Page ever referred "to the morality of that act" of document destruction? Ciresi asked. "No, sir," Tuttle replied.

On February 17, 1975—ten days after the adverse jury verdict in Wichita—Forrest convened a day-long emergency defense strategy session. Even though it was a legal holiday (George Washington's birthday) for other Robins employees, the meeting was attended by Zimmer, Jack Freund, five more vice-presidents, four other executives, Roger Tuttle, and Patricia Lashley.

Lashley has testified that she alone took notes—which she said she never transcribed—and also that the executives turned over to her for safekeeping Shield documents "pertinent to the meeting."

Then the notes and documents vanished. Lashley's testimony about this, at depositions during the winter and spring of 1984, and at another deposition in August 1984, was bizarre.

Lashley said in her initial testimony on February 20, 1984, that the notes and papers were at that time in an untitled manila file folder in a locked document retention center, or "library." She listed the keyholders as Robins's law department, headed by Forrest, and the two Shield law firms in Richmond.

Seven weeks later, on April 19, she said she had since gone to the library, pulled the file folder—and found it empty.

What happened? Ciresi asked. "I don't know," she replied. When had she last seen the notes in the folder? "I have no idea." Had she destroyed the notes? "I may have."

Five weeks after that, on May 23–24, Lashley said the only person she had told of the disappearance was Thomas Kemp, a San Francisco lawyer who was representing her and Robins, and whose law firm also represented Aetna in Shield matters. She also swore she had made no inquiries about the disappearance, had given no thought to whether the notes still existed, and had made no effort to find them.

On August 17, Dale Larson, Ciresi's partner, began to take a new deposition restricted to missing papers. Lashley, as a result of advice she said she had gotten at a high-level meeting with Robins executives and outside counsel, was represented by Kemp and also by two "personal" attorneys whose fees were paid by Robins. Lashley confirmed that she had previously testified to finding the file empty. Was the testimony true? "No," she said.

Larson reminded Lashley of her earlier statement that "there were things in that file," and asked, "Was your testimony accurate?" A tumultuous scene followed in which Lashley replied angrily, "I don't remember whether it was or not as I sit here right now, and you can have it." With that, she rose and left the room.

Her personal lawyers said she was "not capable of continuing," and Kemp accused Larson of "browbeating" her. Larson said, "You ought to talk to her about telling the truth, counsel." He then obtained a court order to resume the deposition three days later, only to be told by her lawyers that a psychiatrist had ruled out her return to the stand at that time.

The mystery was deepened by McGuire, Woods attorney Jon A. Mueller, who was assigned in September 1982 to review Shield files to determine which documents might be exempt from disclosure by virtue of the lawyer-client and work-product privileges. First in an affidavit in July, and then in testimony at a hearing in August, he swore that he had found two papers in a file labeled "Feb. 17, 1975, 9:30 A.M." These were a page from a 1970 calendar and a letter from a lawyer.

No one explained how Lashley's notes could have been missing from the folder in 1982, present in February 1984, and missing again in April 1984, or how two such unrelated pieces of paper as the calendar and the letter could have been all there was in the file. Forrest testified in the latter month, "I haven't got the foggiest notion where Ms. Lashley's notes are."

There were other mysterious disappearances. On February 28, 1984, the day of her initial testimony, Lashley mentioned a tape of the Conference on Septic Spontaneous Abortion held by Robins on February 15, 1974. The day-long conference had been held in an auditorium equipped with electronic gear used to train salesmen. A decade later, in her initial testimony, Lashley insisted to Michael Ciresi that she did not know, and had never tried to establish, the tape's whereabouts.

In St. Paul on the same day, February 28, 1984, Larson and Robins attorney Charles Q. Socha of Denver were negotiating to settle seven of eight Shield cases pending before Judge Lord. During a break, Larson took a phone call from Ciresi and heard the news about the taping. Larson testified later that he had told Socha, "My God, I've just learned that there's a tape of the septic abortion conference." He said Socha replied, "Oh, yeah, I've listened to that tape. You won't get much out of that." Larson added that as Socha walked away, he asked but got no reply to this question: "Why haven't we heard that before?"

A stream of denials followed. On April 19, Lashley testified that McGuire, Woods paralegal Cynthia Hendren had searched for the tape but told Lashley that it did not exist. In July, at a hearing held by United States District Magistrate Patrick J. McNulty in Duluth, attorney Kemp insisted variously that Robins had told him the same thing, that there "never were" such tapes, or that "we don't think" they exist.

In August 1984, McNulty held a three-day hearing in Minneapolis at which Robins was asked to show cause why it should not be punished for document destruction and loss. Socha denied the charge: "I told Mr. Larson I had not heard anything about any tape of a septic abortion conference, and it sounded like more of Mike's [Ciresi's] bullshit."

Also at the show-cause hearing, Ellen Preston, who had run the conference, casually made a disclosure that had never come out in previous lengthy interrogations: she and other Robins officials had discussed but rejected taping the meeting. She certainly would have known if a tape had been made because "I was sitting there the whole time," she testified. "I don't believe it was taped unless . . . it was taped surreptitiously by someone with mikes that were not in evidence."

And there were more disappearances and misplaced documents. Harris Wagenseil, while a law partner of Thomas Kemp in San Francisco, represented Robins in at least one hundred Shield lawsuits over a five-year period. Ciresi has described him as "a principal architect" of Robins's defenses. Wagenseil left in mid-1983 to become the in-house counsel of Cummins Motor Company in Columbus, Indiana. When he moved on August 1, he shipped approximately twenty boxes of Shield papers from San Francisco to his new home in Indiana.

The boxes went into storage, along with some old furniture, in the basement. The papers were presumably secure because they were covered by what lawyers call a non-destruct order. A United States District Judge, Robert G. Renner of St. Paul, had signed the order several months earlier, on February 29. It commanded Robins to notify promptly "all its attorneys . . . and other persons who now have access to" Shield documents not to "damage, mutilate, or destroy" any that have "potential relevance" to Shield litigation.

The order aside, Wagenseil ascribed sentimental value to the papers, testifying at the show-cause hearing that he had them shipped halfway across the continent because they represented "a piece of my life." In view of the order, a letter from Michael Berens, a Minneapolis attorney for Robins, sent to Judge Renner on May 25, 1984, was a surprise. The key passage:

On March 22 and 23, 1984, in ignorance of the nondestruct Order, Mr. Wagenseil's wife, with his consent, discarded his Dalkon Shield papers as part of general spring cleaning.

In the absence of clarification of the Court's Order, Robins interprets the word "attorneys" to mean current attorneys. Robins, therefore, assumes that the Order did not apply to Wagenseil. . . .

Robins said in a separate court paper that it "did not notify past attorneys" and that the loss of Wagenseil's papers was attributable to what Thomas Kemp termed "an inadvertent falling through the cracks."

Griffin B. Bell, who was United States Attorney General in the Carter administration, had been representing Robins for some months and was its lead counsel in the show-cause hearing. "We have not destroyed anything," Bell assured McNulty. Nor, he told the magistrate, has Robins acted "in bad faith."

Bell did concede that Robins had not told Wagenseil of Renner's order until May 4, when Wagenseil mentioned the spring cleaning in a phone conversation with a company attorney. Only then did Robins realize that the order applied to former attorneys, Bell said. Even so, Bell told McNulty, Judge Renner's order was "ambiguous in the extreme." The magistrate told the former attorney general, "I don't consider the document ambiguous in any respect."

At the same show-cause hearing, Wagenseil and his wife, Susan, portrayed the carting away of the papers as "just one of those things." After contracting (in November 1983) to buy a house in the country, they had sought a real-estate agent's advice on how to sell the Columbus house. The agent had recommended a sprucing-up, including a cleanup of the basement. Was this "spring cleaning"? Wagenseil was asked. "Sure," he said.

On the eve of the cleanup, Wagenseil, a Rhodes scholar and Harvard Law School graduate, flew to Philadelphia, where he was a weekend graduate student at the Wharton School of Finance, and phoned Susan to report his safe arrival. She, he testified, told him, in effect, "I'm throwing out that stuff in the basement. Do you have any problem with that?" He said he told her, "No, go ahead." Susan Wagenseil testified that she then had two teenagers who were moving the furniture put the boxes in a van and haul them to the local dump.

Plaintiffs' lawyer Roger Brosnahan pounced on the couple's account, asking Wagenseil, "You moved old furniture to the new house and you took 'a piece of your life' to the dump?" The response was, "We took furniture to the new house, and we threw out . . . a lot of stuff in the basement." Brosnahan reviewed the sequence of events to suggest that the timing of the documents' destruction wasn't just a matter of spring cleaning, and taking aim at the purported date of the basement clean-up, put this chronology into the record:

> In November 1983 in Minneapolis, state District Judge Jonathan Lebedoff ordered Robins to disclose in writing any knowledge it had about any "unpublished" string studies.
>
> In February of 1984, Lebedoff rebuffed a Robins effort to dodge the order, telling the company that it must "fully and completely answer. . . ."
>
> In March—on the eve of the spring cleaning—Lebedoff denied a Robins request to reconsider his order.
>
> The next day, Robins went to the federal court house to ask Judge Renner to vacate, modify or clarify his non-destruct order (he refused and was upheld on appeal).
>
> Later in March, as a result of Lebedoff's actions, it became known for the first time that in extreme secrecy, Robins and Aetna had commissioned several researchers to test the string for wicking.

Wagenseil, after claiming that his missing papers were "completely valueless" to Shield litigants, admitted the following under questioning by Brosnahan and McNulty:

- The boxes had contained notes and possibly other papers that related to the secret string tests and were subsequently covered by two document-production orders, Lebedoff's and another issued by Judge Lord, as well as by Renner's non-destruct order.
- Acting for McGuire, Woods, he had arranged four of the tests, and had made reports on them to the law firm and to William Forrest.
- He had not known of the desperate efforts by plaintiffs' lawyers to find out if Robins had commissioned string tests, and with what result.
- Renner's non-destruct order had not come up in a phone conversation he had with defense counsel Socha—a personal friend who had known of the order—between February 29, when Renner signed the order, and March 22, when the boxes went to the dump (earlier in his testimony, Wagenseil had denied having such a phone conversation altogether).
- After Robins had received Lebedoff's November 1983 order to disclose any knowledge it may have had of unpublished string tests, no one from the company or McGuire, Woods had contacted him about the order—"and I'm not surprised."

The show-cause hearing in 1984 turned out to be but a single climactic moment in a long story of document suppression and legal stalling tactics by Robins. In December 1975, Frank G. Theis, a United States District Judge in Wichita, began to preside over proceedings for which more than a thousand federal and several hundred "tagalong" state cases were consolidated. The purpose of this multidistrict litigation was to coordinate pretrial "discovery" of documents and testimony into a single package of relevant and admissible evidence for trials of lawsuits alleging Shield-caused injuries.

In June 1976, Theis issued an order to Robins to produce "all files, correspondence, memoranda," and other matter "which pertains in any way to the Dalkon Shield, including, but not limited to, its design, purchase, testing. . . ." In response, Robins produced more than 100,000 documents. In an affidavit in July 1984, Theis said, "I was satisfied that appropriate discovery had been made, that only privileged documents had been withheld, and that all relevant evidence in the possession of A. H. Robins and its attorneys had been made available to the plaintiffs."

In August 1981 and again in September 1982, however, plaintiffs' lawyers, led by Bradley Post, asked Theis to reopen the discovery proceedings because they had found evidence that Robins had held back documents covered by the 1976 production order. The judge held a hearing on the requests, and in November 1982, he granted them. As a result, Theis said in the affidavit, "I was again satisfied that all relevant and nonprivileged materials had been produced."

Theis was to be disillusioned once more. Over the years, Judge Lord had consolidated Shield cases and assigned them to Judge Donald D. Alsop, who ultimately presided over five completed trials. By December 1983, twenty-one new Shield cases had been awaiting trial for almost three years, and Lord asked all of the counsel for advice about consolidating them. The upshot was that Lord grouped twenty of the cases, took them over himself, and for three months thereafter supervised the litigation on almost a day-to-day basis.

Soon after Lord became involved on December 9, plaintiffs' lawyers in Robins, Zelle, Larson & Kaplan told him that they had reason to doubt the adequacy of depositions taken from E. Claiborne Robins and certain other officials in the 1970s, and that updating was essential.

On January 23, 1984, in the new round of depositions that followed, plaintiffs' lawyers complained that Claiborne Robins's deposition was bogged down because of his claimed inability to recall any conversation about the Shield with his top executives.[4] "Robins Sr. did state that his recollection would be refreshed by minutes of the company's board of directors' meetings," Lord said in an order, but the company "refused to provide those minutes."

Two days later, after a legal tussle, the company yielded the minute books for Lord to review in chambers. The books, Lord wrote in the order, revealed that both Robins Sr. and his son, chief executive officer E. C. Jr., not only attended nearly every board meeting during their tenure in office but also demonstrated a detailed knowledge of the corporation's affairs. These were crucial revelations, given the fact that both of these officers claimed lack of knowledge due to both poor recollection of events and limited participation in the concerns of the company.

Meanwhile, the plaintiffs' lawyers phoned from Richmond to protest that other Robins officials were unreasonably delaying their depositions. With that, Lord offered to go to Virginia himself to get the depositions moving. Both sides agreed, and he flew to Virginia the next day, January 26. At the company's insistence, its headquarters was the site of the depositions of Claiborne Robins, Sr., and Frederick Clark, the retired medical director. Lord described the scene:

> Company employees milled about, leaving plaintiffs' attorneys no privacy in which to confer with each other. Live microphones further intruded on any discussions between the plaintiffs' attorneys. Chairs were positioned so that attorneys for the deponents sat shoulder-to-shoulder, knee-to-knee with their clients; a nudge by an attorney could—and did—silence the deponent without anyone else in the room picking up the signal. The deposition room itself was small and poorly ventilated. Heat from lights used to videotape the depositions raised the room's temperature to more than eighty degrees.
> Yet this was the environment in which the company chose to conduct the depositions of two of its officers, both of whom were suffering from heart disease. When the court suggested that the depositions be moved to the quiet and calm of the Richmond courthouse, the company objected and resisted.

Later the proceedings moved back to Minneapolis. After that, "often several times in a single day," plaintiffs' lawyers reiterated their requests for documents. "The pattern is the same," Lord wrote. "The defendant either appears to accept the court's orders without objection and then fails to abide by them, or recoils at the slightest hint of a new directive and asks for additional time to prepare its response." Lord said the plaintiffs' counsel may be correct in viewing the company's nationwide defense strategy as a "war of attrition."

At a hearing on February 7, 1984, Earle D. Getchell, Jr., a McGuire, Woods partner and its reputed expert on Shield document discovery, assured Lord that "everything not currently in the MDL [multidistrict litigation] that these plaintiffs asked for is privileged" or "totally irrelevant." Alexander Slaughter, the law firm's national coordinator of Shield cases, heard Getchell make the claim and knew it was inaccurate; he conceded this under oath later. "Some" documents that should have been produced for Judge Theis's proceeding had not been, he testified, admitting that he "did not correct" Getchell.

In any event, Getchell's assurance did not convince Judge Lord, and so the next day, February 8, he signed a comprehensive new order for McGuire, Woods and Mays, Valentine to produce all safety-related Shield materials. Unlike Theis, however, Lord had not left it to the defense to decide unilaterally which documents to exempt as privileged. Instead, he had named lawyers Peter N. Thompson and Thomas C. Bartsh "special masters" and dispatched them to Richmond to assure compliance.

Lord also sent Magistrate McNulty to Richmond to supervise the special masters and to make the depositions move ahead. Only five days later, McNulty wrote a status report in which he expressed incredulity at what he had found. It was not merely that the law department was not passing its information on pelvic inflammatory disease to the medical department; the doctors were not telling the lawyers of what they were learning about PID in Shield wearers. Discoveries of this kind led him to write:

> The court has corroborated its impression, of a deliberate attempt to conceal rather than reveal. . . . It is small wonder that this court has developed concern for the means and method of locating, identifying and presenting for *in camera* inspection documents which have been ordered produced by A. H. Robins Company. The documents in these files have not

only escaped production during twelve years of litigation, but the A. H. Robins [Company] *has not to date even searched these files to ascertain what they contain.*

In an order the next day, February 16, McNulty protested anew that while Robins had for a dozen years been claiming the lawyer's work-product privilege for all of its unproduced records, it had never examined its files to determine whether in fact the documents that they contained were legally exempt from disclosure:

> An impenetrable wall has been erected around the A. H. Robins Company which demonstrates a collapse of voluntary unsupervised discovery procedures. . . . To this date, not a single document has been produced to the masters for examination. Instead, this court has been involved in a day-to-day and hour-by-hour process of definition, of redefinition, of defining and refining, further redefinition, and of discussion as to the propriety of production, the methods of production, the methods of examination, the persons who should be allowed to view, and many other technical hindrances.

McNulty designed his order of February 16 to overcome the massive resistance to discovery. For example, he said that the masters and Roberta Walburn, Lord's clerk, "are to be afforded access to files and file repositories, after examination by defense counsel, and permitted to spot check files for the purpose of identifying the type and nature of documents contained."

In June, the special masters filed separate reports on how they had fared. They said that after sixteen days in Richmond, and after eight days of working under McNulty's order, they had gotten basically nowhere. Bartsh estimated that Robins claimed privilege on *"approximately two to three truck loads of documents"* and that about 20 percent were not privileged. "There is no question that [Lord's] order required the production of thousands of documents which had not been previously produced," he wrote. Thompson said that in one box of papers, which defense attorneys had labeled "nonresponsive" to Judge Lord's document-production order, he had found documents that Judge Theis, in his affidavit, would term "the focal point of much of the document discovery effort before me."

Yet, by summer, thanks to the pressures applied by judges and plaintiffs' lawyers, large numbers of previously undiscovered documents surfaced. Among them were *nearly 5,800* that Robins admits were not exempted from disclosure by the work-product privilege and that were covered by Judge Theis's orders for the Wichita proceeding. An index of previously undisclosed documents was itself 568 pages long.

On July 2, Robins, Zelle, Larson & Kaplan filed a motion charging that the loss or destruction of evidence showed "a lack of good faith, willfulness and gross negligence" in violation of Judge Renner's non-destruct order. The law firm's Michael Ciresi asked McNulty, sitting in for Renner, to order eight persons to show cause why they should not be held in contempt of court. They were William Forrest, described by Claiborne Robins, Jr., as one of the company's "two most instrumental" persons "in the Dalkon Shield situation"; Patricia Lashley, the self-described "funnel . . . through which all information is channeled within the Robins Company concerning the Dalkon Shield"; Alexander Slaughter, who coordinated dozens of Shield defense law firms for McGuire, Woods, and who was said by Forrest to be one of the two best-informed persons about Shield-related documents (Lashley being the other); William Cogar and Clifford Perrin, partners in Mays, Valentine; William R. Norell, a Robins in-house attorney, and Jon Mueller and Cindy Hendren, the McGuire, Woods attorney and paralegal. The result was the three-day show-cause hearing held by McNulty in August. (By late August 1985 he had still not held anyone in contempt.)

On July 3, the day after the motion was filed, Judge Theis signed his affidavit, which was submitted in connection with a separate proceeding. He said that Robins's nonproduction of thousands of documents, as reported by the special masters,

appears to be contrary to the representations made to me by counsel for A. H. Robins. . . . It would appear to me that representations made to me concerning the completeness of discovery during the MDL proceedings are open to serious question. While there may possibly be explanations and justifications, this does not appear in any of the materials that have been furnished to me. It would seem, in the light of the disclosures by the Masters, that serious questions exist [as] to whether or not counsel who appeared before me, or their client, should be disciplined. . . . The frustrations and confusions which I have at times experienced in the eight years I have been shepherding this discovery appear to have been part of a pattern of that which occurred before Judge Lord.

Robins, accusing Theis of bias, asked him to disqualify himself from presiding over Shield proceedings. He refused, and the company appealed. The Tenth U.S. Circuit Court of Appeals rejected the appeal, without a hearing, in a one-sentence order on March 19, 1985.

It took a decade of costly litigation, court orders, and extraordinarily resolute judges to force a recalcitrant A. H. Robins to disgorge documents without which large numbers of Shield victims could not hope to obtain simple justice in the courts. Yet no one knows how many more victims would have obtained justice were it not for the disappearance of many more documents. Desperate to suppress the truth, Robins tried to silence first one judge and then another. Even so, enough evidence emerged to get the company and several of its lawyers—nominal officers of the courts—into deeper and deeper trouble.

13

The Tide Turns

In 1983, the manufacturer and the insurer of the Dalkon Shield saw grim omens appear in three cities.

In St. Paul, federal juries made two awards of punitive damages to Shield victims, one for $1,750,000 and another for $50,500. These dealt a heavy blow to the A. H. Robins Company, partly because it had no insurance coverage for exemplary damages, and partly because the awards would inevitably encourage other victims to seek to punish the manufacturer.[1]

In Philadelphia, a federal jury, barred from awarding punitive damages to a Shield user who had suffered a pelvic infection and loss of her ability to bear children, set a record for compensatory damages: $5.15 million.[2] This was bad news for Robins, but perhaps worse for Aetna Casualty & Surety Company, which, in its 1977 agreement with Robins, had undertaken to pay the bills for *all* awards of compensatory damages—even those arising from "the supplying of false and misleading information."

From the vantage point of Robins and Aetna, however, a development in Minneapolis on December 9 was the most ominous of all: the six federal judges of the District of Minnesota assigned twenty-one Shield cases to Miles W. Lord, the activist, blunt-spoken Chief Judge. Over the next three months, Lord would be intensely and personally involved in trying to expedite Shield litigation, which was clogging the federal and state courts of Minnesota.[3]

Lord had been nominated for a judgeship by his friend Hubert H. Humphrey, then a senator from Minnesota, and appointed by President Lyndon Johnson. On the bench, he won the hearts of some and the enmity of others with his pro-environment decisions, particularly in a case in which the Reserve Mining Company was accused of polluting Lake Superior. Eventually, the Eighth U.S. Circuit Court of Appeals removed him from that case, accusing him of "gross bias" against the company. For Lord's admirers, the court's action and accusation, which Lord denied, were omens of bias against a judge who was willing to stand up to large corporations.

"I think my job as a judge is to see that justice is done," Lord told Barry Siegel of the *Los Angeles Times.* "The whole object is to get at the truth, and I try to do that. I worship the truth. If you just don't read the lawbooks, you can get lots done."[4]

"The accumulation of corporate wrongs is in my mind a manifestation of individual sin," Lord said in a speech to the Minnesota Council of Churches in 1981. "Many people denounce crime in the street, but few examine crime in the skyscraper," he told the churchmen. "Even Hitler, when he was butchering people, articulated a reason to his madness. We don't even do that."* Admirers as well as critics call him "the last breath of frontier populist justice," Siegel reported. *Time* called him "a resolute populist."[5]

Lord quickly set about to remove every possible obstacle to the production of documents and the taking of new depositions; Robins was equally determined to replace any obstacles he might remove with new ones. On February 6, 1984, his patience worn thin, Lord assigned the special masters, Thomas Bartsh and Peter Thompson, to go to Richmond to expedite pretrial discovery. It took Robins only three days to retaliate; accusing the judge of abusing his "power and discretion," the company asked the Eighth Circuit to disqualify Lord from presiding over the litigation. If Robins's purpose was to get Lord off the case, it succeeded. The next day, February 10, the judge ended his participation in discovery until such time as the appeals court would rule. But if the company's aim was the more important one of impeding the discov-

*See Appendix A.

ery process, the move was a failure. Lord directed Magistrate Patrick McNulty to take over discovery. "As the arguments against production of the documents exhaust themselves, the tribunal itself becomes the target," Lord said in the order. "This court has tasted of this cup before; it has had its fill."[6]

The appeals court rejected Robins's appeal swiftly, on February 16, putting Lord irrevocably in charge. Now Robins's options were reduced to two: go to trial before a judge it had tried to disqualify and who condemned crimes committed in corporate boardrooms, or try to buy its way out of the pending cases with expensive settlements.

By late February, Robins had settled fourteen cases. On February 28, the company agreed to a package settlement of the seven remaining cases in which the lead counsel was Robins, Zelle, Larson & Kaplan: the two still pending before Lord, plus five others pending in other courts. The offer was for $4.6 million— a larger sum than the women had originally sought. Furthermore, Robins made concessions in connection with the "truckloads" of unproduced documents that Robins, Zelle wanted to examine in connection with its three-hundred-odd other Shield cases in various courts. The company consented, for example, to segregating the documents it claimed to be privileged from those for which it claimed no exemption.

Although Lord had been an indispensable catalyst for the February 28 settlement, and finally for the agreement, he remained troubled by the relatively narrow scope of the prospective three-hundred-case settlement. To be sure, it was an acceptable outcome for the women represented by Robins, Zelle; but if thousands of other Shield victims were to have a chance to achieve comparable results, each judge in their cases would separately have to reopen pretrial discovery. Another point rankled Lord, believing as he did that corporate executives should be personally accountable for immoral corporate conduct: The officers of the family-controlled Robins company were still pleading ignorance, still denying wrongful acts, still refusing to recall the Shield from the tens of thousands of women still at risk.

On February 24, counsel for Robins and for the plaintiffs told Lord that they were on the brink of settling the seven cases. But as a condition of settlement, Robins, Zelle demanded that three senior officers of the company appear before the judge to certify it as binding. Lord knew by then that he had to phase himself out of Shield litigation because Robins, by hiring a Minneapolis law firm in which his son-in-law was a partner, had made it impossible for him to hear additional cases. And, of course, he had reason to be distrustful of Robins. In the negotiations that followed, he won the consent of defense counsel to the appearance of the officers. At that point he decided to draft a statement to the officers with the intention of having them read it silently in his presence, so that they could never again deny knowledge of the dangers of the Shield.

The judge took great care with the statement, worrying over it for several days and showing it to three other judges. Finally satisfied with it, he decided to request the presence in the court-room of three top Robins executives: president E. Claiborne Robins, Jr., senior vice-president for research and development Carl Lunsford, and vice-president and general counsel William Forrest. "Robins junior and senior had never been in a courtroom all these years," Lord told Siegel. "I thought, 'Isn't it time to bring them to the reality of what's happening?' "[7]

On Monday, February 27, the judge told counsel that he wanted the officers to be in court on the morning of February 29 (the elder Robins's health did not allow him to appear). He also disclosed that over the weekend he had prepared some remarks for delivery to the officers. The only question left was how harsh his statement would be.

The officers appeared before Lord on the morning of February 29. He asked each one to read to himself a copy of his 1981 speech to the ministers, and also a copy of his statement, which he labeled a "speech." In the latter, they found an excoriation (Lord said he hoped it would "burn its mark into your souls") and a plea to "face up to your misdeeds."[*]

After they had finished reading, Lord began to ask them questions. He asked Lunsford, for example, about the Robins Company's practice of inquiring into the private lives of women who

_____
*The text of Lord's statement appears in Appendix B.

had brought suit. All three stood mute, on the advice of counsel. They did not ask for time to prepare a response. Neither then nor later did they challenge the accuracy of the reprimand. Shortly, Robins attorney Charles Socha objected to the proceeding and asked Lord to stop it. With that, Lord read his speech into the record. "It is not enough to say, 'I did not know,' 'It was not me,' 'Look elsewhere,'" Lord told them. "Time and time again, each of you has used this kind of argument . . . pretending to the world that the chief officers and the directors of your gigantic multinational corporation have no responsibility for the company's acts and omissions. . . . You, Dr. Lunsford, . . . have violated every ethical precept to which every doctor under your supervision must pledge as he gives the oath of Hippocrates," Lord said. "You, Mr. Forrest, . . . have not brought honor to your profession. . . ." When women filed claims, he told all three men, "you introduced issues that had no relationship whatsoever to the fact that you planted in the bodies of these women instruments of death, of mutilation, of disease. . . . You target your worst tactics for the meek and the poor."[8]

The officers maintained a stolid silence that bespoke disdain; Shield victims in the courtroom wept. But beyond the searing words, as the defense soon learned, were troubling ripple effects: national publicity, more lawsuits generated by the publicity, and a resultant heavier drain on the Robins and Aetna treasuries.

As a final act, Lord approved the settlement agreement, writing on it two words: "So ordered."

After the hearing, William Forrest denounced Lord; Claiborne Robins, Jr., did the same at Robins's annual meeting. On March 30, Robins appealed to the Eighth Circuit to strike the words "so ordered," on the ground that Lord lacked authority either to approve or disapprove a private settlement. Because the appeal did not protest Lord's courtroom reprimand, plaintiffs' lawyers assumed that was the end of the matter. After all, if Robins had wanted to assert that the speech had denied due process of law to the three officers and that it should therefore be stricken from the record, the company had but to say so, either in the "so ordered" appeal or in a separate one.

But instead, Robins's attorneys invoked the Judicial Conduct and Disability Act, a 1980 law that Congress had enacted to provide recourse against judicial officers who have problems such as alcoholism, drug addiction, and senility, or who engage in conduct "prejudicial to the effective and expeditious administration of the business of the Courts." It is difficult to see how the law could be applied to Miles Lord. He was not—and was not accused of being—a drunk, an addict, or a black-robed dodderer (he was then a vigorous sixty-four years old). Nor could he be accused of impeding the operation of the federal courts in Minnesota; rather it was *Robins's* obdurate conduct that had caused Shield litigation to stagnate not only in Minnesota, but in courthouses across the land. In sum, if anyone was prejudicing "effective and expeditious" administration, it was the company.

Robins had retained Griffin Bell, the former U.S. Attorney General, to help coordinate the counterstrike against Lord, and two complaints were filed on April 24, fifty-five days after Lord's speech and twenty-five days after the "so ordered" appeal. The complaints—typed on simple government forms—made these principal accusations against Lord: he had blindsided the three officers; he had methodically destroyed their personal and professional reputations and thus denied them due process of law; he was "biased and acting as an advocate for the plaintiffs" and so was ethically required to disqualify himself; he had given a gratuitous judicial approval to the settlement. The requested remedies were the expunging of Lord's speech from the record and "a judicially fashioned remedy of comparable notoriety," that is to say, a public rebuke.

As provided by the 1980 law, the complaint forms were filed with a committee of the Eighth Circuit's judges, the Judicial Council, which is headed by Chief Judge Donald P. Lay. Commonly, such committees investigate complaints, find them meritless or improper end-runs around the judicial process, and throw them out. The complaints against Lord were obvious attempts to circumvent the process. At the same time, to dismiss them out of hand would have been to take a slap at Bell, who was himself a former judge of the Fifth United States Circuit Court of Appeals, and who personally had signed the forms. So the complaints survived, and Judge Lay notified Lord that a Special Investigative Committee of the Judicial Council—five circuit and district judges—would hold a hearing on them.

Now the ball was in Lord's court. The conduct law gave him a choice between a secret hearing or an open one. He chose to become the first accused judge to opt for an open hearing. In doing so, he converted what Robins had hoped would be a triumph won in secrecy into what would become instead a self-inflicted public-relations debacle. Instead of one former judge arguing behind closed doors to other judges, some of them reputedly hostile to Miles Lord, there would be a hearing massively covered by print and television reporters from the national press.

The five judges, led by Donald Lay, held the hearing on July 9 and 10, 1984, in a St. Paul courtroom. Lord sat on a bench with his four grown children. His attorneys were Ramsey Clark, who had been Attorney General of the United States in the Johnson administration, and Joe A. Walters of Minneapolis. Bell's co-counsel included Charles Kirbo, who had been a confidant of President Carter.

Bell's core argument was that Lord had deprived the officers and the company of due process. He called only one witness, Alexander H. Slaughter, the partner in McGuire, Woods & Battle who had played a principal role in coordinating the Shield defense law firms. Under cross-examination, Slaughter admitted to Walters that some documents were "not produced that should have been." Bell used only two of the three hours he had been allotted.

For Lord, three judges (in testimony and statements read for them), and two independent expert witnesses warned that Robins's use of the 1980 law threatened the independence of the judiciary.[9] Federal judges Paul Magnuson and Robert Renner, who sit in St. Paul, said in a joint statement: "We must be free to act untrammeled by fear, answerable only to the Constitution and our consciences. That freedom from fear, which is the essential ingredient of our independence as judges, is threatened by proceedings such as these which grow out of a judge's actions in litigation."

Robert J. Sherman, former Chief Justice of the Minnesota Supreme Court, testified that subjecting judges to discipline "for good-faith comments in open court" would have "an extremely repressive impact on the administration of Justice." Lord himself, in a statement, said that he had decided to read his speech aloud only after the officers' "demeanor of undisguised disdain for the court compelled me to. . . ." In closing arguments, Clark called the complaints a "sinister" abuse of the 1980 law and said that a victory for Robins would send a signal to large corporations and other wealthy and powerful litigants that they could use the same law to chill judicial independence.[10]

Bell, under questioning by the judges, made a devastating admission: Robins had been perfectly free to seek redress for its grievances and those of the officers through the normal appeals process. Thus, Bell stripped from his clients and himself any credible defense for having invoked the 1980 law. The very next day, July 11, Judge Lay announced that the investigative panel, which was to have made a report promptly, would delay it until a three-judge panel of the Eighth Circuit disposed of Robins's "so ordered" appeal. Now it was—or should have been—the turn of Judge Lay to be embarrassed. Why hadn't he and his Judicial Council told Robins at the outset to stay within the appellate process?

On October 29, 1984, Robins announced its multimillion-dollar program to remove Shields from women still wearing them. This was eight months after Lord, in the courtroom reprimand, had pleaded with the officers to end their "monstrous mischief" by recalling the Shield. In an interview that day, the judge said that "fourteen years too late is better than never." He expressed dark feelings about why Robins had decided at last to begin a campaign similar to the one he had sought. "On its surface, it may appear that this company has belatedly developed a concern for the women whose health it purports to protect," Lord said. "I fear, however, that the eyes of the company executives have not lifted above the bottom line." He termed the campaign "an attempt to save them money in the long run," pointing out that the company's "carefully worded statement avoids admitting wrongdoing [while serving] to help it in future litigations." If his courtroom plea for a recall program had helped to lead the officers to their decision, "it was well worth the anxiety, discomfort, or inconvenience" that the complaints caused him and his family, Lord continued, saying he would await the apology of Claiborne Robins, Jr., Carl Lunsford, and William Forrest. None came.

Four days later, on November 2, the three-judge panel of the Eighth Circuit unanimously ordered Lord's reprimand expunged from the record, denouncing it as "a governmental attack on their [the officers'] good name, reputation, honor and community standing," which denied them due process and "fundamental fairness." The panel, led by Chief Judge Lay, also reversed Lord's "so ordered" action. The judges found no fault with the company, the officers, or, for that matter, themselves for not having dismissed the complaints out of hand. Their only criticisms were of the judge they had put on trial.

Even so, the decision in itself implicitly validated Lord's basic contention that recourse to the 1980 law was improper. And although Robins succeeded in having Lord's speech expunged from the record, it did not get a "remedy of comparable notoriety." It is the speech, finally, and not the ruling, that will be remembered.

The company said it was "satisfied that justice has been done." Lord, for his part, said he was "greatly pleased that the A. H. Robins Company has failed in its attempt to personally punish me for reprimanding that company for its misdeeds," adding: "A. H. Robins never seriously contested the truth of my remarks, nor did the Court of Appeals question the accuracy of my statement. The jurors in Minnesota and across the nation have found the company to have acted with willful indifference to the rights and safety of women. I am sure that the law will come to the position of holding corporate officials accountable for the misconduct of their corporations." He continued, "I have no idea how I will pay the attorneys' fees and expenses occasioned by this unwarranted intrusion into my personal life." He estimated that he owed between $70,000 and $100,000.

One formality remained: the original special investigative committee that had held the hearing in St. Paul in July still had to deal with the complaints filed under the 1980 law. On December 26, in a tersely worded decision, the committee dismissed the misconduct complaints brought by A. H. Robins and its officers against

Lord, noting that the issues had been fully resolved by the Eighth Circuit panel. As Ramsey Clark said, "Our grave concern was that all of this corporate power could be used to put a judge on trial rather than the defendant . . . but in terms of both truth and justice Lord has prevailed."

During this time, Roger Tuttle had been leading a quiet academic life in Tulsa, and he had fended off plaintiffs' lawyers who had hoped to take his deposition. Yet the ambivalence he had felt in the document-destruction saga nine years earlier still lingered. After all, the Shield episode was laden with ethical, moral, and religious implications, and Tuttle was a teacher of legal ethics at Oral Roberts University. He had even put his ambivalence on display in September 1983 in a small showcase, the *Oklahoma Bar Journal,* where he published "The Dalkon Shield Disaster Ten Years Later—A Historical Perspective." His tone was professional and sober. One lesson to be learned from this experience, Tuttle concluded, "is to place less emphasis on the profit motive in any high risk area as important as human health."

In the spring of 1984, Robins, Zelle lawyers subpoenaed Tuttle for a deposition in Minneapolis. This time, having been moved by Lord's speech a few months before, he did not resist. But in June, just as Tuttle was about to fly to Minnesota, Robins moved to seal his lips. Meeting privately with a judge of the Tulsa County District Court, company counsel alleged that Tuttle had volunteered to testify and had violated his attorney-client relationship by publishing the article. The judge then signed a temporary restraining order (TRO) to prevent Tuttle from so much as disclosing that he had worked for Robins. The TRO was effective pending a hearing on Robins's petition for a permanent injunction. Along the way, the company indicated to Tuttle that it would try to have him disbarred. Four days later, the plaintiffs' lawyers intervened, accusing Robins of improperly interfering with the orders of the United States District Court in Minnesota. By then, another Tulsa judge was in charge of the case. After a closed two-day hearing, he vindicated Tuttle by dissolving the TRO, dismissing—with prejudice—Robins's petition for the lifelong injunction, and freeing him to testify for four days in Minneapolis, starting on July 30.

Tuttle's testimony—particularly his charge that general counsel Forrest had ordered him to arrange the destruction of Shield documents—created a national sensation.[11] It also brought Robins and Aetna a new cycle of publicity and lawsuits.

For Robins, the growing number of awards of punitive damages had become a plague. In the February 29, 1984, package settlement, Robins had to pay $2,050,000 to dispose of two jury awards of punitive damages, including $1.5 million to Brenda and Robert Strempke. On June 4, the Colorado Supreme Court upheld the record $6.2 million award of punitive damages to Carie Palmer, the woman in Elkhart, Kansas, who had suffered a severe pelvic infection that left her unable to bear children. Strikingly, Robins paid the award rather than appeal. On June 6, a jury made a $1.4 million exemplary award to Melissa Mample, the cerebral-palsied child in Boise, Idaho, whose mother had given birth with a Shield in place. By June 30, juries had awarded punitive damages in eight cases, totaling $17.2 million. Shield victims who specified only the exemplary awards had filed suits in excess of $12 billion more. In the first six months of 1984, new lawsuits were being filed at a rate of more than four a day.

For relief, Robins turned to the United States Senate, where the Commerce Committee had before it a bill to establish national uniform standards for the liability of manufacturers whose products are alleged to have caused avoidable disease and injury to consumers and workers. In addition to President Reagan, two large coalitions of about three hundred businesses and trade associations supported the bill, whose principal sponsor was Senator Robert W. Kasten, Jr. (R–Wis.). Over a period of four years starting on January 1, 1979, their political action committees (PACs) gave $626,918 to members of the Commerce Committee.[12] A new committee member, Paul S. Trible, Jr.—a Republican from Robins's home state of Virginia—received $117,593, the largest single share of the total. Robins did not have a PAC, and the sums Trible received in personal contributions from Robins officers were small.

Trible was elected to the Senate in 1982, with the aid of a $5,000 contribution from the Association of Trial Lawyers of America, a leading opponent of the Kasten bill. In a statement to

ATLA members at the time, Trible said: "Product liability law has traditionally been a matter for state regulation, and ought to remain so. The rights of those wronged in product liability cases must be preserved. . . . Any proposal to modify current liability law requires the most serious study. I pledge to keep your thoughts and concerns in mind."[13]

Yet in early 1984, it was Paul Trible who introduced an amendment under which a manufacturer of any kind would have to pay punitive damages only once—to the first litigant to persuade a jury that the company had been grossly negligent or had recklessly disregarded safety. In Robins's case, that litigant was Connie Deemer, who had won the first Shield punitive award in 1975 in Wichita, and who had been paid $75,000. Punitive damages "threaten to engulf American business," Trible claimed at a subcommittee hearing on March 5.

A few days later, a Trible spokesman told me that the senator had introduced the amendment—which critics called "the Robins bail-out"—after being contacted by Robins. The committee incorporated the Trible proposal into the bill and, on March 27, 1984, approved it.

On July 30 in Minneapolis, Roger Tuttle made his document-destruction charge against general counsel Forrest. On August 1, Forrest and Robins's federal-government lobbyist, Cyrus C. Tichenor III, received the senator and Trible's deputy legislative director for a half hour at the company's Washington office. Under questioning about the meeting, Forrest revealed that he had met with Trible and his staff "from time to time over the past year," had "encouraged" the senator to sponsor the amendment, and had given him "an outline of those provisions or concepts that should be included."

Trible's amendment aroused the anger of women's groups, trial lawyers, consumer advocates, and unions. Newspapers—one of them in Trible's home state—published harsh editorials. "When Trible does a triple back-flip off a high board on behalf of a special interest, he pretends to be a reformer," the *Philadelphia Daily News* said. "So far up to this summer, the Dalkon Shield has cost Robins $233 million. You can imagine how much Trible's bill could be worth in the long run."[14]

Sensing the threat to his political future, Trible, then thirty-seven years old, first said he would weaken his amendment and then dropped it altogether. The bill did not come up before the Senate went out of session.

Defeated in the legislative branch in Washington, Robins turned to the judicial branch in Richmond. On October 24, 1984, the company asked United States District Court Judge Robert R. Merhige, Jr., to consolidate more than 3,500 pending punitive-damages cases into a class action under which payments would be made from a single limited pool of funds. The motion, signed by Griffin Bell, termed the need to litigate the cases separately across the country "inherently unworkable and unfair" to both the women and the company. How 3,500 cases could be handled, fairly if at all, in a single proceeding was left to the imagination. Trial lawyers geared up for another long legal battle, citing a 1982 decision in which the Ninth United States Circuit Court of Appeals in California reversed a lower court that had allowed creation of a class of Shield victims for punitive damages. Merhige held a hearing in mid-December, and denied Robins's request on July 23, 1985.

If the motion for a class action put a temporary cloud over the hopes of Shield victims and their lawyers, an order issued by Magistrate McNulty in July 1984 put a cloud over Robins. The order empowered Robins, Zelle to take the depositions of the company's outside directors. Up to that time, these three men— pillars of the community—had been insulated from the litigation, despite having acquired inside knowledge of Shield matters at the highest level of the company.[15] For Robins, Zelle, which had tried continuously to crack the secrecy of the board of directors, and which was eager to settle its remaining 198 Shield cases, the order was a trump card. The outside directors were obviously anxious to avoid being interrogated under oath about what they knew, and when they knew it. The potential for embarrassment was high, particularly for E. Bruce Heilman, the university president who in 1982 had pronounced Claiborne Robins one of God's "most essential instruments." It is reasonable, therefore, to assume that not only did Robins fear the testimony that the outside directors might give, but that the directors, in their turn, pressured the company to make certain that they would never have to testify at all. These assumptions would seem to explain why Robins, in negotiations with the law firm beginning in October, indicated a willingness to settle the 198 cases. As Roger Brosnahan of Robins, Zelle said in an interview, the company felt it had to "raise the white flag."

On November 14, after a month-long series of consultations with Robins, Zelle's clients, Brosnahan and Ciresi announced at a press conference in Minneapolis that they had settled the 198 cases. All of the women had suffered pelvic infections, loss of fertility, and other injuries. Eleven had become pregnant and gone to term, giving birth to defective children, including one who is blind, a second who has cerebral palsy and is mentally retarded, and a third who is hydrocephalic. Two bore children who died. The total amount was $38 million, for an average of close to $192,000—nearly quadruple the previous average; the range was said to be between $5,000 and $3 million. "We feel that the clients are very fully and adequately compensated in each case," Brosnahan said.

About 160 of the women live in Minnesota, where there were more than a thousand Shield lawsuits—more than in any other state but California. The company said that the escalation in the price of settling the 198 cases was "directly attributable to Robins's belief that Judge Miles Lord's public attacks and utterances over the past several months have so inflamed and prejudiced potential jurors that a fair and impartial trial for Robins in Minnesota is no longer possible." By contrast, Brosnahan credited Lord with having "opened up the discovery process." Thanks to Lord and others on the Minnesota bench—especially judges Jonathan Lebedoff and Donald Alsop—"the system worked" in Minnesota, although there had been a time when Shield cases "threatened to drown the system." The dockets now were nearly clear.

The settlement agreement was unprecedented, partly because of unique provisions designed to facilitate settlements of thousands of other Shield suits pending around the nation. For example, Robins agreed that all the Robins, Zelle depositions and other discovery materials would be available to all other plaintiffs' lawyers.[16] "We hope that the agreement signals a change in the attitude of A. H. Robins from one of extending the litigation, and trying cases one at a time, to an attitude of trying to get this bad chapter in their history behind them," Brosnahan said. "And we hope it means they are going to try to fully and adequately compensate the victims of the Dalkon Shield."

Although Robins was increasingly embattled, its status as a large, international conglomerate with many and diverse other lines of business and some thirty foreign subsidiaries protected it financially. This was reflected in the company's report for the three months ending June 30, 1984. Because of a 430-percent increase in Shield litigation expenses, the company said, net earnings fell 70 percent, to $4,069,000. But sales rose 11 percent to $151,992,000—the best second quarter in Robins's history.

Still, the Shield took its toll. On March 5, 1985, the company announced that it was trying to set up a reserve for Shield claims, and until preparations were complete, it would be unable to determine the financial results of its 1984 operations, address the matter of a first-quarter dividend, hold the annual meeting on the scheduled date of April 23, or set a new meeting date.

On April 2, Robins held a press conference in Richmond to announce the creation of a $615-million reserve fund for paying Shield claims until the year 2002. The payment through December 31, 1984, having been $314.6 million, the total now would approach the $1 billion level. G. E. R. Stiles, senior vice-president and financial officer, revealed that a study by an outside consultant indicated that the Shield may have injured roughly 87,000 or 88,000 of the 2.2 million American women who wore it, that the ultimate total of those who would sue or file claims would be approximately 20,000, and that the $615 million would suffice for compensatory damages for all existing and expected claims. But Stiles left considerable doubt that the $615 million would be adequate, mainly because it allowed neither for punitive damages —although billions of dollars in such damages were being sought —nor for lawsuits by foreign Shield users, who by 1985 had begun to sue Robins in American courts.

Even without such future woes, the $615-million fund caused Robins to report a 1984 net loss of $416.6 million, a sum larger than the company's net worth, and large enough to wipe out all shareholder dividends through the end of 1986. But Stiles did have cheerful news for the stockholders: the reserve would generate tax benefits of $126 million, so the actual cost of the reserve to Robins would be only $489.1 million. In other words, American taxpayers, who already had to foot substantial bills for the health and court costs generated by the Dalkon Shield, now would have to pick up a tab of $126 million in the form of higher taxes. In addition, 1984 sales had increased 12 percent over 1983 to a record $631.8 million, and operating earnings had gone up 21 percent to yet another record—$128 million. And there were other consolations; Robins stock was holding up reasonably well on the New York Stock Exchange, and its reputation was holding up in Richmond. As a Norfolk newspaper reported:

In this city, there is scant talk about the cloud that hangs over Robins. Indeed, others here offer sympathy, as if the problems were more a family matter than a public issue.

Residents here describe the company as a benevolent employer and generous contributor to charitable and civic endeavors.

"I think most people view the company the same way they view the [Robins] people—favorably," said Justin T. Moore, Jr., chairman of Richmond Renaissance and chairman of Dominion Resources, Inc., the utility holding company also based in Richmond.

Residents recall that the Robins family, which still owns more than half of A. H. Robins Co.'s stock, has donated $100 million to the University of Richmond, where the new field house and athletic complex is named the Robins Center.

And they recall that the company's chairman, E. Claiborne Robins, helped organize "Businesses Who Care," a coalition of Richmond corporations that has encouraged companies to increase their contributions to charitable and cultural activities.

And they recall that the senior Robins and his son, E. Clairborne Robins, Jr., who is president and chief executive officer of the company, have been active in the Richmond Renaissance, a two-year-old effort to rejuvenate the city's downtown.[17]

But the setbacks for Robins continued into 1985. Not the least of them was the increasingly prominent attention of the press.[18]

On January 21, the Eleventh United States Circuit Court of Appeals in Miami ruled that Dr. Louis Keith, the long-time Robins consultant and Northwestern University professor of OB-GYN, might have committed perjury, and the FBI began an investigation.

On February 21, special masters Peter Thompson and Thomas Bartsh, who had been sent to Richmond a year earlier to seek compliance with Judge Lord's document-production order, filed a report. Their summary began:

> We conclude that Plaintiffs have established a strong *prima facie* case that A. H. Robins Co., Inc., has, with the knowledge and participation of in-house counsel, engaged in an ongoing fraud by knowingly misrepresenting the nature, quality, safety, and efficacy of the Dalkon Shield. The ongoing fraud has also involved the destruction or withholding of relevant evidence.

Bartsh and Thompson, by then in possession of about 15,000 pages of documents that were produced for *in camera* inspection, said that Dr. Hugh J. Davis, the developer of the Dalkon Shield, "by now in our view is neither a credible witness nor a scientist."

They said of the four studies cited in the eight-page "Progress Report" advertisement that Robins published in the final four months of 1972: "Robins officials knew that the results of the studies were inaccurate and misleading." And they said that Roger Tuttle's unveiling of the W. Roy Smith memo on copper—"a key document"—"substantially corroborates the essence of his story that Robins lawyers have pulled documents from files so that they would not be produced in litigation."

On May 3, 1985, in Wichita, a Sedgwick County jury awarded punitive damages of $7.5 million—a new record in Shield litigation—and $1.1 million in compensatory damages to Loretta Tetuan, thirty-three, who lost her uterus and ovaries after wearing a Shield for nine years.

On May 29, also in Wichita, Judge Theis made a ruling consistent with that of the special masters in Minnesota. He held that a *prima facie* case had been established "for the purpose of the crime or fraud exception to the attorney-client privilege and the work-product doctrine."

On July 23 in Richmond, as noted, Judge Merhige denied Robins's request for a class action for punitive damages.

Finally, on August 21, a startling development followed in Merhige's court, one that caused the price of a share of Robins's stock to fall to $8 from a 1985 high of over $24, and one that made most every front page in the country. The company asked Merhige to let it reorganize under Chapter 11 of the Bankruptcy Code, so that it could be protected from lawsuits by creditors—Shield victims, above all—while it devised a plan to pay its debts. Robins did not claim to be financially shaky. Rather, it invoked "the continuing burden of litigation," much as the financially healthy Manville Corporation had done in 1982, when it pioneered in using Chapter 11 as a refuge from lawsuits, brought in its case by victims of asbestos-related diseases.

The next day, Merhige suspended proceedings in thousands of Shield lawsuits, saying that "everything is stayed in every court." Many plaintiffs' lawyers denounced Robins for a "sham" and "unjustified" action that would let it pay everyone to whom it owes money except Shield victims.

On August 23, a motion to dismiss Robins's petition was filed by the National Women's Health Network, which twice had sought worldwide Shield recalls—in a 1981 court action and in a 1983 FDA petition. As of this writing one day later, the outcome of Robins's actions is uncertain. Many bankruptcy experts assert that the Manville gambit provides no legal basis for denying Shield plaintiffs individual trials for punitive damages. Whether sucessful or not, Robins's move to declare bankruptcy is only the latest in a long series of efforts to avoid restitution.

In 1974, when the news of spontaneous septic abortions and lawsuits came flooding in, the A. H. Robins Company had a choice: to cut its losses or to tough it out.

Cutting its losses would have meant forthrightly telling women and the medical profession—everywhere—that it had, without malign intent, marketed a defective and hazardous IUD. It would have meant a multimillion-dollar advertising campaign seeking the removal—at its own expense—of Dalkon Shields from more than 4 million women in order to avert great harm to tens of thousands of them. It would have meant, in sum, contrition, compassion, and plain good sense. But instead Robins chose to tough it out. That meant trying to stem the tide of litigation by suppressing, "losing," and destroying documents, testifying falsely, invading Shield victims' privacy, using university experts dishonestly, and warring against federal judges. It meant inflicting lasting damage on the company's reputation with the medical and legal professions, and with the general public as well. It meant shelling out hundreds of millions of dollars to victims and to an army of defense lawyers, to the point of shaking the company's financial stability. And all to what end? To delay a removal campaign for more than a decade; and thereby to condemn tens of thousands of women to terrible harm. The Chapter 11 filing, E. Claiborne Robins, Jr., said, was necessary "to protect the company's vitality against those who would destroy it for the benefit of the few." This from a man whose corporation had destroyed women for the benefit of itself.

Epilogue

What does the Dalkon Shield catastrophe teach us? Not that the A. H. Robins Company was a renegade in the pharmaceutical industry. Yes, Robins—knowingly and willfully—put corporate greed before human welfare, suppressed scientific studies that would ascertain safety and effectiveness, concealed hazards from consumers, the medical profession, and government, assigned a lower value to foreign lives than to American lives, behaved ruthlessly toward victims who sued, and hired outside experts who would give accommodating testimony. Yet almost every other major drug company has done one or more of these things, and some have done them repeatedly or routinely, and continue to do so. Some have even been criminally prosecuted and convicted, and are recidivists.

Nor does the Shield catastrophe teach us that the pharmaceutical industry is unique. Cigarette companies profit from smoking, the single greatest cause of preventable disease and death. Knowingly and willfully, automobile manufacturers have sold cars that would become rolling incinerators in rear-end collisions; chemical companies have sold abroad carcinogenic pesticides that are banned here; makers of infant formula have, in impoverished Third World countries, deprived babies of breast milk, the nearly perfect food; assorted industries have dumped poisonous wastes into the environment; coal companies have falsified records showing the exposure of miners to the particles that cause Black Lung; military contractors have supplied defective weapons to the armed services.

No, the lesson of the Dalkon Shield catastrophe is not that Robins alone behaved in an immoral or unexpected fashion, but that, first, the corporate structure itself—oriented as it is toward profit and away from liability—is a standing invitation to such conduct; second, the global scale of contemporary marketing has made hazardous corporate activities more perilous to ever larger numbers of people; and, third, all the deterrents and restraints that normally govern our lives—religion, conscience, criminal codes, economic competition, press exposure, social ostracism—have been overwhelmed.

Consider two scenarios. Each involves a corporate executive of, say, a tire company, who drives to work through a school zone posted with twenty-mile-per-hour speed limit signs.

In the first scenario, he drives fifty miles an hour, in clear-cut violation of the law, and—unintentionally—kills a child and is arrested and prosecuted for manslaughter. Even if he isn't incarcerated, his life has been darkened in an instant. His career is a shambles. His wife and children, though altogether innocent, are also paying a terrible price.

In the second scenario, the executive drives carefully, arrives at the office, and deliberately puts on sale millions of tires that he *knows* will blow out with extraordinary frequency. What fate awaits him?

It is highly improbable that he will face arrest, denunciation in church, or the wrath of newspaper editorialists or columnists. If there is publicity, it will be fleeting and confined to the news columns, particularly in a climate in which business executives, thanks in part to the President of the United States, are widely perceived as victims of regulatory persecution. In fact, the stockholders may give him a bonus. The workers and the community may thank him for saving jobs. If he has invested in the right election campaigns, the White House may name him to a regulatory agency. If he has been generous in his philanthropy, a university may name a building for him, or a service organization may honor him with an award for distinguished service.

And, most likely, he will believe it to be just and right that he be punished if he strikes a child in the school zone, but unjust and wrong if he is punished for putting out unsafe tires in the presumed best interests of the corporation.

I do not feel, and hope I do not seem to be, self-righteous. I am not holier than thou—or than the executive I have hypothesized. But it is, I think, fair to wonder where one may find the believer who will argue that God does not see into the executive suite; where it is written in the Bible that a sin is cleansed if committed for a corporation; where our ethical heritage instructs that for one to inflict injury and death knowingly is impermissible—unless one does it by remote control, via a paper entity. It is also fair and necessary to wonder why such questions are rarely raised and discussed.

Some putative deterrents and restraints have become part of the problem. The political process is a case in point. The electorate does not elect Presidents, or perhaps anyone else, on the basis of issues such as unacceptable corporate conduct. If new laws are needed to curb such conduct, obstacles arise at once, because our legislators have made themselves increasingly dependent for election funding on the interests that need to be curbed, not on the voters. In the Carter administration, Senator Edward Kennedy won the approval of the Judiciary Committee for proposals to strengthen the weak "reckless endangerment" provisions of the federal criminal code, but despite strong backing from the Department of Justice, these life-protecting proposals were never adopted. In the Reagan administration, the Justice Department did not so much as propose such a strengthening. This omission went virtually unnoticed in the press, which frequently defines news in ways that assure that such matters will be ignored or not given attention commensurate with their importance to human life.

Government regulation, by itself, provides insufficient and erratic protection, in part because it is subject to political pressure from both Congress and the corporations themselves, and in part because of the lethargy of entrenched bureaucracy. Thus, despite the evidence produced by trial lawyers that rotting tail strings put large numbers of women at risk, the Food and Drug Administration did *nothing* to protect Shield wearers for nine years, from the time the Shield went off the market in 1974 until 1983, when a study done by the Centers for Disease Control incriminated the device. The FDA never acted on a petition filed by the National Women's Health Network in April 1983 for a recall—to be paid for by Robins—to ensure retrieval of the Shield "from all women who currently wear it" and for imposition of criminal penalties. Of course, I am not saying we should abandon government regulation, but only that we must recognize its limitations. As it stands now, it often provides the illusion, but not the substance, of adequate protection.

Nor has organized religion come to grips with its proper role as moral guide in this problem of corporate crime. The extraordinarily popular electronic evangelists are the most retrograde in this respect. Dr. William C. Martin of Rice University in Houston, a former minister of the Churches of Christ and now a professor of sociology, told me:

> I have listened to radio and television evangelists for over twenty years. I may have missed something, but I can't recall a single instance of their having addressed the issue of sin or crime or malfeasance committed by otherwise moral people as a consequence of their occupational roles.
>
> Traditionally, of course, they have concentrated on the well-known catalogue of personal sin—alcohol and drug abuse, illicit sexual behavior, gambling, and so forth. In recent years, they have railed at the shortcomings of institutions, but they seem to think these problems can be cured simply by staffing the institutions in question with born-again Christians.
>
> For whatever reason, they show little evidence of being aware of the structural factors—for example, the need to show a profit, the desire to keep or improve one's position in the institution, pressure from one's superiors, the pervasiveness of the values of competition and success, the socializa-

tion into the norms one finds on entering a new position, or the distance between one's decisions and those who are harmed by them—that cause or permit an otherwise moral man or woman to act in immoral ways.

Television evangelists, of course, are not unique in their naïveté. Business and government leaders have often failed to recognize their complicity in corporate actions or situations that are fundamentally immoral or unethical. From lynch mobs to extermination camps, having others to share the guilt can move apparently decent individuals to behave in frightening ways.

Jerry Falwell, in a signed article in *Newsweek* in 1981, said: "There is something worse than war, and worse even than speaking out. It is silence! The grossest immorality has been perpetuated not by those who carried it out, but by those who remained silent and did nothing. We may not always be right, but we will never stand accused of doing nothing." Never?

From Martin's point about the behavior of individuals in groups, it is worthwhile to return once more to Edward A. Ross, who brilliantly and prophetically portrayed the dangers of the corporate milieu. In 1907, in *Sin and Society,* he wrote:

There is nothing like distance to disinfect dividends. Therefore the moral character of the stockholders makes very little difference in the conduct of the affairs of the corporation. . . .

It feels not the restraints that conscience and public sentiment lay on the businessman. It fears the law no more, and public indignation far less, than does the individual. You can hiss the bad man, egg him, lampoon him, caricature him, ostracize him and his. Not so the bad corporation. The corporation, moreover, is not in dread of hellfire. You cannot Christianize it. You may convert its stockholders, animate them with patriotism or public spirit or love of social service; but this will have no effect on the tenor of the corporation.

In short, it is an entity that transmits the greed of investors, but not their conscience; that returns them profits, but not unpopularity.

The problems Ross identified have become commonplaces of corporate behavior. In 1929, Alfred P. Sloan, Jr., defined his responsibilities as president of General Motors. He was responding to Lammot du Pont, president of E. I. du Pont de Nemours & Company, who urged him to use safety glass in Chevrolets, GM's least expensive cars. Lammot du Pont's company stood to profit because it made safety glass, but his interest was nonetheless congruent with the interest of the public.

Sloan resisted. "Accidents or no accidents, my concern in this matter is a matter of profit and loss," he told du Pont. Despite GM's "large return," he wrote, it "should not adopt safety glass for its cars and raise its prices even a fraction of what the extra cost would be. I can only see competition being forced into the same position."

In 1932, du Pont revived the issue, telling Sloan that Ford was using safety glass in its windshields. This was Sloan's reply:

> That is no reason why we should do so. I am trying to protect the interests of the stockholders of General Motors and the Corporation's operating position—it is not my responsibility to sell safety glass. . . . You can say, perhaps, that I am selfish, but business is selfish. We are not a charitable institution— we are trying to make a profit for our stockholders.

It was not that Sloan had no conscience, but that he defined personal and business ethics separately. Would such a dedicated corporate officer find it difficult to reconcile his dedicated quest for profit with his conscience? With going to church? With what he confessed? I don't know, but I doubt it; and if he did not, is that not troubling?

Modern society cannot function without the large organization. It organizes our great endeavors; it brings us great good. The need today is to stop the individuals who run corporations from inflicting harm. This will not be done by weakening or eliminating existing deterrents and restraints, such as federal regulation; our hopes lie in strengthening them and adding new ones.

Since 1979, two congressmen, George Miller (D–Cal.) and John Conyers (D–Mich.) have been seeking legislation that gets to the heart of the problem. It says, in terms of legal art, that a corporate manager who discovers an imminent hazard to the safety or health of the work force, in a process or a product, must report it to the appropriate federal agency within thirty days; if he does not do so, he risks prosecution and, on conviction, imprisonment. No new bureaucracy would be needed.

This approach is conceptually *right*. It reconciles the need for the corporation with the need to infuse personal accountability into corporate officials who are exposed to relentless corporate pressures to "go along to get along." It embodies the powerful moral command in Leviticus 19:16: "neither shalt thou stand idly by the blood of thy neighbor."

For the foreseeable future, no legislation embodying such a moral command stands a chance—at the federal level. Not so long as Ronald Reagan is President. Not so long as the likes of George Bush may succeed him. Not so long as Congress allows special interests to control election financing. And not so long as most Americans remain content to live with the paradoxical proposition that harm knowingly and willfully inflicted on them is to be punished, even by death, if done for personal reasons, but is to be unpunished, not even by a day in jail, if done for corporate reasons.

But even in this political climate, growing numbers of Americans have awakened to the paradox. They have become aware, in part through the repercussions of the Shield disaster, of the impossibility of reconciling personal responsibility with corporate immunity; they know that the proposition is fraudulent. As the public mood becomes more receptive to efforts to hold individuals accountable for corporate actions, I also believe, prosecutors, governors, and legislators in many states will make such efforts, and will earn public approval for doing so. Already, Illinois has convicted of murder three company owners who, the state alleged, knowingly and willfully exposed deceived and helpless workers to lethal chemicals.

The now-defunct company, Film Recovery Systems, Inc., of the Chicago suburb Elk Grove Village, hired uneducated, poor, illegal immigrants to recover silver from used X ray film, using open vats filled with a solution containing lethal cyanide. The liquid came from barrels carrying prominent, forceful warnings, but many of the workers did not speak or read English. The cyanide supplier repeatedly warned company officials of the danger, but they neither cautioned the workers nor acted on their numerous complaints of illness. In 1983, one of the workers—Stefan Golab, sixty-one, an illegal Polish immigrant—died of cyanide inhalation.

The State's Attorney office of Cook County, invoking an Illinois law normally used to prosecute arsonists who set fire to occupied buildings, charged five Film Recovery owners and executives with murder and reckless conduct for having "knowingly created a strong probability of death."

Circuit Judge Ronald J. P. Banks, sitting without a jury, held an eight-week trial. In June 1985 he found three of the officials guilty—the first known conviction of American corporate executives in connection with a job-related death. On July 1, Banks imposed twenty-five-year prison sentences for murder on president Steven J. O'Neil, plant manager Charles Kirschbaum, and foreman Daniel Rodriguez. The judge also imposed concurrent 364-day jail sentences for each of fourteen reckless-conduct charges. Defense attorneys said they would appeal.

In language reminiscent of Judge Lord's denunciation of Robins executives for having refused to recall the "depth charge in the womb," Banks likened the conduct of the defendants to that of a person who would let a time bomb continue to tick away on an aircraft. "Every day people worked there," he said, "it kept ticking away."

Such prosecutions must proliferate, and state officeholders and candidates must make passage of tougher laws an issue. The press and clergy, too, will have to take the stand that a person's criminal and immoral conduct is criminal and immoral, period, and that no counterargument exists. Then, once the issue has broad popular support at the state level, reform at the national level will become inevitable.

Appendices

A: SPEECH OF JUDGE MILES W. LORD

"The Church's Claim on the Corporate Conscience: Toward a Redefinition of Sin": excerpts from a speech by Miles W. Lord, Chief U.S. District Judge for Minnesota, before the Minnesota Council of Churches, November 12, 1981.

Sin has been variously defined as "transgression of the Law of God," "moral failure," "a breaking away from God and from the rest of humanity," "the state of estrangement or alienation," and so on. Each of us has his own particular favorite and I suspect we could spend this whole time arguing the finer points of each one. But the point I want to emphasize *here* is that for most of us, sin is thought of in very *individual* terms. Sin, to use some of the definitions I just proposed, is the *individual's* transgression of the Law of God, the *individual's* moral failure, the *individual's* estrangement or alienation. I submit to you today, however, that it manifests itself in another quite powerful way which I would like us to consider together for a while.

This [corporate] individual we've created is, in the eyes of the law, a person who has been, rightly or wrongly, afforded the rights and privileges and immunities that are accorded to natural-born people—those who *do* have a heart, a soul, and a conscience. However, the corporate individual, unlike the person, does not have the legal or moral responsibilities imposed upon it. Many people denounce crime in the street, but few examine crime in the skyscraper.

But, just as the mugger in the street can cause problems as a member of our human family, so can the corporate individuals cause problems as they coexist with us, operating and exerting their influence on humanity. The mischief they can create is multiplied and magnified manyfold since the act of one is the act of many. Ordinarily, in the eyes of the law (that is, the criminal law) in dealing with the conduct of individuals, the law is very fearful of the consequences of two or more individuals operating together to break the law—so much so that it is illegal for persons to band together and agree to accomplish an illegal result. This amounts to a conspiracy. The illegal agreement itself is the crime. And yet, when a person is allowed to have a corporate charter by merely laying down seventy-six dollars, any number of people can get together and operate as a single entity and, except in very rare instances, the conspiracy laws do not apply. You need no further explanation than that to begin to understand the dangers inherent in corporate activity. The law has recognized that more than one person acting together multiples the danger to society, except in the instance of the corporate structure where many people can be gathered together and the law looks only at the final results as the corporation acting as one person. It has been said that the corporation has no soul, it has no heart, it has no conscience, and yet its acts are the composite of the individual acts of many people.

Corporate officers and officials can begin to operate with the highest ideals and principles, with aspirations to do great things for their corporation and society. Yet they are constantly subjected to a strong single influence. Perhaps millions of people unknown to the officers and directors are looking daily at the *Wall Street Journal* or the local newspaper to determine how their stock is doing. The progress of their stock is governed by the profit-and-loss statement. That is almost their total index as to how the corporation is doing. If the corporate officers direct their corporation into violating the law to make profit, and they are caught and pay a fine, that's looked upon as a nuisance, a nonrecurring obligation it says in the books, and an unfortunate incursion by outsiders. The corporate official, the individual who is caught with his fingers in the pie and making antitrust arrangements, polluting, or making unsafe goods, or other arrangements which are contrary to the law, suffers almost no disgrace either in the eyes of his corporate officials and employers, or [in those of] the the public at large, but rather his conduct is looked upon as being the norm, but for the fact that some nosy government investigator looked in and blew the whistle on him. These people are not punished, demoted, or fired. If they are, it is in such a way that they suffer no economic consequences therefrom. Some of our largest corporations actually have mechanisms whereby any fines or punishment or expenses incident to defending their officers from criminal activity in the name of the corporation are reimbursed to the employee by the corporation itself. And thus our legal efforts to correct corporate misbehavior by fining the responsible individuals are nullified. The odds are in favor of their getting off.

Let me give you an example from my own experience. If you're going to pollute, do it on a grand scale—form a corporation. You can have sixty or 100,000 employees. Very seldom do the government or the law-enforcement people accuse the individual within a corporation of the act of conspiracy. They say no, it is the act of the corporation. The corporation is a "person" and can only act through its agents. Therefore, the actors are all one person and are not charged as conspirators. It makes for a disparity under the law, because we find the government proceeding against small groups all over for the crime of conspiracy, but they don't go after the corporation. Even when several corporations work together, there is often immunity from the conspiracy claims.

The current thought is that you should maximize the profit: you should buy cheap and sell dear. The country—the well-being and the very existence of the government—can depend on how we do on Wall Street. Buy as cheap as you can and sell as dear as you can and have something left for yourself. That is the American way. I have done all right by it. But it is a kind of fancy way of saying that your country is run by selfishness and greed. If you just look at it in its barest elements, that is what it is.

Now is that a very good system to turn loose to control the long-term destiny of mankind? Having selfishness and greed control our environment, control our workplaces, decide that which we are going to breathe, what we are going to eat, what we are going to drink, whether or not we go to war? You read horror stories daily about the unfit and unsafe foods, drugs, air, and water to which we are exposed. Who is doing these things and why are they being done? By and large, it is corporate activity.

The corporation which is doing most of the acting isn't ordinarily trying to attract the philosopher or the scholar. It sees the corporate goal as making money, while the average corporate leader looks disdainfully at the cry of those who don't have a job—the Chicano, the black or the poor minorities of any kind. You know, the minorities have a little slogan. They say: We would like to be excused for crimes of survival.

The poor people say that if we have to commit a crime to get groceries or clothing or to heat our houses, we should be forgiven. But the cry from that stratum of society is by and large ignored by the courts or the government or the businessman. The leaders give little heed to those unfortunates who choose to exist by committing a crime even though it be a crime of survival. Yet we see that time and again the corporations are making that same cry—the cry which does not work for the poor, but which works well for the corporations.

The corporations say we cannot stay in business unless we do the thing we're doing. If we did something wrong in terms of turning out bad products for people to eat, or a drug that poisoned instead of curing them, we cannot be responsible. We have done so much good for this country; we provide for so many people. We cannot survive unless we get away with this. It is a crime of survival. So we come around full circle.

The people who can best afford to pay for the crimes of survival are getting away with it. The people who need the crimes of survival are not getting away with it. I am not sure either of them should get away with it.

Unfortunately, with the corporations we sometimes find people who are turning out foods or fibers or drugs and selling a product that is harmful and we can't find out exactly who's doing it. Let us attempt to ascertain who is responsible. If you go to the research department, you might find that somebody tested it on rats and wrote it up in a report. Where the report went, you'll never find out. Certainly, the people in the production department didn't know about it when they began the production. The sales department was never told. And it would be unthinkable to believe that one of the higher corporate officials got hold of information to the effect that what they were selling as a cure was actually poisoning people. The board of directors is the last to know. There is something wrong with the system. Their officers are not expected to compute the incalculable damage to the world as a part of the cost of production.

But, they say, the corporation does what it is designed to do. It uses its political muscle and its economic power to achieve a maximum return on the investment—not next year, not the year after, not ten years from now, but today. The name is instant profits.

For example, you could set a little plant up right here in Minneapolis. You could manufacture something with ten or fifteen people on the payroll, make $50,000 a year, spew poisonous waste into the earth or into the air. That would cause ultimate damages in the billions, but the profit system says there's a right to do that, absent government control

—and there are those who say today that we should "get off business's back."

But let's get back to the balance sheet. Within the narrow confines of the balance sheet, the corporation is doing well. That is all that counts. If the product is unsafe or actually poisonous, it may be known by others, but not by the corporation officials. But suppose one of the men in the industry learns what is happening. He doesn't like the fact that it is happening, so he goes out and tells somebody. He might tell a government official or a newspaperman about what he found. Now, what do you think *his* ultimate fate will be? He will be hounded from that company. "He's disloyal. He's a troublemaker. He's a squealer." What you are expected to do in industry is to follow the code of the underworld: *omerta* —silence. That code requires that *you never squeal,* no matter what happens. You go to jail, you do your time, you take your punishment, but you do not squeal. To me, it is rather sickening to see that code enforced in our business circles. If a person is run out of an industry because he squealed, ordinarily a job in another similar industry can't be found. He is often foreclosed from positions on college faculties. He violated the code.

I recently heard a case involving the Chemistry Department at the University of Minnesota. The case itself involved alleged discrimination against women, but we covered the grant procedures in the department. Of the forty chemists in that department, there was not one ecologist, and all grants were received to invent new polymers or to enhance productions; not one grant was dedicated, nor was one penny spent, to determine the effects of the products upon humanity. Not one penny. Turn it out. If it is useful, use it. Let somebody else worry about how humankind should protect itself from it. There is a great deal of orientation in academia toward the profit motive.

In the olden days—you know, golden olden days—if you killed somebody, if you produced something that would hurt somebody, you were stopped. If you poisoned someone's cattle, you were stopped. If you burned all of the surface off someone's land, you were stopped. Not today. Today we have cost-benefit analysis, where you weigh how much a human life is worth. Funny, I always thought life was a sacred and priceless thing.

The cost-benefit analysis is an amazing tool. You can get an economist to put a price on a human life and then you weigh that against the benefit. When you put a price on the priceless, all is lost. Economists can do anything they wish with figures. If the pollution is pervasive and many people are killed or injured, the corporation asks the government to step in and take over. They can have a Black Lung Bill passed, as was done for coal, or they can have a White Lung Bill, as is about to be done for asbestos. They are now talking about Brown Lung for cotton. So you may go ahead and poison, and if it gets bad enough, the federal government will take action. If it doesn't get bad enough, you can deny all responsibility. So we don't have much sense about how we do this cost-benefit analysis. There is no rhyme or reason to it. We sort of play Russian roulette. And this sentence of death and debilitation isn't imposed upon us by some foreign power. We are doing it to ourselves by the cost-benefit-analysis approach. We are ashamed to acknowledge the stark reality of it. What we are doing is to trudge along with no clear plan as to where we are going, or which individual will be sacrificed.

You know, even if a group of people were alone in a lifeboat and had to sacrifice one person to save water and get a little raw meat, it would probably pick on some old doodler, who had lived beyond his time anyway. Even Hitler, when he was butchering people, articulated a reason to his madness. We don't even do that. We go along and make those sacrifices in easy stages.

We actually have government officials who claim they are polluting and laying waste to our national parks in the name of God. It occurs to me that the church might develop an ethic which would say that pollution, contamination, and desecration of our environment are sins and that we should not look to the Second Coming immediately, but should plan for future generations.

We had been moving along over the past ten or fifteen years, starting with Earth Day, initiated by Senator Gaylord Nelson. We had begun to develop an environmental ethic and to start to try to protect our people from drowning in their own sewage and effluent.

Now, all at once, we have elected a leader of our country who turns the opposite way—who says, echoed by his advisers, "Well, we must give some breaks to the rich. You haven't seen any breaks for the rich lately." "The rich haven't been getting any breaks out of social welfare." I agree with them that we must mine the coal. We must cut some of the forest. We must develop the oil. We have to live and we have to grow. All these things are necessary, to a degree, but strict controls should be imposed by the government in order to minimize the damage to the environment. Under the present administration, it is concluded that business knows what's best for our people, and that the competition for resources can dictate their preservation.

Jobs and people who hold them are the most potent hostages available to industry. A fairly recent congressional enactment calls for environmental-impact statements. Environmental-impact statements were designed to prevent the commencement of industries which have as their ultimate result the desecration of the environment. The impact statement looks at the long-term damage to the environment from a perspective before the damage is done. The alternative, which works much better for the industry and which can frustrate governmental control, is to start slowly, hire ten workers, and thereafter use these few jobs and the prospect of more as leverage upon the public. As soon as ten people are employed, the stage is set. It is literally impossible to stop or to control them. "It will cost jobs and depress the economy," they proclaim.

They call an economist. The payroll is hypothetically recycled through each of the local business enterprises in the community, and projections of prosperity and affluence created by these ten jobs will go a long way toward paying off the state debt.

For example, if you pay one hundred dollars to the grocery store operator for groceries, the grocer pays it to the store's suppliers, who buy gas and tires and so on. One hundred dollars keeps changing hands until it is $50,000 worth of benefits. With ten jobs gone, you have lost hundreds of thousands of dollars right there. All they are doing, after all, is pumping stuff in this little creek or killing a few babies, and we've got too many babies.

President Reagan said the other day that even coal has a right to rights. Well, coal has veins; maybe it is something like a person. But, now, do you realize that if we enforce these environmental standards and don't let them tear up the sod and the topsoil, that some coal might not be mined? Can't you see that little piece of coal down there? It says, "Gosh, President Reagan is going to let me be mined."

We are all for the environment. Every one of us. We talk about it and we think about it, we act on it, but one of the things you affect when you start to move on the polluters is jobs. Jobs will be lost.

I've been around a long time. It is not easy to tell anyone they can't have a job because they are producing poison. It is not easy to tell a bank robber that he has to change his way of making a living.

You're probably saying to yourself right now, "What kind of a bird is this speaker? He's really anti-corporation, isn't he?" If you are saying this, let's examine not my thinking, but your thinking.

You undoubtedly applauded when the President and the Chief Justice

of the Supreme Court announced that we have to crack down on criminals who are making our country a less safe place in which to live. People
are being mugged, slugged, and drugged by criminals. You perhaps
agreed when the President said these bad actors must all be put in jail.
We must search them. We must use any kind of evidence against them.
We must streamline the jailing of individual criminals.

While you applauded these efforts by the President or the Chief
Justice, you felt proud and you did not think that they were un-American.
You didn't think of them as being anti-criminal, but rather pro-people
—"stand up for the good guys." Merely denouncing these actors who
kill, maim, cheat, rob, and steal does not earn us the title of being "anti"
anything. However, as I call attention here to the fact that a great deal
of this kind of conduct is carried on in the corporate form, I will find
myself being called anti-corporation, anti-business, or worse. The mere
fact that a person is an individual who may work for a corporation does
not mean that he is being denounced, any more than being a member
of the public makes someone a criminal. What is being denounced here
are those people and institutions that are doing wrong. If, as an individual participating in this wrongdoing, the shoe fits, I might suggest that
it is perfectly appropriate for you to wear it so long as you recognize your
reason for being so alarmed.

As I told you, some of our finest people are selling poison, but they
shouldn't be allowed to do it. The corporation shouldn't be allowed to
do it. One of the ways that you stop them is to publicize it.

I am firmly convinced that if the newspapers followed corporate civil
trials as closely as they follow the trial of an individual charged with a
crime, the disclosures made in the course of this coverage would change
the manner in which business is done in America. These practices can
only be carried on by management, shrouded in secrecy. The stockown-
ers themselves would often rebel if they knew of some of the dirty tricks
being done in their names for the sake of dividends.

The corporate officials who are responsible as the actors in the main
are decent people. It seems that the system they get caught up in causes
them the trouble. They are kind and honorable in their personal relationships, their personal mores. They attend church, they do charitable
deeds. Almost any corporate president or official would walk miles to
help a little child who is hungry or injured or who is hurting. But he or
she could then walk back to the office and approve a plan that would
dump tons of poison into the drinking water of that same child.

So, *you* move in. But what are you going to do? You're not a prosecu-

tor or a governmental official or an adversary in a civil case. You're
something better; you're the pastor, the confidant, the trusted friend.

The corporate officer or official sits in the front pew of your church.
He or she serves on the church's board of directors, the session, the
board of deacons. And, most important of all, the officer's name is
prominent on your list of donors.

While it would be fun for me to watch, and exciting for you to do, I
am not recommending that you denounce your local corporate crook from
your own pulpit. I suggest that under these circumstances you continue
to do what you have been doing—that is, to make a cost-benefit analysis.
If you lose that important and influential member and his financial
support, you will not be able to carry on the good work of saving the souls
of those who are dying of his misdeeds. I suggest that, on a wide scale
and within a broad framework, the church itself should do as was
recently done by Archbishop [John R. Roach of St. Paul] in relation to
the nuclear arms race: examine the morality of the result and condemn
the individual actors.

They say that we cannot legislate morals. I think we can. You have
often said that a person can rise no higher than his ideals. You, as church
leaders, can change the nation's way of thinking. You can raise their
ideals and shame the wrongdoer.

Every religious person should know that the church holds that person
individually responsible for participating in group wrong. The old con-
cept of individual responsibility should be applied. The soldier doing the
killing is not acting in the name of God. Even the man who opens the
spigot to turn loose poisonous smoke, fumes, or liquids cannot justify his
action by saying he was ordered to do so. It is, at least, his duty to report
the wrongdoing. The engineer and the production manager who continue
to produce dangerous machines cannot justify knowingly doing that
because they were given orders. The nutritionist who turns out non-
nutritional foods and the chemist who turns out dangerous drugs are
doing wrong. They are acting against God's wishes; they cannot morally
justify their actions by saying that they were ordered to do it, even if
others are doing it in concert with them.

THOU SHALT NOT STEAL applies to every corporate official who sells
shoddy, dangerous, or unusable merchandise in the name of profit.

THOU SHALT NOT KILL applies to the corporations and agencies of those
who are killing and maiming through industrial pollution. This is done
by individuals, by corporate leaders who must someday appear in somebody's church. They should appear with the same attitude of contrition

and humility which accompanies every other sin. They should ask to be forgiven and they should promise to mend their ways in the future.

And to the rest of us who do our own kind of sin, the important thing is that it must be recognized as *individual* sin. Responsibility must be assigned to each individual who participates—to each member who constitutes part of the corporate body.

If, in the process, you are alienated, ridiculed, scorned, or cursed by those who are the subject of this discussion, you may find great comfort in one of your favorite passages from the Sermon on the Mount.

> Blessed are they which are persecuted for righteousness' sake: for theirs is the kingdom of heaven.
> Blessed are ye, when men shall revile you, and persecute you, and shall say all manner of evil against you falsely, for my sake.
> Rejoice, and be exceeding glad: for great is your reward in heaven: for so persecuted they the prophets which were before you.

You need only take the scales off your eyes and see that it is the individual who would destroy, pillage, and ruin our earth and the people on it. It is up to you, for after all, when Cain asked God the question, we all had the answer: Yes, we are our brother's keeper.

B: COURTROOM STATEMENT OF JUDGE MILES W. LORD

Following is the prepared text of the courtrom statement made by Miles W. Lord, Chief U. S. District Judge for Minnesota, on February 29, 1984, to three officers of the A. H. Robins Company who were before him: E. Claiborne Robins, Jr., president and chief executive officer; Carl D. Lunsford, senior vice-president for research and development, and William A. Forrest, Jr., vice-president and general counsel.

Mr. Robins, Mr. Forrest, and Dr. Lunsford: After months of reflection, study, and cogitation—and no small amount of prayer—I have concluded it perfectly appropriate to make to you this statement, which will constitute my plea to you to seek new horizons in corporate consciousness and a new sense of personal responsibility for the activities of those who work under you in the name of the A. H. Robins Company.

It is not enough to say, "I did not know," "It was not me," "Look elsewhere." Time and time again, each of you has used this kind of argument in refusing to acknowledge your responsibility and in pretending to the world that the chief officers and the directors of your gigantic multinational corporation have no responsibility for the company's acts and omissions.

In a speech I gave several years ago (in the document which I have just asked you to read), I suggested to the hundreds of ministers of the gospel who constitute the Minnesota Council of Churches that the accumulation of corporate wrongs is, in my mind, a manifestation of individual sin.

You, Mr. Robins, have been heard to boast many times that the growth and prosperity of this company is a direct result of its having been in the Robins family for three generations. The stamp of the Robins family is upon it. The corporation is built in the image of the Robins mentality.

You, Dr. Lunsford, as director of the company's most sensitive and important subdivision, have violated every ethical precept to which every doctor under your supervision must pledge as he gives the oath of Hippocrates and assumes the mantle of one who would help and cure and nurture unto the physical needs of the populace.

You, Mr. Forrest, are a lawyer—one who, upon finding his client in trouble, should counsel and guide him along a course which will comport with the legal, moral, and ethical principles which must bind us all. You have not brought honor to your profession, Mr. Forrest.

Gentlemen, the results of these activities and attitudes on your part have been catastrophic. Today as you sit here attempting once more to extricate yourselves from the legal consequences of your acts, none of you has faced up to the fact that more than nine thousand women have made claims that they gave up part of their womanhood so that your company might prosper. It is alleged that others gave their lives so you might so prosper. And there stand behind them legions more who have been injured but who have not sought relief in the courts of this land.

I dread to think what would have been the consequences if your victims had been men rather than women, women who seem through some strange quirk of our society's mores to be expected to suffer pain, shame, and humiliation.

If one poor young man were, by some act of his—without authority or consent—to inflict such damage upon one woman, he would be jailed for a good portion of the rest of his life. And yet your company, without warning to women, invaded their bodies by the millions and caused them injuries by the thousands. And when the time came for these women to make their claims against your company, you attacked their characters. You inquired into their sexual practices and into the identity of their sex partners. You exposed these women—and ruined families and reputations and careers—in order to intimidate those who would raise their voices against you. You introduced issues that had no relationship whatsoever to the fact that you planted in the bodies of these women instruments of death, of mutilation, of disease.

I wish to make it absolutely clear that I am specifically directing and limiting my remarks to that which I have learned and observed in these consolidated cases before me. If an incident arises involving another product made by the A. H. Robins Company, an independent judgment would have to be made as to the conduct of your company concerning that product. Likewise, a product made by any other company must be judged upon the individual facts of that case.

Gentlemen, you state that your company has suffered enough, that the infliction of further punishment in the form of punitive damages will cause harm to your ongoing business, will punish innocent shareholders, and could conceivably depress your profits to the point where you could not survive as a competitor in this industry. When the poor and downtrodden in this country commit crimes, they too plead that these are crimes of survival and that they should be excused for illegal acts which helped them escape desperate economic straits. On a few occasions when these excuses are made and a contrite and remorseful defendant promises to mend his ways, courts will give heed to such a plea. But no court would heed this plea when the individual denies the wrongful nature of his deeds and gives no indication that he will mend his ways. Your company, in the face of overwhelming evidence, denies its guilt and continues its monstrous mischief.

Mr. Forrest, you have told me that you are working with members of the Congress of the United States to ask them to find a way of forgiving you from punitive damages which might otherwise be imposed. Yet the profits of your company continue to mount. Your last financial report boasts of new records for sales and earnings, with a profit of more than $58 million in 1983. And all the while, insofar as this court is able to determine, you three men and your company still engage in the selfsame course of wrongdoing in which you originally commenced. Until such time as your company indicates that it is willing to cease and desist this deception and to seek out and advise victims, your remonstrances to Congress and to the courts of this country are indeed hollow and cynical. The company has not suffered, nor have you men personally. You are collectively being enriched by millions of dollars each year. There is as yet no evidence that your company has suffered any penalty whatsoever from these litigations. In fact, the evidence is to the contrary.

The case law indicates that the purpose of punitive damages is to make an award which will punish a defendant for his wrongdoing. Punishment traditionally involves the principles of revenge, rehabilitation, and deterrence. There is no evidence I have been able to find in my review of these cases to indicate that any one of these factors has been accomplished.

Mr. Robins, Mr. Forrest, Dr. Lunsford: You have not been rehabilitated. Under your direction, your company has in fact continued to allow women, tens of thousands of them, to wear this device—a deadly depth charge in their wombs, ready to explode at any time. Your attorney, Mr. Alexander Slaughter, denies that tens of thousands of these devices are still in the bodies of women. But I submit to you that Mr. Slaughter has no more basis for his denial than the plaintiffs have for stating it as truth, because we simply do not know how many women are still wearing these devices, and your company is not willing to find out. The only conceivable reasons you have not recalled this product are that it would hurt your balance sheet and alert women who already have been harmed that you may be liable for their injuries. You have taken the bottom line as your guiding beacon, and the low road as your route. This is corporate irresponsibility at its meanest. Rehabilitation involves an admission of guilt, a certain contrition, an acknowledgment of wrongdoing, and a resolution to take a new course toward a better life. I find none of this in the instance of you and your corporation. Confession is good for the soul, gentlemen. Face up to your misdeeds. Acknowledge the personal responsibility that you have for the activities of those who work under you. Rectify this evil situation. Warn the potential future victims and recompense those who already have been harmed.

Mr. Robins, Mr. Forrest, Dr. Lunsford: I see little in the history of this case that would deter others from partaking of like acts. The policy of delay and obfuscation practiced by your lawyers in courts throughout this country has made it possible for you and your insurance company, Aetna Casualty and Surety Company, to delay the payment of these claims for such a long period that the interest you earn in the interim covers the cost of these cases. You, in essence, pay nothing out of your pocket to settle these cases. What other corporate officials could possibly learn a lesson from this? The only lesson could be that it pays to delay compensating victims and to intimidate, harass, and shame the injured parties.

Mr. Robins, Mr. Forrest, Dr. Lunsford: You gentlemen have consistently denied any knowledge of the deeds of the company you control.

Mr. Robins, I have read your deposition. Many times you state that your management style was such as to delegate work and responsibility to other employees in matters involving the most important aspects of this nation's health. Judge Frank Theis, who presided over the discovery of these cases during the multidistrict litigation proceedings, noted this phenomenon in a recent opinion. He wrote, "The project manager for Dalkon Shield explains that a particular question should have gone to the medical department, the medical department representative explains that the question was really the bailiwick of the quality-control department, and the quality-control department representative explains that the project manager was the one with the authority to make a decision on that question." Under these circumstances, Judge Theis noted, "it is not at all unusual for the hard questions posed in Dalkon Shield cases to be unanswerable by anyone from Robins."

Your company seeks to segment and fragment the litigation of these cases nationwide. The courts of this country are now burdened with more than three thousand Dalkon Shield cases. The sheer number of claims and the dilatory tactics used by your company's attorneys clog court calendars and consume vast amounts of judicial and jury time. Your company settles those cases in which it finds itself in an uncomfortable position, a handy device for avoiding any proceeding which would give continuity or cohesiveness to this nationwide problem. The decision as to which cases to try rests almost solely at the whim and discretion of the A. H. Robins Company. In order that no plaintiff or group of plaintiffs might assert a sustained assault upon your system of evasion and avoidance, you time after time demand that able lawyers who have knowledge of the facts must, as a price of settling their cases, agree to never again take a Dalkon Shield case nor to help any less experienced lawyers with their cases against your company.

Minnesota lawyers have filed cases in this jurisdiction for women from throughout the United States. The cases of these women have waited on the calendar of this court for as many as three years. The evidence they will present at trial is predominantly generic evidence concerning the company's actions, which is as easy to produce in Minnesota as anywhere else. Yet your company's attorneys persist in asking that these cases be transferred to other jurisdictions and to other judges unfamiliar with the cases, there to wait at the bottom of the calendars for additional months and years before they they have their day in court.

Another of your callous legal tactics is to force women of little means to withstand the onslaught of your well-financed, nationwide team of attorneys, and to default if they cannot keep pace. You target your worst tactics for the meek and the poor.

(I should point out that the Faegre & Benson law firm, local counsel for your company in the consolidated cases before me, has a high reputation for fair play, integrity, and fidelity to the court. Faegre & Benson, and other local firms retained for trials across the country, are not responsible for the overall strategic decisions of your company.)

Despite your company's protestations, it is evident that these thousands of cases cannot be viewed in isolation, one at a time. The multidistrict litigation panel of the federal court system found these cases to have sufficient similarity on issues of fact and law to warrant their reference to a single judge who, for varying periods of time, conducted discovery, depositions, and proceedings designed to devise an efficient method of handling these cases. In each of these thousands of cases, the focal point of the inquiry is the same: the conduct of your company through its acts and omissions. Indeed, Judge Gerald Heaney of the Court of Appeals for the Eighth Circuit recently urged judges in Minnesota to work together to devise a coordinated system for dealing with all of their Dalkon Shield cases.

These litigations must be viewed as a whole. Were these women to be gathered together with their injuries in one location, this would be denominated a disaster of the highest magnitude. The mere fact that these women are separated by geography blurs the total picture. Here we have thousands of victims, present and potential, whose injuries arise from the same series of operative facts. You have made no effort whatsoever to locate them and bring them together to seek a common solution to their plight.

If this were a case in equity, I would order that your company make an effort to locate each and every woman who still wears this device and recall your product. But this court does not have the power to do so. I must therefore resort to moral persuasion and a personal appeal to each of you. Mr. Robins, Mr. Forrest, and Dr. Lunsford: You are the people with the power to recall. You are the corporate conscience.

Please, in the name of humanity, lift your eyes above the bottom line. You, the men in charge, must surely have hearts and souls and consciences. If the thought of facing up to your transgressions is so unbearable to you, you might do as Roger Tuttle did and confess to your Maker, beg forgiveness, and mend your ways.

Please, gentlemen, give consideration to tracing down the victims and sparing them the agony that will surely be theirs.

C: COUNTRIES WHERE THE A. H. ROBINS COMPANY
SOLD THE DALKON SHIELD

Argentina	Honduras	Panama
Australia	Hong Kong	Paraguay
Austria	Iceland	Peru
Bangladesh	India	Philippines
Belgium	Indonesia	Portugal
Brazil	Iran	Puerto Rico
Canada	Iraq	Samoa
Chile	Israel	Saudi Arabia
Colombia	Italy	Singapore
Costa Rica	Jamaica	Somalia
Cyprus	Japan	South Africa
Denmark	Jordan	Spain
Dominican Republic	Kenya	Sri Lanka
Ecuador	Kuwait	Sudan
Arab Republic of	Laos	Suriname
Egypt	Lebanon	Swaziland
El Salvador	Lesotho	Sweden
Ethiopia	Liberia	Switzerland
Finland	Libya	Syria
France	Luxembourg	Taiwan
Federal Republic of	Malaysia	Tanzania
Germany	Mexico	Thailand
Ghana	Netherlands	Tunisia
Great Britain	Nicaragua	Uganda
Greece	Nigeria	Venezuela
Guatemala	Norway	Virgin Islands
Haiti	Pakistan	Zambia

Notes

Preface

1. The Moral Majority president debated Judy Goldsmith, president of the National Organization for Women, at the National Press Club in Washington, and I paraphrased Suzanne Garment's report in her *Wall Street Journal* column on February 15, 1985. She quoted Falwell: "The unborn are the last disenfranchised minority with no civil rights. . . . We only want equal rights for the unborn—their constitutional guarantees." The Lynchburg connection aside, anyone holding these views might appropriately speak out on fetus-killing by the Dalkon Shield.

2. Ross, Edward A. *Sin and Society: An Analysis of Latter-Day Iniquity, with a Letter from President* [Theodore] *Roosevelt* (Boston: Houghton Mifflin, 1907), 29–30. Roosevelt told Ross in characteristically muscular prose:

"You define 'sin' as conduct that harms another in contradistinction to 'vice,' by which we mean practices that harm one's self; and you attack as they should be attacked the men who at the present day do more harm to the body politic by their sinning than all others. With almost all that you write I am in full and hearty sympathy. As you well say, if a ring is to be put in the snout of the greedy, only organized society can do it."

Introduction: The Toll

1. In industrialized nations, PID accounts for about 50 percent of all tubal pregnancies and for 30 to 40 percent of all infertility, as well as for numerous miscarriages. In recent years in the United States, more than 850,000 women

annually get PID, and about 200,000 of them go to hospitals. PID death rates in the Third World, where medical treatment is commonly inferior, scarce, or nonexistent, are far higher.

2. As will be seen later, some physicians experienced pregnancy rates in multiples of 5 percent while others reported fractions of 5 percent. Bradley Post, the lawyer in Wichita, Kansas, who has spent much of a decade gathering and analyzing facts about the Shield, assumes 5 percent to be a reasonable estimate overall, and, on that base, calculated an "excess" of 11,000 fetal deaths.

3. An unidentified company attorney told the *Richmond Times-Dispatch* that a grand total of thirty-six Shield deaths had been alleged in lawsuits, complaints, and "voluntary reportings." But, the newspaper said on June 23, 1985, the attorney cast doubt on the figure, saying that it "cannot be verified and may include some double counting."

4. The manufacturer's records, obtained by plaintiffs' lawyers, were the source of figures on the numbers of Shields made and sold. Appendix C is the company's listing of the countries.

5. *Minneapolis Star and Tribune,* November 1, 1984.

6. *New England Journal of Medicine,* April 11, 1985. See also the news stories of the same date in the *Wall Street Journal* and the *Washington Post.*

7. As will be recalled, it was PID entirely in pregnant women that precipitated the suspension of Shield sales in June 1974. Why did great waves of PID in nonpregnant women come only later? The reason was that in the second trimester, the expansion of the womb had progressed to the point that it tended to tug into it lower and contaminated portions of the tail string—segments that would remain outside the bacteria-free uterus in women who were not pregnant or who were in the first trimester.

8. *Minneapolis Star and Tribune,* April 16, 1984. The staff writer was Delia Flores.

9. In the *Richmond Times-Dispatch* of February 3, 1985, staff writer Thomas R. Morris said he had been told by the lawyer who filed the suit in the Standeford death that before she died, "a doctor had drained '1,000 cc or so of pus, enough to fill a mayonnaise jar.' "

10. The initial reactions were predictable denunciations of Lord and assertions of innocence of wrongdoing. Claiborne Robins, Jr., at the annual meeting of stockholders on April 24, charged that Lord had "no basis" for his "poisonous attack." He added: "Look at our progress that has been built on integrity, fair play, and good products. Ask if this company would jeopardize its future and its product lines by marketing a device it knew to be faulty."

11. In the fall of 1984, a plaintiffs' lawyer gave me a copy of Dr. March's letter to Robins about Mrs. Berlin's death. The letter clearly indicated that she had been fitted with a Shield in 1976—two years after Robins had suspended domestic sales and almost as long after it had recalled used Shields from supply pipelines. Seeking an explanation, I phoned March, but he said, "All I intend now or ever to say is what I said in the letter, period."

I. THE ROAD TO RICHMOND

1. *Hugh J. Davis, M.D.*

1. I told the Pill story fully in my book *The Pill: An Alarming Report* (New York: Fawcett, 1969, and Boston: Beacon, 1970). Both versions are out of print, but the Beacon hardcover is in many libraries.

2. With tens of millions of women on the Pill, and with tens of millions more about to start or stop using it, oral contraception became the greatest *uncontrolled* medical experiment in history. These were *healthy* human beings taking potent drugs twenty or twenty-one days a month. But leaders of the medical profession and the FDA, powerfully aided by an overall disgraceful press performance, made it extremely difficult for the public to receive straight information and to make balanced and informed judgments about the Pill's safety. The report of the Medical Research Council on May 5, 1967, was a classic case of medical experts—on whom the public must rely—trying to tell the truth while simultaneously trying to conceal the truth, with the press mindlessly going along.

An Associated Press story began, "The British Medical Research Council says birth control pills may have caused the deaths of twenty women in Britain last year, but riding in a car would have been twice as risky as taking the pills." A UPI report stated that "British medical researchers said today birth control pills are not 100 percent safe. But they said the Pill is far safer than a walk across a busy street." Reuters: "A report in the British Medical Journal linked the deaths of twenty women in Britain last year [with birth-control pills] but said the risk was small compared to the number of deaths in childbirth or in traffic accidents."

The unspoken rationale for such absurd comparisions—what woman rides in a car as a mode of birth control?—was a desire to avoid panic. Commendable, but where was that desire when women were driven *to* the Pill by what amounted to panic in the medical profession and in the news media?

The MRC story rated twelve lines of type in *The New York Times,* which, in the first sentence of an article seven months later, on January 7, 1968, enshrined the Pill as the "perfect" contraceptive.

3. U.S. Department of Health, Education, and Welfare, Food and Drug Administration. Medical Device and Drug Advisory Committees on Obstetrics and Gynecology. *Second Report on Intrauterine Contraceptive Devices* (Washington, 1978).

4. See note 3 above.

5. *The American Journal of Surgery,* n.s. 38, no. 3 (March 1938): 631–34.

6. A. Curtis. *Textbook of Gynecology* (Philadelphia: W. B. Saunders Co., 1943).

7. Weilerstein, Ralph W. "The Hazards of Intrauterine Pessaries: An Evaluation." *Western Journal of Surgery, Obstetrics & Gynecology* 65 (May–June 1957).

8. U.S. Department of Health, Education, and Welfare, Food and Drug

Administration. Advisory Committee on Obstetrics and Gynecology. *Report on Intrauterine Devices* (Washington, 1968).

9. In January 1968, the Food and Drug Administration's Advisory Committee on Obstetrics and Gynecology made a report on IUDs that I reviewed for this book. It did not mention the reports I have cited, not even in a formidable 340-entry bibliography of clinical literature. This puzzled me until I noticed that the starting date for the bibliography was 1959—two years after last of the negative reports cited.

10. On February 21, 1985, Thomas C. Bartsh and Peter N. Thompson, who had been appointed by the United States District Court in St. Paul as "special masters" to investigate certain matters in connection with Dalkon Shield litigation, filed one in a series of periodic reports with federal judge Robert G. Renner. At one point, the report dealt with the contention of plaintiffs' counsel that the failure to reveal "Davis' role in the invention of the Dalkon Shield and the fact that the Dalkon Shield was derived from another IUD designed by Davis, the Incon Ring, [was] an initial fraud perpetrated on the Patent Office." The report said that the plaintiffs' lawyers had "indicated that they would supplement the record with specific evidence establishing the nature and scope of this fraud. They have not done so. We note that the deliberate omission of a joint inventor from the patent application invalidates the patent."

11. Lerner, in a June 1, 1973, letter to Davis, enclosed a check for $10,000 "as my donation to Johns Hopkins University for support of research on IUDs as we discussed on the phone." At a deposition, lawyer Bradley Post pointed out to Lerner that the donation followed completion of Davis's research on the Shield, speculating that perhaps Davis had sought the money to "placate" Hopkins. This exchange followed:

LERNER: No, sir; had nothing to do with placating Johns Hopkins.
POST: Sir, you did say in that document, "Good luck in your efforts. . . . "

12. Dr. Ernst Grafenberg (the inventor, in 1930, of the Grafenberg Ring) was unknowingly prescient about the potential hazards of an IUD "tail string" of the sort that would prove so dangerous in the Dalkon Shield. As Dr. Howard J. Tatum, a famed obstetrician-gynecologist, wrote in "Milestones in Intrauterine Devices" in *Fertility and Sterility* 39, no. 2 (February 1983), Grafenberg "vehemently espoused" the doctrine that no IUD should have a tail "because of its propensity to enhance microbial invasion."

13. A woman on a sequential regimen took estrogen-only tablets during part of her menstrual cycle and combination estrogen-progestogen tablets during the remainder. The sequentials were eventually taken off the market after compelling evidence was found indicating that the chemically unopposed estrogen heightened the risk of cancer.

14. The 199,000 figure is in an internal company memo of August 16, 1973, from Robert A. Hogsett to Kenneth E. Moore, Shield project coordinator.

15. Seaman, Barbara. *The Doctors' Case Against the Pill* (New York: Wyden, 1969).

16. Tietze, Christopher J. "Intrauterine Contraception: Recommended Procedures for Data Analysis." *Studies in Family Planning* suppl. 18 (April 1967).

17. Mitchell made the statement on September 10, 1962, at a conference on blood clotting in Enovid users, sponsored by the birth-control pill's maker, G. D. Searle & Company. Searle had played the same dangerous game as Davis by making a case for the oral contraceptive's safety based on women who had used it for twenty-five months, while ignoring the dropouts (Mintz, *The Pill: An Alarming Report*, 57–60).

18. An account of how Davis became a supposed authority on oral contraceptives was provided by Dr. John E. Tyson, professor and department chairman of OB-GYN at the University of Manitoba in Winnipeg, to the *Toronto Star* for a story on October 25, 1980. Tyson, who joined Hopkins's OB-GYN department in 1966 and directed its endocrine clinic from 1967 to 1979, assisted Davis in his Shield trials. Tyson told reporter Gillian Cosgrove that Davis was invited to argue the negative in a debate on the safety of the Pill at the 1969 convention of the American College of Obstetricians and Gynecologists in Miami. Cosgrove wrote:

> To make himself an overnight expert, Davis turned to Tyson, who had been studying the metabolic effects of oral contraceptives.
>
> Tyson pointed out that downgrading the Pill could be a conflict of interest since Davis had a financial stake in the Dalkon Shield. Davis went to Miami anyway. . . .
>
> Tyson . . . says: "Of course he was foolish to get involved in a conflict of interest situation, but I believe that everyone has the right to choose the way they go down the tube."

19. Davis, Hugh J. *Intrauterine Devices for Contraception: The IUD* (Baltimore: Williams & Wilkins, 1971).

20. House Subcommittee of the Committee on Government Operations, *Regulation of Medical Devices (Intrauterine Contraceptive Devices)*, 93d Cong., 1st sess. (May 30, 31; June 1, 12, 13, 1973).

21. Senate Select Committee on Small Business, Subcommittee on Monopoly, *Competitive Problems in the Drug Industry*, 91st Cong., 2d sess., pt. 15 (January 14, 15, 22, 23, 1970).

22. I tried to interview Davis, but he told me in the second of two brief phone conversations in 1983, "I don't think there's anything to be gained by hashing and rehashing events of ten to twelve years ago."

2. Thad J. Earl, M.D.

1. The Dalkon Corporation's incorporation papers and annual reports to the State of Connecticut named only three persons: Irwin S. Lerner, president and

a director; Robert E. Cohn, secretary, treasurer, and a director, and Fanny H. Lerner, a director. State records show that the corporate name was changed on May 17, 1972, to D.L.K., Inc., further obscuring Davis's connection.

2. Roger L. Tuttle, a former Robins attorney, told the author that the company's sales force of more than five hundred was "the most aggressive . . . in the industry." Robins's records show that the salesmen's salaries, bonuses, and commissions increased from $8.7 million in 1970, the year before it began to sell Shields, to $10.2 million in 1974, the year in which it stopped selling them.

3. Clark wrote this memo ("Notes on visit to Dr. Hugh Davis, Baltimore, on 6/8/70") on June 9, 1970.

4. Memo from William A. Forrest, Jr., vice-president and general counsel, dated February 28, 1975, marked "CONFIDENTIAL," and addressed to Robins's defense counsel. The title was "Chronological History of Acquisition and Marketing of DALKON SHIELD by A. H. Robins Company."

5. See Note 4 above.

II. A. H. ROBINS BUYS THE DALKON SHIELD

3. A. H. Robins

1. The brochure is entitled "1866 / A. H. Robins / 1978." The introduction says: "Roscoe E. Puckett, Jr., Manager of Public Information, has probed the memory of E. Claiborne Robins, grandson of the founder and, since 1933, architect of the Company's development into a diversified multinational corporation with more than 5,500 employees and annual sales of well over a quarter of a billion dollars."

2. "Remarks by E. C. Robins, Jr.," 21st annual meeting of stockholders, A. H. Robins Company, Richmond, Virginia, April 24, 1984.

3. A parallel exists in Indianapolis, home of Eli Lilly and Company, a major pharmaceutical house, and of the Lilly Endowment, an immensely wealthy charitable foundation. A hand attached to almost any nonprofit activity—artistic, cultural, religious, athletic, civic—can hardly be outstretched in Indianapolis and Indiana without quickly clenching on a grant from the Endowment.

4. Interview with columnist Guy Friddell, *Richmond Times-Dispatch*, May 24, 1982. Friddell pronounced Robins "as self-effacing as he is generous."

5. *Richmond Times-Dispatch*, November 27, 1969.

4. Anatomy of a Decision

1. For example, Ralph W. Weilerstein, M.D., "The Hazards of Intrauterine Pessaries: An Evaluation," *Western Journal of Surgery, Obstetrics & Gynecology* 65 (May-June 1957): 157–60. Dr. Weilerstein, associate medical director of the Food and Drug Administration, said in his abstract:

"One hundred and seventy-nine patients suffered severe illness or injury due to intracervical or intrauterine contraceptive pessaries. The reported effects included *infection and its complications, imbedding,* irritation, *perforation, migration, coincident ectopic pregnancies, and cervical carcinoma.* " I have italicized the medical conditions not noted by Dr. Clark. That IUDs cause cancer of the cervix is, however, most unlikely.

Weilerstein continued: "These cases were compiled from responses to a Federal Food and Drug Administration questionnaire, Bureau of Medicine, to geographically selected Diplomates of the American Board of Obstetrics and Gynecology. The consensus of this group of informed experts overwhelmingly condemns the continued distribution of intracervical and intrauterine pessaries."

Indeed, as noted in Chapter 1, 101 of 129 of the Diplomates who responded opposed continued distribution of IUDs, while 18 more opposed use of the devices except under "certain qualifying circumstances. . . ."

Dr. Clark recorded no inquiries to the FDA, the American College of Obstetricians and Gynecologists, or OB-GYNs at the Medical College of Virginia, a ten-cent phone call away in Richmond.

2. The National Academy of Sciences–National Research Council later found that in the quarter-century between enactment and amendment of the drug law, only 12 percent of all of the medicines that entered the market fulfilled all of the claims made for them. Indeed, the FDA told the Senate Subcommittee on Monopoly on January 18, 1971, that 15 percent fulfilled none.

In *Pills That Don't Work,* Sidney M. Wolfe, M.D., and Christopher M. Coley listed 610 prescription drugs found by the NAS-NRC not to have been shown to be effective but still being sold in 1979!

"Neither you nor, in some instances, even your doctor realize that one of every eight prescriptions filled—169 million prescriptions costing over $1.1 billion in 1979—is for a drug not considered effective by the government's own standards," the authors said.

The book's Appendix B listed the "1979 Top Less-Than-Effective Prescription Drugs (All Among the Top 200 Drugs in the U.S.)." Leading the list was A. H. Robins Company's Dimetapp, with 14.8 million prescriptions and retail sales of $67 million. Robins's Donnatal (8.97 million prescriptions, retail sales of $31.7 million) ranked third; its Dimetane Expectorant-DC (1.6 million, $8.5 million) ranked twenty-ninth.

The book is a powerful rebuttal to the advocates of repeal of the efficacy requirements in the drug law, including President Reagan and the economist Milton Friedman, who wants to abolish the FDA altogether (along with the National Institutes of Health).

The Health Research Group, of which Dr. Wolfe is the director, published the book in 1980. The HRG is part of the advocacy organization Public Citizen, and is located at 2000 P Street, N.W., Washington, D.C. 20036.

3. U.S. Department of Health, Education, and Welfare. Food and Drug Administration. Advisory Committee on Obstetrics and Gynecology. *Report on*

Intrauterine Contraceptive Devices. Washington, 1968. The four deaths are noted on page 32 of the report; Dr. Scott's ominous assessment of the litigation potential is on page 45.

4. Russel J. Thomsen, M.D. "Agency for International Development and the Dalkon Shield Intrauterine Contraceptive Device." Unpublished report dated March 7, 1985.

5. In a report in *American Family Physician,* Earl said he had inserted 536 Shields in a study covering 4,633 woman-months. Since the average of 8.64 woman-months was 56 percent longer than Davis's claimed 5.54, Earl's claimed 0.5-percent failure rate, if credible, was all the more impressive. That Earl should have reported a 0.5 result—not, say, 0.4 or 0.6—raises eyebrows because it happened to coincide with the figure predicted much earlier at an international meeting by none other than Hugh Davis. "Within a year," Davis told the Sixth Congress of Gynaecology & Obstetrics in New York, "we should have an intrauterine contraceptive device with a pregnancy rate of 0.5 percent or less."

Dr. Russel J. Thomsen, in a report on the Shield for the Agency for International Development in March 1985, productively illuminated the chronological sequence:

Davis made his prediction of a 0.5-percent rate close to the February 1, 1970, revelation in the *American Journal of Obstetrics and Gynecology* of his supposed 1.1-percent actual rate.

Four weeks after that issue of the *Journal* appeared, Davis and coauthor Dr. John Lesinski repeated the prediction of a 0.5-percent rate and the claim of an achieved 1.1-percent rate in an article submitted to the same journal.

"These claims were widely disseminated through the *Journal of the American Medical Association* in an article entitled 'Virtually Failsafe IUD Seen in Year,' " Thomsen wrote. The first sentence of the unsigned article, in JAMA's "Medical News" section on May 18, 1970, recited Davis's claim of a "0.5-percent or less" pregnancy rate "within a year." The article also cited the Davis study that found the claimed 1.1-percent rate but put a figleaf in front of the name of the device, calling it the "D Shield."

The Davis-Lesinski article submitted to the OB-GYN *Journal* ("Mechanism of Action of Intrauterine Contraceptive Devices in Women") appeared in September 1970.

Earl's report ("The Shield Intrauterine Device") appeared in the September 1971 *Family Physician,* but, of course, had been submitted long before then.

Conceivably, it was a coincidence, even if a promotionally useful one, that the Shield developer's prophecy of a 0.5-percent pregnancy rate should be fulfilled by the Shield's overt promoter at an opportune moment, while sales were soaring, and while almost no one knew of their ownership interests in the device.

6. A few weeks after the visit, however, one of the patients suffered a perforated uterus. In one deposition, Earl said he had reported this to Robins,

"because I reported anything that I felt was significant"; in a later deposition, he testified he had not reported the perforation. His article in *American Family Physician* (see note 5 above) fifteen months later did not report a perforation.

Perforations were a tough subject for Hugh Davis, too. In 1974, he swore he had seen three or four perforations in Shield wearers; in 1976, he swore he had seen none. "Was that false testimony [in 1974]?" he was asked. "It was not," he testified.

7. On May 29, Smith and Morton briefed fellow executives, including president William L. Zimmer III.

On June 1, a larger in-house meeting was held, partly to have a general discussion of the Shield with two medical consultants on hand: Solon Davis and a colleague at MCV, Dr. John Board, husband of Dr. Anne Board, a member of the company's medical department.

On June 2, a third meeting took place, which consisted in part of Earl screening what he called a "physician education" film in which "I demonstrated how I inserted the device and how the device was used in my practice. . . ." On June 4 or 5, Forrest and six other executives visited Dalkon's offices in Greenwich, Connecticut. The purpose, the general counsel said in his memo, was to look at the corporation and its facilities, discuss numerous matters relating to the Shield, and have Irwin S. Lerner, the president and listed inventor of the Shield, "confirm information furnished by Dr. Earl."

8. A persuasive explanation of the assumed "even better" than 1.1-percent effectiveness rate is that the three men were lunching on June 9—on the day, and perhaps at about the time, that Dr. Clark was writing the memo in which he divulged to Dr. Freund the pregnancies of twenty-six women in Davis's study, rather than the five that Davis had cited in his paper.

9. Forrest's chronology entry for July 20 said that "Dr. Clark called Dr. Grody to arrange a meeting on August 10, 1970. Contracted with respect to his clinical study (?) initiated by Dalkon Corporation . . . very enthusiastic about Shield."

Grody offered to study the Shield for Robins for a large but unspecified fee, but Dr. A. N. Chremos, director of clinical pharmacology, rejected his offer. Grody's "own written admission of primary monetary considerations would render his findings as an investigator suspect because of the possibility of bias," Chremos wrote. "I would not be ready to capitulate at this moment by paying him this sum he has demanded as a consultation fee. The fee far exceeds the limit . . . usually commanded by the most well-known authorities in the profession.

"There is no doubt in my mind that the best interests of the A. H. Robins Company dictate that we disengage ourselves from any association with Dr. Grody . . . ," Chremos said.

Chremos's treatment of Grody rises to footnote importance only because of subsequent events. In a deposition in 1976, Dr. Clark said that he agreed with Chremos's appraisal and, indeed, had taken his advice. But, he admitted, he had then hired Grody four years later, in August 1974, to come before a panel of advisers to the Food and Drug Administration to help defend the Shield as a safe and effective IUD.

Two weeks after the FDA hearing, Clark sent Grody a letter of thanks "for your interest and willingness, for your excellent presentation. . . . Attached are two checks, one for $1,840 made out to the Greater Hartford OB/GYN Group, P.C., and the other for $122.85 made out to Marvin H. Grody, M.D., both representing remuneration for expenses incurred in assemblage of your data on the Dalkon Shield and presentation at the August 21 hearing."

III. THE LAUNCH

5. Deceiving Doctors

1. The Shield itself consisted of only two parts, a plastic matrix, molded by Pee Wee Molding Company of Brooklyn, N.Y., and the nylon string, supplied by a West German firm. In the first "Dalkon Shield: Orientation Report," R. W. Nickless said on June 29, 1970: "One fast worker with good manual dexterity can 'tie' 1,000 Shields a day." Tied Shields were put in sterile packages with an inserter and labeling.

2. In a memo ("Manufacturing Proposal for the Dalkon Shield") on December 16, 1970, Stuart L. Petree and E. Carlton Gammon recommended that Chap Stick produce Shields, terming the labor market there "more favorable than [in] Richmond." However weak unions are in Virginia, they are weaker in Lynchburg than in Richmond. The memo put the Shield unit cost of "Labor & Overhead" at nine cents at Chap Stick as well as at the Dalkon Corporation in Stamford, Connecticut, compared with fifteen cents at the main Robins plant.

3. Note the absence of documentation for the cleverly phrased claims made by A. H. Robins in the following Q-and-A in "The Dalkon Shield: Some Questions and Answers," a brochure it made available to the press in 1983 "to provide background information and, hopefully, correct some of the common misconceptions concerning this product. . . ."

"To what extent was the safety and efficacy of the Dalkon Shield tested prior to marketing by Robins?

"The Dalkon Shield was a *well-tested* product prior to marketing by Robins. The product was already on the market when purchased by Robins with some 27,000 devices having been sold. *Robins was able to draw on the experience of several thousands of users in evaluating the Dalkon Shield prior to national marketing including data from five formal studies.* Toxicity and biopsy results were also *considered* as was the large amount of generic IUD data then available. The *generic* information available to Robins prior to marketing exceeded that theretofore available when other IUDs were introduced." [Emphasis added.]

4. I computed the ratios from data in a Food and Drug Administration memo

prepared for a meeting of outside OB-GYN advisers on June 11, 1974. On the basis of "inspection reports and telephone discussions with representatives of the firms involved," the memo gave the following figures in a table on "Annual Domestic IUD Distribution":

	Shield	Saf-T-Coil	Lippes Loop
1971	1,081,000	180,060	409,176
1972	883,500	178,995	411,952
1973	604,400	230,561	492,912
Totals:	2,568,900	589,616	1,314,040

Counting Shields distributed in the first half of 1974, until domestic sales were suspended on June 28, Robins said in its 1983 press brochure (see note 3, above) that it had distributed 2,861,078 units "within the United States," that an estimated 2.2 million were inserted, "and that 1,709,213 were sold as Government service agency sales, direct export sales, overseas subsidiary sales and Canadian sales."

5. The unidentified writer in the *Medical World News* said that Davis "has tested the Shield in nearly *1,000* women. 'Expulsion rate has been almost zero during sixteen months' experience,' he said. 'And the device has provided *98.9 percent protection* against pregnancy [i.e.—lo and behold!—a 1.1 percent failure rate].' " [Emphasis added.]

6. "The Dalkon Shield: A Preliminary Market Study," August 1970. The executives who received the report—none of them physicians or scientists— were C. E. Morton and Ernest L. Bender, Jr., vice-presidents; John L. Burke, general sales manager; R. W. Nickless, product management coordinator in the pharmaceutical division, and Dale R. Taylor, director of market planning and development.

7. Memo of June 11, 1970.

8. Williams & Wilkins executive Sara Finnegan, as noted in an earlier chapter, refused to disclose sales figures or comment on any aspect of the book. The Spanish edition was doubtless pushed in Latin America, where Davis, fluent in Spanish, was influential in several birth-control programs.

9. Lester W. Preston, Jr., "Dalkon Shield Distribution Data," January 28, 1974.

10. Here is a sampling culled from physicians' complaints to Robins that were relayed by its salesmen, or that were made directly, over a twenty-month period in 1971–72:

February 3, 1971: Salesman John P. Kypriotis of Tiverton, Rhode Island, reported on a doctor who had inserted about fifty Shields, "Out of this number he has had four pregnancies [8 percent], but even more upsetting is that he has had to remove about 20 percent of the Shields."

April 20: OB-GYN John H. Belton of St. Catherines, Ontario, wrote of having made fifty-eight insertions followed by four pregnancies (6.8 percent).

June 15: Salesman Victor R. Grayson of Mishawaka, Indiana, reported that Dr. Philip Sarrel, of Yale, said in a speech that "he had experienced a 50-percent pregnancy rate [in, as it turned out, twelve patients]."

July 26: Salesman Robert T. Brooks reported that in Anniston, Alabama, Dr. R. C. Aliq had "six pregnancies in less than one hundred insertions," and Dr. L. S. Smith, Jr., "had five . . . in less than one hundred insertions.'

September 2: OB-GYN Phillip Minor of Richmond, Virginia, "reported that he and his partner have inserted approximately 65–70 Dalkon Shields over the last six months and six pregnancies (at least 8.6 percent) have occurred to date. . . ."

October 10: OB-GYN Kenneth J. Chapman of Columbus, Ohio, told salesman Gordon V. Lanum that he had inserted fifty-six Shields "and has recorded his seventh pregnancy [12.5 percent]."

November 24: Dorothy Urich, a registered nurse supervising the Planned Parenthood Center in Morristown, New Jersey, wrote that three pregnancies followed twenty-nine insertions (10.3 percent).

March 12, 1972: Dr. Owen K. Youles of Valdosta, Georgia, said he had inserted Shields in about seventy women; of the thirty-four for whom he had records, six became pregnant (17.6 percent).

October 26: Dr. Roy Holly, chief of OB-GYN at the Jefferson University Hospital in Philadelphia, reported four pregnancies following twelve Shield insertions (33.3 percent).

11. Robert S. Murphey, "Minutes of Meeting of 7/15/71 on Dalkon Shield." The three physicians in the discussion were Ellen J. Preston, the Shield monitor; Anne W. Board, who worked with her; and A. N. Chremos, director of clinical pharmacology.

12. In a deposition on December 22, 1976, Ellen Preston said that she didn't know whether Robins had tried to get Ostergard onto the FDA advisory panel. In a deposition about six months later, on June 8, 1977, she said, "I believe we nominated him as a candidate, yes."

13. Post then showed Preston a copy of his memo bearing a handwritten note to him from Dr. Freund: "Mr. Al Young would like to chat with you about this —at your convenience. Jack." Had Preston had a chat with Young? Preston testified he could not recall.

> Q: And if, in fact, Dr. Freund has testified that he did order you to either continue to process Dr. Ostergard's data or not to put the suspension in effect, you don't have any reason to believe that statement is inaccurate, do you?
> A: Well, I'd like that question again.
> [The court reporter reads the question back.]
> A: Now, I'm really trying to understand you.
> Q: The statement by Dr. Freund—

A: That his statement would be inaccurate?

Q: Yes.

A: Well, it would appear to be inaccurate. It appears to be in conflict with what I just testified to.

Q: Well, I want you to assume now that Dr. Freund has testified that he issued an order for you to continue processing Dr. Ostergard's data or not to suspend analysis activities. Will you assume that? . . . You don't have any reason to believe that isn't true, do you?

A: No, sir.

14. House Subcommittee of the Committee on Government Operations, *Regulation of Medical Devices (Intrauterine Contraceptive Devices)*, 93d Cong., 1st sess. (May 30, 31; June 1, 12, 13, 1973): 306–24.

15. See note 14 above, pp. 61–62 and 116–123. "By the way," Thomsen testified, the "Progress Report" ad "is not the worst advertisement for IUDs. By far the worst one, in my opinion, is the recent one put out for the LEM. . . . This brand-new IUD has just been marketed with full advertising and distribution by Searle & Company. . . . Its promotion and advertising is based upon what is surely one of the most pathetic IUD clinical studies I have ever seen. The study involves only 606 patients with only 209 having the device for twelve months. And nearly 20 percent of the 606 women were actually lost to follow-up. The admitted complication rate for the LEM based on this pathetic study is 25 percent. And that is the advertising basis for the LEM."

16. See note 14 above, p. 120.

17. See note 14 above, p. 303.

18. The Tietze guidelines were set out in "Intrauterine Contraception: Recommended Procedures for Data Analysis," *Studies in Family Planning* suppl. 18 (April 1967).

19. The total number of woman-months underlying the twelve-month figure was 16,390—4.6 times as many as in Hugh Davis's allegedly year-long study that Robins would continue to cite—and would advertise twenty-one months later in Australia and New Zealand.

20. In an interview in 1983, however, Tietze told me that the 15-percent rule had long since become overly "generous" and that the permissible loss to follow-up should not exceed 10 percent or so.

6. Deceiving Women

1. *Code of Fair Practices in the Promotion of Drug Products.* Pharmaceutical Manufacturers Association, 1100 Fifteenth Street, N.W., Washington, D.C. 20005.

2. Wilcox continued:

Beyond the *Ladies' Home Journal* we are, if necessary, equally prepared to work with *McCall's, Redbook, Glamour* and other magazines with large

readership among women. . . . There are other important outlets which
should be considered. There are, for example, several nationally syn-
dicated medical columnists. . . . We are ready to start as soon as you give
the word. And we look forward to doing a bang-up job together.

3. *American Family Physician* published in September 1971 an article in
which Earl claimed a breathtakingly low—and not-to-be-believed—0.5-percent
pregnancy rate in a fifteen-month study. As noted in an earlier chapter, he did
not divulge that he was then Robins's highest-paid consultant, at $30,000 a
year, and was receiving royalties on every Shield sold.

4. *Mademoiselle* declined to discuss the episode with me, emphasizing that
the current editors and staff members were not at the magazine at the time of
the Wilcox-Chremos visit.

5. Seaman, Barbara. *Free and Female: The Sex Life of the Contemporary Woman*
(New York: Coward, 1972; Fawcett, 1973).

6. Two of the papers were the *Southeastern Times* in Clarkston, North Carolina, and the *Ivanhoe Times* in Minnesota.

7. This is a persisting abusive practice, and it takes many forms. See Morton
Mintz and Jerry S. Cohen, *Power, Inc.: Public and Private Rulers and How to
Make Them Accountable* (New York: Viking Press, 1976): 282–87.

8. "The Dalkon Shield: A Preliminary Market Study," an internal report by
David E. Jones and George J. Mancini of the A. H. Robins Marketing Research
Department, August 1970.

9. House Subcommittee of the Committee on Government Operations, *Regulations of Medical Devices (Intrauterine Contraceptive Devices)*, 93d Cong., 1st
sess. (May 30, 31; June 1, 12, 13, 1973): 118.

7. Dodging the FDA

1. House Committee on Interstate and Foreign Commerce, *Medical Device
Amendments of 1976*, 94th Cong., 2d sess., February 29, 1976, Rept. 94–853.

2. This summary was drawn from my brief history of food and drug legislation
in *The Therapeutic Nightmare* (Boston: Houghton Mifflin, 1965), and the updated
version, *By Prescription Only* (Boston: Beacon, 1967), 37–52.

3. Wiley, Harvey W. *Harvey W. Wiley: An Autobiography* (Indianapolis:
Bobbs-Merrill), 206.

4. See note 1 above.

5. Barnett's letters were filed in United States District Court in Wichita,
Kansas, in 1985.

6. Staff writer Thomas R. Morris, in a story on March 31, 1985, said: "If
the Defiance discrepancies are substantiated, they could cast doubt on Robins'
contention that wearers of the Dalkon Shield were no more likely than any other
American women to contract . . . PID."

IV. TROUBLE

8. The String

1. A. H. Robins. *Interim Report to the Food and Drug Administration on the Dalkon Shield Removal Program.* April 3, 1985.

2. As it turned out, doctors in increasing numbers would complain that the string broke when they tugged on it because it had rotted. Commonly, they had to use surgery to remove the matrix.

3. Identified in Robins records as Kunststoffwerk Alfred Huber of Offenburg/Baden.

4. In March 1971, Crowder, upon finding that Chap Stick was making the Shield, went to Julian W. Ross, his superior, "thinking he was not aware of it, and asked whether any provision had been made for [its] quality control. He told me that he had been meaning to discuss that with me . . . and that he wanted me to be in charge of the quality control . . . at Chap Stick. . . . I examined some of the Shields' string, inserters, some of the components. I found that a shipment of the components had been received from Dalkon Corporation and were in the warehouse and I took a cursory look at the components. I asked Mr. Ross about specifications, literature, whatever was available. At that time specifications were not available."

5. Memo to Dr. Ellen J. Preston, August 6, 1971.

6. Memo to Dr. Oscar Klioze, September 2, 1971.

7. Memo to W. Roy Smith, October 11, 1971.

8. Letter to Dr. John Jennings, associate commissioner of the Food and Drug Administration, February 27, 1975.

9. Crowder set off more confrontations in which Ross recycled his "previous outbursts" and warnings that "my conscience didn't pay my salary" by writing memos about problems with the string, or by "challenging the use or shipment or sale of some product that I regarded as possibly dangerous." He testified that when he "objected strongly to the use of those contaminated products, he [Ross] made further reference to having told me previously that my conscience could pay my salary and he would see if he could give me a chance for it to do so."

Two weeks later, on September 6, 1978, Chap Stick told Crowder to leave with a letter that, he said, cited "departmental reorganization based on economic motives or something to that effect." He said in his deposition that he feels "very positively" that Robins wronged him, but also said, "I don't feel bitterness." Ross declined to be interviewed.

10. Tatum had a persistent critic: Theodore M. King, vice-president for medical affairs of Johns Hopkins University since the spring of 1983. For the eleven preceding years, Dr. King had headed the OB-GYN department in the School of Medicine. Hugh Davis, a long-time department member, left in 1982. King was briefly a paid consultant to Robins before his promotion. In early

1983, plaintiffs' lawyer Nicole Schultheis asked him at a deposition: "Is a multifilament string, such as was used in the Dalkon Shield, more likely to be a pathway for bacteria than a monofilament string?" He replied, "I don't really think so."

11. Drs. Harvey L. Bank and H. Oliver Williamson of the Medical University of South Carolina used an electron microscope to examine five undamaged strings from Shields that had been worn for at least two years without signs of infection. They reported in 1983 that bacteria had passed through allegedly impervious knots and were thriving inside the entire length of the strings.

Robins did not have and did not seek access to an electron microscope, although one was close at hand at the Medical College of Virginia. In September 1974, after Tatum's use of an electron microscope had implicated the string in PID, Dr. Donald R. Ostergard offered access to one "to study the string." The offer was discussed in a meeting on September 23 that was attended by Robins's general counsel as well as company doctors. In a memo on the meeting, Allen J. Polon, who had been Shield project coordinator for nearly a year, wrote: "At this time we do not feel that this type of work would be helpful."

12. Robins executives have defended themselves by casting doubt on Crowder's competence, mainly by insinuation. "I don't know anything about him," Claiborne Robins testified in 1984. Not knowing anything about him did not prevent Robins from calling Crowder "a disgruntled former employee . . . I think that anything that he said would be suspect." Frederick Clark testified, also in 1984, "It was not my understanding that Mr. Crowder was a scientist or a research worker. . . ." Clark admitted, however, that neither he nor anyone else he knew of at Robins had questioned Crowder's qualifications when he was responsible for quality control at Chap Stick.

13. This committee consisted of Claiborne Robins, William Zimmer, and six other executives.

9. Insidious Infections, Insidious Cover-ups

1. An even larger award of punitive damages, $7.5 million, was won by Loretta Tetuan, thirty-three, of Topeka, Kansas, on May 3, 1985. A mother of two, she had worn a Shield for nine years when, in 1980, she suffered a pelvic infection followed by surgical removal of her uterus and ovaries. A Sedgwick County jury in Wichita also awarded her $1.4 million in compensatory damages, for a total of $8.9 million, but withheld about $300,000 because, before becoming ill, she had rejected a doctor's advice to have the Shield removed. Tetuan's lawyer was Bradley Post. The company said it would appeal.

2. In January 1968, the FDA's Advisory Committee on Obstetrics and Gynecology submitted a *Report on Intrauterine Contraceptive Devices*. The report said that some IUD makers clearly alerted physicians to possible "pelvic inflammatory disease." By contrast, the "Progress Report" used the vague

word "infection" and used it only once—in tiny type at the end of the five-line "Adverse Effects" paragraph, the next-to-the-last paragraph on the last of eight pages.

Robins reviewed a copy of the FDA report before buying the Shield. The Lippes Loop provides a contrast. In 1965, Dr. Jack Lippes, the inventor, reported twenty-three diagnoses of PID in 1,673 wearers. Among the twenty-three were eight "tentative" diagnoses "unsupported by laboratory corrobora-tion." Even so, years before the Shield went on sale, Ortho Pharmaceutical Corporation, the manufacturer, took care to disclose all twenty-three cases in the labeling for physicians.

3. On April 27, Preston reported a sharp increase to Dr. John Board, saying she had "been advised of a dozen cases, at the very most." Had she included the four Marchand cases, her total would have been only six or seven.

On September 5, she reported a 50-percent *decrease* to Dr. J. Stewart Tem-pleton, Robins's medical officer in England. "One thing that has been a little disturbing recently is the accumulation of some half dozen or so cases of serious septic abortion associated with the Shield," she told him in a letter. Yet Clark's chronology lists fourteen reported cases by June 30—eleven weeks earlier.

4. Christian, C. Donald, "Maternal Deaths Associated with an Intrauterine Device." *American Journal of Obstetrics and Gynecology* 19, no. 4 (June 15, 1974).

5. Hatcher, who is also a pediatrician and a consultant to the CDC, said in an interview in March 1985 that "I was learning, like a lot of people, about the problem of [spontaneous] septic abortions" and had come to the conference "in a troubled mood."

He said he had also been troubled because of a serious problem with the Shield in women who had never borne a child and who had suffered a perfora-tion of the uterus: insufficient barium in the plastic allowed it to elude detection by X ray, greatly complicating the task of pinpointing its whereabouts in the abdominal cavity. As a result, Hatcher said, he had phoned Ellen Preston to urge that the nullip Shield be taken off the market, She told him, he said, that Robins was not going to recall it.

6. They had concerns in addition to the Shield's apparent leading role in spontaneous septic abortions. One was that Robins's Shield complaint file—which the company had withheld from FDA inspectors until Representative Fountain turned on the heat on June 12, 1973—indicated an 8.8-percent pregnancy rate—eight times the widely advertised rate.

7. It is unclear why high FDA officials found it essential to take the unusual step of declining to repose full trust in the panel on devices, of which the Shield was one, in favor of involving the Bureau of Drugs OB-GYN committee—particularly when that committee's chairman, Dr. Theodore King, was a col-league of Shield developer Hugh Davis.

V. TOUGHING IT OUT

10. *Witnesses for the Defense*

1. In interviews, Tuttle told me: "I was unaware of (a) the amount of money that was paid by Robins for the device, and (b) the split-out of that money [among Dalkon's owners], and (c) of the ongoing obligation of Robins to pay royalties. And this information was deliberately withheld from my knowledge, and I said so under oath."

At the deposition, Michael Ciresi asked Tuttle if he had ever told his boss, William Forrest, "that Dr. Davis had lied under oath." Tuttle replied that he had told Forrest after he learned the facts in October 1974, and that Forrest's response was, "basically, 'deal with it' . . . it was my problem. I was responsible for the litigation."

Later, Tuttle testified, he "remonstrated" with Davis, telling him "that he'd cut me adrift once and I didn't want it to happen again, and that irrespective of how embarrassing it may be . . . he had to testify honestly and accurately." Davis's response was "pretty much . . . garbage in, garbage out," Tuttle recalled. "He could explain why black was white and conversely. It didn't satisfy me. . . ."

2. One need not be very precise to find this false: Not having been sworn, Davis could not have committed perjury even if he had not committed truth.

3. Fishbein told me she had advised Hopkins officials, including Dr. King, to refuse my requests for interviews, but she provided written answers to my questions. She said she was the sole spokesman because Hopkins was a defendant in Shield lawsuits. However, a check of court records in Maryland by *Washington Post* reporter Paul W. Valentine unearthed no Shield lawsuit naming the university. Fishbein confirmed—three months later—that Hopkins was not a defendant in any pending Shield suit. But, she said, she must hold to a "cautionary approach" because future plaintiffs might some day make Hopkins a defendant.

4. Also in 1974, in August, Davis was invited to testify before FDA advisers considering the safety and effectiveness of the Shield. On his own, court papers indicate, he lobbied them. He billed Robins for expenses of $4,826, including $1,447 "for telegrams and telephone calls on behalf of A. H. Robins."

5. Kennelly also called it "fundamentally unfair for such an accusation to be made without providing Dr. Keith a hearing. If such a hearing were held, we anticipate that it would be demonstrated that Dr. Keith did not commit perjury." A spokesman for Northwestern told me, "From the university's perspective, we do not agree that Dr. Keith committed perjury."

6. Three of the attorneys in this episode had been on the federal bench themselves. Robins's judicial stars were Griffin B. Bell, a former attorney general and former judge of the Fifth Circuit, from which the Eleventh evolved, and Sidney O. Smith, a former district judge. Bronson, Bronson & McKinnon chose Harold R. Tyler, also a former district judge (and a former deputy attorney

general). As of late August 1985, there had been no decision in this case; nor was the outcome of the FBI investigation known.

7. G. K. Hall & Company of Boston, which published *Intrauterine Devices*, said it sold about two thousand copies. The book drew applause in prestigious medical publications ("Must reading for every physician who practices family planning or counsels women in that area," said a reviewer in the *Journal of the American Medical Association*).

8. The complaint named as defendants the Charles A. Fields Foundation, Ltd., which was established in honor of the late chairman of OB-GYN at the Chicago Medical School, and two of its trustees. One was Keith. He became the foundation's part-time, $3,000-a-month president in April 1979, four months before it registered under the Illinois Charitable Trust Act. Keith testified in 1984 that he had also been medical director of the foundation and that it no longer existed.

The foundation ran an abortion clinic in Madison, Wisconsin. The complaint accused Keith of "self-dealing," partly by participating in foundation decisions to award three grants totaling $26,000 from which he "personally benefited." Each grant was for a book of which Keith was an author. One was *Intrauterine Devices*. For it, the complaint alleged, the foundation funneled $11,000 through MRC.

Keith denied any improper activities and said he had resigned from the foundation in March 1981. Berger, a trustee of the foundation when it registered in Illinois, was not a defendant. A judge dismissed the complaint in April 1983 on the ground that the alleged violations had occurred before the foundation had begun to do business in Illinois.

11. Dirty Questions, Dirty Tricks, and the Secret Life of Aetna Life

1. In a May 1983 letter, senior associate counsel Robert P. Walton spelled out NYU's position. Under "universally accepted canons of ethical and professional responsibility," he wrote, "information pertaining to ongoing litigation . . . is more appropriately initially disclosed in the course of discovery conducted by the parties to the litigation. . . ."

On telling Cornell of NYU's position, I learned that it was far from being "universally accepted." A spokesman told me that NYU had paid Cornell something less than $10,000, mainly for the subcontracted analyses of string bacteria done by Dr. O'Leary.

2. General counsel Forrest, who had helped to negotiate the agreement, revealed some of the background in February 1984, when Michael Ciresi questioned him at a deposition. The pact "arose as a result of a dispute that we were having regarding punitive damages and whether, in fact, the insurance policies covered a claim [based] on award of punitive damages," Forrest testified. Aetna had "said that they might be inclined to deny coverage," he added.

Forrest also hinted at why Aetna may have been so inclined: Robins had not passed to Aetna documents on defects in the Shield string, on wicking, or on related problems. Robins had begun to accumulate the documents in 1970; Aetna apparently saw them for the first time in early 1975, when they surfaced in Shield pretrial proceedings in Wichita, Kansas.

In August 1984, Ciresi questioned Forrest about an internal Aetna memo containing previously closely held information.

The memo concerns a tense, two-day defense strategy meeting in mid-June 1977 in Richmond. In attendance were Aetna and Robins executives, members of a law firm representing the reinsurers, and partners in Robins's two leading Shield law firms, Mays, Valentine, Davenport & Moore, and McGuire, Woods & Battle.

The memo reveals that at Aetna's request, Robins had been paying for some of the settlements made by the carrier, that Robins's potential exposure to punitive damages could be as high as $75 million to $80 million, that Aetna regarded Shield trials as potentially "disastrous," and that the insurer was expecting a "surge of litigation" in the six-month period ending September 30, 1977.

3. It was brought out later that Aetna limited its liability by buying "reinsurance" from other carriers. Aetna declined to discuss its relationship with Robins.

4. By contrast, the company's reports to stockholders have listed its costs "in respect of claims" as follows: $4.6 million in 1980, $3.3 million in 1981, $7.1 million in 1982, and $18.7 million in 1983 (the year of E. Claiborne Robins, Jr.'s testimony).

As if this weren't confusing enough, the company turned over documents to Robins, Zelle indicating that as of ten days after Claiborne Robins, Jr., testified, September 30, 1983, *Aetna* had paid out about $144 million to dispose of Shield cases, plus about $60 million in defense costs, for a total of $204 million. Yet A. H. Robins's report to stockholders for the quarter ended on that date said: "The company and its insurer have paid out in the aggregate approximately $164 million in disposing of . . . claims." How Aetna had paid out $204 million (according to Robins) while Aetna and Robins together had paid out $40 million *less* (also according to Robins) is unexplained and possibly inexplicable. One is forced to wonder what impelled Claiborne Robins, Jr., to testify as he did in the light of two documents the reliability of which is not in question.

The interim pact of March 1977 disclosed that Aetna had "paid the expenses of defending cases to date and . . . *will continue to defend the aforesaid Dalkon Shield cases and all similar cases filed in the future. . . .*" The agreement also said that Robins would continue to pay punitive damages. Long before Claiborne Robins, Jr.'s 1983 testimony, the manufacturer had in fact paid punitive damages.

The memo on the June 1977 Aetna-Robins strategy meeting, noting that five hundred or so claims had been closed up to that time, said that "contributions from Robins were requested *and made on fifteen cases amounting to $600,000.*" [Emphasis added.]

5. By the conservative count of Barbara Feinman, a *Washington Post* researcher.

6. In 1974, the year in which domestic Shield sales were suspended, Robins had obtained numerous complete medical records on women who had suffered spontaneous septic abortions. Could Clark cite a single Shield adverse-reaction report that Robins had sent to the FDA in that year? "I cannot specifically offhand," Clark said.

7. Harris Wagenseil, the former Robins counsel in San Francisco, testified before Magistrate McNulty in August 1984 that he had arranged four of the secret tests for McGuire, Woods, had reviewed interim results "continually" with the law firm, had made (oral) reports to it, had sent the final written reports to it, and had never reported to Robins's medical department.

12. The Vanishing Documents

1. Ending up "utterly frustrated" with a client that was "harder on me than the opposition," Tuttle said that he ruminated about what might happen if government were to hold corporate officers personally responsible for criminal corporate conduct. Finally, in early 1975, he vented his feelings at a medical department meeting. In his deposition in 1984, he testified to having spoken "to the effect that Dr. Freund ought to be on his knees nightly praying to his God and mine . . . and thanking Him that he was not in that position where he would be subject to such penalty, because surely he would be doing hard time if the truth was ever known."

In answer to Michael Ciresi's question about Freund's response to this, Tuttle replied, "He was outraged, stomped out of the meeting, and never spoke to me again as long as I was with the Robins company." "What did the other participants in the meeting say?" Ciresi asked. "I think there was stunned silence. . . . I think that I shocked everybody," Tuttle answered.

2. Defense counsel objected vehemently to much of Tuttle's testimony—mostly on grounds of the confidentiality of the attorney-client relationship and of the attorney's "work product"—and Tuttle himself several times objected on the same grounds. But United States Magistrate Earl Cudd, who was presiding, overruled most of both men's objections.

3. Tuttle testified that following the defeat in Wichita, Forrest attended a meeting with Aetna officials and fired him a few days later, saying "that Aetna had demanded my [Tuttle's] scalp. . . ." Tuttle appealed to Zimmer, and Forrest relented, leaving Tuttle on the payroll but forbidding him to have anything more to do with the Shield.

4. Paralegal Lashley testified that, in compliance with a document-discovery order issued by Judge Lord, a search was made of the offices of E. Claiborne Robins, Sr., and his secretary. The search turned up not one piece of Shield-related paper, not even a phone message, she said.

13. The Tide Turns

1. Robins settled the two cases in 1984 for a total of $2,050,000—$49,500 more than the plaintiffs had sought.

2. The verdict was appealed but then settled, for a sum said to be much less than $5.15 million, but still substantial.

3. By late 1983, four of Minnesota's eight federal judges were trying Shield cases simultaneously. In Hennepin County District Court (Minneapolis and environs), Shield trials were costing county taxpayers an estimated $7,000 a week.

4. Siegel's fine portrait of the judge ("Miles Lord: Champion or Zealot") appeared June 28, 1984.

5. "A Panel Tries to Judge a Judge." *Time,* July 24, 1984.

6. It bears noting that numerous federal and state judges in at least five states have been angered and frustrated by the litigation tactics of Robins and McGuire, Woods & Battle. In addition to Minnesota and Kansas (Judge Frank G. Theis), the states in which the cases have been heard are Florida, New Jersey, and South Carolina, though the presiding judges were less outspoken than Miles Lord.

Florida: In a 1981 case in Dade County, Robins was six months late in filing answers to written questions, and disobeyed two pretrial orders. Judge Jon I. Gordon struck down the company's legal defenses and ordered the case to trial solely on the issue of the amount of damages. Robins appealed but lost. Gordon had "ample evidence" for refusing "to be the victim of [Robins's] shell game tactics," Judge Woodrow M. Melvin wrote in the appeals court opinion.

Also in Florida, plaintiffs' lawyer Sidney L. Matthew was trying to compel Robins to produce its secret string studies. In a pretrial proceeding on July 6, 1984, in Pensacola, Senior Federal Judge Winston E. Arnow ordered Robins to produce the documents. The company stalled for more than two months, first with a motion that the judge dismissed as "meritless," next with a thinly veiled dare to Arnow to hold executives and/or counsel in contempt, and then with motions in the Eleventh United States Circuit Court of Appeals that were summarily rejected. "Robins drags [its] heels every time we turn around," Arnow said. Finally, in late September, Arnow set specific deadlines for document production. Robins said it could, after all, comply, but asked for and got a temporary protective order that prevented Matthew from using or disclosing the materials to anyone—particularly other Shield litigants. On November 30, Arnow not only dissolved the order, but showed his disdain for Robins's delaying tactics by ordering the company to reimburse Matthew for the expenses he had incurred in opposing those tactics.

New Jersey: In a 1983 case, Federal Judge Stanley S. Brotman criticized Robins's "nonresponsive," delay-causing submissions and denied a defense motion to bring in outside counsel under the "indirect control" of McGuire, Woods. The outside counsel included Washington lawyers William J. Cassidy, Jr., of Hogan & Hartson and Charles P. Goodell, Jr.

South Carolina: Federal Judge C. Weston Houck told a June 1984 hearing in Charleston that he wanted the Robins counsel in Richmond who had prepared written questions for a plaintiff "to sign them" so that he couldn't come in later and say "he didn't have anything to do with it and [local defense counsel Julius W. McKay] is the one that failed there." The Robins counsel in Richmond was "trying to keep from producing any information he can," Houck said. "I don't think that is right."

7. See Note 4, above.

8. The quoted words are from the transcript of Lord's remarks in court on February 29, 1984.

9. The other witnesses were experts on judicial administration and legal ethics: Ernest C. Friesen of California Western School of Law and Monroe G. Freedman of Hofstra University. Friesen testified that Lord's speech could be viewed as an effort to fulfill the purpose of the 1980 law by making the judicial system work better. Freedman said that "anything less than a full and ambiguous vindication would not only be an injustice to Judge Lord, but also a serious impairment of the independence of the federal judiciary."

10. Clark also charged that the officers' complaint made "serious deceptive statements." His principal example centered on an accusation intended by the officers to demonstrate Lord's alleged bias: the judge had been preparing his reprimand "for 'months.' " Clark said there was "no support for that." In reply, Bell did no more than read aloud the pertinent portion of the opening paragraph of Lord's speech: "Mr. Robins, Mr. Forrest, and Dr. Lunsford: After *months of reflection, study and cogitation—and no small amount of prayer*—I have concluded it perfectly appropriate to make to you this statement. . . ." [Emphasis added.]

The complaint form, signed by Bell as well as the officers, carries this instruction on its first page: "Any false statement of a material fact in this complaint may serve as the basis for prosecution and conviction for perjury."

11. Tuttle's damaging testimony left Robins groping for ways to try to discredit him. On May 6, 1985, the company persuaded a federal magistrate in Tulsa to compel Tuttle to testify exclusively on document-destruction matters. In doing so, Robins insisted that no news reporters be admitted to the deposition. None is known to have been told of the proceeding, which lasted for nine hours, and none attended.

As expected, Robins tried to show that Tuttle had fabricated the document-destruction episode. But he stood fast and recanted nothing. In a shabby move nine days later, on May 23, Robins held a press conference in Richmond at which two of its outside lawyers, Terrence M. Bagley and James S. Crockett, Jr., tried to sell a totally self-serving account of the evidence produced by the deposition to reporters who, as Robins knew, had neither attended the Tulsa proceeding nor read the transcript.

The tactic failed in the case of the *Richmond Times-Dispatch* because of staff writer Thomas R. Morris's diligence in interviewing James R. Eagleton, Tuttle's lawyer in Tulsa, and in finding out how Tuttle had responded—under oath—to the Robins allegations. According to Morris, Tuttle flatly denied the allegation that he back-dated a memo about the destruction and insisted that the destruction did in fact take place, although he was in El Paso at the time. As for the propriety of the destruction, Tuttle acknowledged that Forrest told him to be sure that the destruction conformed to the company's record-retention program—a program which for the most part came into existence in 1972 and was updated at about the same time as the destruction. But, according to Morris, Tuttle, steadfastly refused to accept Robins's efforts to sanitize the destruction as an "innocent effort" to carry out the company's record-retention policy.

At the very least, Morris's balanced May 24 story—too intricate and lengthy to be recycled here—cast grave doubt on the validity of the allegations. Another point should be noted. Bagley told the news conference that Robins intended to request Federal Judge Frank Theis in Wichita to strike Tuttle's 1984 deposition. But as of this writing—nearly three months later—no such request had been made.

12. The tabulation was made by Congress Watch, a unit of Public Citizen, Inc., a consumer activist organization in Washington, founded by Ralph Nader. The tabulation was disclosed by the *Washington Post* on March 25, 1984.

13. *Washington Post,* August 7, 1984.

14. *Philadelphia Daily News,* September 12, 1984.

15. The other outside directors: Carroll L. Saine, chairman of Central Fidelity Banks, and Stuart Shumate, retired president of the Richmond, Fredericksburg & Potomac Railroad Company.

16. These provisions make Robins, Zelle available, at the request of the company and plaintiffs' counsel, to evaluate the remaining complaints with a view toward recommending acceptable settlements. The law firm would be paid on an hourly-fee basis. Another provision transferred all pending Shield court orders and discovery materials in the law firm's Shield cases to Federal Judge Robert G. Renner in St. Paul, so that, as Brosnahan said, they "will be available to other plaintiffs' lawyers in the country."

Brosnahan declined to specify the fees his firm will be paid, but said it shunned the practice of some plaintiffs' lawyers of increasing their percentage in high-risk cases.

17. *The Virginian-Pilot* and the *Ledger-Star,* February 10, 1985.

18. The *Richmond Times-Dispatch,* which for too long had treated the Robins

family reverentially, began to do some solid, straight news reporting. The *Dallas Times-Herald* of February 17, 1985, published a well-researched report by William P. Barrett that occupied a large chunk of the front page and four full inside pages. My five-part series in the *Washington Post* began to run on April 7, 1985.

Index

INDEX

ABOUT THE AUTHOR

Morton Mintz has been a reporter for the *Washington Post* since 1958. Winner of both the Columbia Journalism Award and the A. J. Liebling Award, he has also been a Neiman Fellow at Harvard University. Among his books are *By Prescription Only* and *The Pill: An Alarming Report,* and, with Jerry S. Cohen, *America, Inc.: Who Owns and Operates the United States.*